Bringing Your
Product to Market

The *Entrepreneur* Magazine Small Business Series

<u>Published:</u>

Bringing Your Product to Market
The Entrepreneur Magazine Small Business Advisor
The Entrepreneur Magazine Small Business Answer Book
Guide to Integrated Marketing
Human Resources for Small Businesses
Making Money with Your Personal Computer
Small Business Legal Guide
Starting a Home-Based Business
Starting an Import/Export Business
Successful Advertising for Small Businesses

<u>Forthcoming:</u>

The Entrepreneur Magazine Encyclopedia of Entrepreneurs
Guide to Raising Money
Business Opportunities on the Internet
Organizing and Promoting Seminars
Working with Consultants and Suppliers
Guide to Professional Services

ENTREPRENEUR MAGAZINE

Bringing Your
Product to Market

DON DEBELAK

John Wiley & Sons, Inc.

New York • Chichester • Weinheim • Brisbane • Singapore • Toronto

Copyright © 1997 by Don Debelak
Published by John Wiley & Sons, Inc.

Library of Congress Cataloging-in-Publication Data:

Debelak, Don.
    Entrepreneur magazine : bringing a product to market / Don
Debelak.
        p.   cm. — (The Entrepreneur magazine small business series)
    Rev. ed. of: How to bring a product to market for less than
$5,000.   1992.
    Includes bibliographical references and index.
    ISBN 0-471-15773-2 (cloth : alk. paper). — ISBN 0-471-15750-3
(pbk. : alk. paper)
    1. New products—Management.   2. New products—Marketing.
I. Debelak, Don. How to bring a product to market for less than
$5,000. II. Entrepreneur (Santa Monica, Calif.) III. Title.   —
IV. Series.
HF5415.153.D43   1997
658.5'75—dc20   96-36095
                                          CIP

Printed in the United States of America

10 9 8 7 6 5 4 3 2

PREFACE

I've yet to meet a person who hasn't thought of a better way of doing something. Some people are inventors who design complicated products, such as inspection equipment, electronic diaries, or complex machinery. Other people think of simple innovations: a Chip Clip, a slap bracelet, or a bicycle clamp that holds a soda. Almost everyone has thought of tiny product variations, such as putting black pumpkin faces on orange garbage bags or adding neon-colored bows to sunglasses. Every year, products from all of these categories are put on the market.

I believe anyone with the right product idea can create a profitable company. Yet, according to business start-up statistics and income tax returns, over 250,000 individuals lose money on product concepts every year. Many of those people spend over $50,000 without ever getting their products in front of customers.

I wrote this book because I don't think people should spend their life's savings on what they *hope* is a million-dollar idea. Instead, I want every person to have a chance to pursue and evaluate an idea for less than $5,000.

Most entrepreneurs give me puzzled looks when I say they can introduce products for very little of their own money. I do understand why people are confused. I too have introduced products (about 15) for midsize to large companies, and, typically, I have spent between $300,000 and $1,000,000 to do that. But I've also worked with several entrepreneurs, each of whom had less than $1,000 of their own money to introduce products, and a good percentage of them also succeeded. Money is not why people succeed; it's their knowledge, skill, and persistence that drive their success.

This book is loaded with examples, and I thought readers might understand the examples better if I explain my background. I had a rather uneventful career until at age 30 I received my MBA from Rutgers University and landed a marketing job with a midsize dental company. This company was fascinating because it was the result of a merger between two classic "backyard" inventors. The first was selling vibrating reclining chairs at the Iowa State Fair when a dentist walked up and asked him if could make this chair work for dental patients. It turned out the dentist had a bad back and couldn't bend around a patient any more. The inventor and his brother created a dental chair in their garage and managed to sell ten chairs in their first year of business.

The other inventor was a dental equipment repairman who invented a better vacuum pump to power the vacuum device dentists place in your mouth. Neither inventor had a college or engineering degree; they just had good ideas. I introduced about ten products for that company and, as I learned the new-product process, I started helping small product entrepreneurs market their ideas.

My next full-time job was with a high school dropout who invented a product that could measure diffusion depths in semiconductor wafers. He was able to build sales to the $800,000 mark but he was unable to introduce a second successful product. This is when I started to take a keen interest in working with inventors to market their product ideas. I realized that most successful inventors didn't really know why they had succeeded. And yet I found that those same successful inventors had actually followed very similar paths. My goal at that time was to capture the steps that inventors actually used and then use that knowledge to help other product entrepreneurs bring their products to market.

Over the last ten years I've worked as an independent new-product marketing consultant and as a part-time new-product consultant with a small business development center. I've worked with hundreds of entrepreneurs, some of whom had less than $100 and some of whom have raised over $1 million from investors and other companies to launch their products. I've found there are far more similarities than differences between introducing a product with and without money. Both present challenges and both call for a careful introduction approach.

Over the last ten months I've worked with a biomedical company, a pipe-coupling manufacturer, an inventor of baby products, and a metal-processing company. Together, these companies are raising $5 million to launch what we all hope will be successful companies. But over the same year I've also worked with inventors of an ironing board caddy, a new tool for braided hair, inclusive art equipment for wheelchairs, and a device that always ties the perfect dress tie. These inventors combined couldn't spend more than $20,000 on their products. But each product has a real chance to make it on the market. The point is not the money, but the product, and how that product meets the market's needs. Once you have the right product, almost anyone, in almost any financial condition, can introduce a product using the introduction strategy I detail in this book.

I am always a little apprehensive when talking to or writing for inventors. Most how-to books emphasize that they disclose an easy path to instant wealth. I've never done that. Instead, I try to detail the hard work and long process involved in taking a product to market. My goal isn't to sell the greatest number of books, but rather to help dedicated product entrepreneurs succeed. Some entrepreneurs are disappointed that they won't be overnight millionaires, but many more inventors have expressed their appreciation for the time I take to help them know how to market their products.

This book covers both marketing a product yourself and licensing an idea. I believe inventors are usually better off marketing their own ideas, although licensing is an avenue many, if not most, inventors prefer to pursue. My views of licensing are very different from those you'll read in most books. The concept of taking an idea to a manufacturer and hoping the manufacturer will agree to a license is a narrow approach that greatly limits your licensing options and minimizes your chances of succeeding. This book covers how to take a much broader approach to licensing, offering manufacturers a series of options that take both you and the manufacturer closer to the licensing decision. My goal is not just to help you sign a traditional license agreement, but to help you get your product on the market with the help of a manufacturer, which can be done in any number of ways.

I've also tried to address inventors' number-one concern and problem: *money.* Product entrepreneurs always have problems raising money. Most of the inventors I talk to either just don't know how to raise money, or they simply don't devote the time and energy needed to raise money. I can't force you to make a more dedicated financing effort, but I can help you learn how to go about raising money. The book covers everything from starting off without any money to raising over a million dollars to launching a major corporation.

One of the important points I make throughout the book is that marketing a new product is a matter of constant adjustments. Product entrepreneurs like to think of creating ideas and then marketing them. Most products have far too many small flaws for that to happen. The question is not, "Does your product pass the go/no-go decisions listed in Part 2?," but rather, "How do you change your product so it will pass?" The go/no-go decisions are not one-time events but starting points. You need to evaluate your product first and then modify it so it will be ready for introduction.

The book includes charts and checklists that you can use to keep your project on track. When you start on a project, make copies of these checklists and put them in your inventor's notebook. You can use them to monitor your progress and guide you through each step of the introduction process. Currently only 1 in 500 to 1,000 inventors launches a money-making project. I hope to help readers—both those introducing their own ideas and those working to license their ideas—to raise their odds of achieving winning introductions to a minimum of 10 to 20 percent.

Readers will find that my advice changes: Sometimes I'll stress how difficult it is to introduce a new product idea, and other times I'll stress how anyone can take the right product to the market. The reason for this apparent conflict is what is sometimes called *the PGL syndrome.* PGL stands for *paranoia, greed,* and *laziness.* Even one of these three traits will doom anyone trying to introduce a product. Paranoia prevents people from receiving the outside input they need; greed pushes them to overlook investors who could be instrumental in their product's success; laziness stops them from creating the extra drive that every product idea needs before it will sell. When I emphasize that product creators have a difficult challenge, I'm encouraging readers to put forth every ounce of effort they have.

One of the book's goals is to help entrepreneurs understand the new-product introduction process. Examples of the right and the wrong moves that other people have made are presented in italics throughout the book. The product creators named don't mind being identified or their stories have been told previously in newspapers or magazines. Others who preferred anonymity have been given fictitious names or first-name-only identification.

The vast majority of the examples given involve products created by individuals. I've modified some of the products discussed, because the creator of the idea wasn't quite ready to put the product on the market and did not want the idea disclosed or asked me for a confidentiality agreement. I have not, however, changed the market situations that these product creators confronted.

Documentation for the statistics given in several places throughout the book can be found in the "Helpful Sources" section at the end of the book.

CONTENTS

PART 2   THE GO/NO-GO DECISIONS

PART 3   SELLING YOUR PRODUCT

INTRODUCTION: THE FIVE CRITERIA FOR SUCCESS

There are five criteria for determining whether a product idea can be successfully marketed:

1. The product is easy to distribute.
2. The technology is simple.
3. The product is perceived to be unique.
4. The benefit is obvious.
5. The product can be sold at four to five times its manufacturing cost.

Your job as an entrepreneur is to be sure your product meets these five criteria. Most of the time original ideas don't start with all the necessary ingredients for success. Your choice then is to drop the idea or, preferably, to reconfigure the idea so that it meets the key criteria. I've found that most ideas can be modified so they have a chance to be successful. One of my goals in this book is to show you how to turn average ideas into winning market introductions. That is a skill that will allow you to turn out new products on a yearly basis.

The importance of the key criteria is illustrated by two inventions: a real estate lock box and foam lock-box cover. Neither product was on the market when my wife and I were shopping for a house in Pennsylvania. The real estate agent drove us from house to house; for almost every showing, she had to go to another realtor's office to get a house key. Sometimes, the key wasn't there, usually because another agent had not yet returned it. I estimate that nearly half our time with her was spent tracking down house keys.

Eight years later, when we were again house shopping, not one minute was lost looking for keys. In those seven years, someone had created the real estate lock box. The box has a U-shaped hook that slides over the back of the doorknob and then locks into the back of an empty box. The front of the box has a combination lock that opens the box's door. The keys to the house are put inside this locked compartment. All a real estate agent has to do is call the seller's real estate office to get the lock's combination. I'm not sure who created this nifty product idea, but it saves real estate agents hours of time.

The real estate lock boxes had one problem. When the front door was opened, the box would swing out a few inches and then bang into the door. This is where Darnell Krell entered the picture. When she and her husband had their house up for sale, she noticed the damage caused by the lock box. When she saw the same damage on virtually every house with a lock box, Darnell created knitted mittens for lock boxes, as an experiment. Real estate agents loved the idea, and Darnell decided to market a molded foam lock-box cover. Her product protected the front door and provided an advertising spot for mortgage bankers and real estate agents.

Darnell worked hard to market her product, but her efforts were aided by the fact that both the lock-box cover and the lock box met the five criteria for successful marketing:

1. The distribution system was obvious and available. Not only were real estate offices and mortgage bankers easy to locate, but they represented a virtually untapped market, because few products were sold exclusively to them.
2. Combination lock and foam molding technology were well known and relatively simple.
3. The products were unique; nothing like them had ever been sold.
4. The products' benefits were obvious to the real estate agents.
5. Lock-type products and foam molded products typically sold at four to five times the cost of these new products.

All the go/no-go decisions discussed in this book are based on the five criteria for successful marketing of a product idea. Can an individual, operating alone, market a product that doesn't meet the criteria? Yes. But the product creator will need more money for advertising, distribution, and/or manufacturing than most people can afford to spend. Meeting the criteria will offer the best chance for a successful introduction and the only chance for marketing a product with a small investment.

My experience is that out of one hundred ideas that might have market potential, only five to ten can be introduced by an individual. Corporations have advantages that individuals don't, such as already developed distribution networks, established research and development (R&D) and marketing departments, and extensive financial resources.

Many times product entrepreneurs are better off dropping ideas that are too difficult to introduce. Dropping ideas allows you to invest your time and money into projects with which you can succeed. But you shouldn't be too quick to drop a good idea. Many times you can work on your idea, make needed changes, and end up with a product that can be sold. Other times, you may be able to compensate for gaps in your product by teaming up with a company. For example, you can overcome difficult distribution problems by having an established company distribute your product, or you can overcome the difficulties of a complicated product by making a joint-venture agreement with a manufacturing company.

The key to using the criteria is to understand that they are the foundation of a successful product. You need to figure out how you'll meet the five criteria before you start spending a lot of money and effort on your idea. Otherwise you may end up investing in a product that won't sell.

Bringing Your
Product to Market

PART ONE

GETTING STARTED

Yoshiro Nakamatsu ("Dr. NakaMats"), who invented the floppy disk, digital watches, and approximately 2,000 other products, is probably the world's leading inventor. Dr. NakaMats believes that the first element of inventing is *suji*, which translates into English as "knowledge." I agree with Dr. NakaMats. Before you start to take a product concept to the market, you need to know and understand the importance of the product introduction process.

Part 1 covers some important questions that you should consider before deciding whether you want to try to introduce a product concept.

- How much time should be devoted to the product?
- How much money will an introduction take?
- How can the needed money be raised?
- How can a product idea be protected, for the lowest possible cost?

1

FACING REALITIES: HARD WORK LIES AHEAD

I'm never sure what to tell people when I'm talking about the reality of introducing a new product. For the people who are afraid to try to take an idea to market, I want to tell them that it is not that difficult to introduce a new product, that it is something anyone can do.

In the summer of 1995 I helped a billing clerk named Sharon DeCarlo generate $35,000 in sales for her ironing board caddy, a product that hangs on the end of an ironing board and has a bar for hanging shirts and dresses. Her total time and investment was less than six months and $200. Sharon didn't think she had a chance to take a product to market. But I told her we could do it—we just needed a prototype, a sales flyer, and a price sheet, to see if the market would buy.

But for every cautious entrepreneur like Sharon, there are other product creators who believe an idea is like a lottery ticket—all the entrepreneur needs to do is cash it in. Well, introducing a new product is not that easy. There may be 200,000 individuals working on product ideas at any one time, and probably only 400 to 500 succeed in introducing their ideas in any given year. I want to tell these entrepreneurs to wake up: No one is going to just give them potfuls of money because they have ideas; instead, they are going to have to do a lot of hard work to turn their ideas into money.

Most people who take an idea to market realize that it will cost money, and in many cases they are ready to spend it. They are ready to spend on prototypes, production quantities, packaging materials, ads, sales materials, and inventory. Unfortunately, most of these inventors lose their money. The secret to a successful product introduction is not having a lot of money to spend, it's having the right product to sell. With the right product, you can use other people's money to help you introduce your product. Getting the right product takes time and effort, but not necessarily a lot of money. Take a look at the conventional product introduction process outlined in Figure 1-1. Product creators have many opportunities to spend money. The convention highlights the major contributor to most new product failures: an assumption, from the very beginning, that the product idea is perfect. There is no effort to check on distribution channels, to get help from people established in the market, or to establish that the product will sell. Not surprisingly, most of these products end up in someone's basement or the neighborhood Dumpster.

RAISING YOUR CHANCES OF SUCCESS

Figure 1-2 is a chart of what I call the *product-to-market approach,* a step-by-step process designed to give you the best chance of success. Each step by itself isn't that hard, but the sequence is critical. You need to stage each part of the process to maximize your odds to get the investors, marketing, and manufacturing help you need. The approach is built on three major points that I believe to be true about the new product process:

1. Most successful products have numerous revisions before introduction.
2. Anyone, no matter what his or her financial position, should be able to introduce a new product.
3. New entrepreneurs can't succeed in the market without help from people experienced in their target market.

I don't mean to imply that money doesn't help. It certainly does make an introduction less work. But it's not impossible to introduce a new product without lots of money. In fact, many new introductions are made by people with little money. They often succeed because they have to ask for help. People with a lot of money frequently just spend it without getting any of the assistance they really need.

The product-to-market concept is a process, something you can use as a guideline for your introduction. Many of the steps can be done easily, while others need a great deal of effort. The most important feature of the

Figure 1-1   The Product Introduction Process—Conventional Approach

1. Ask for friends' advice.
2. Look in a few retail stores for similar products.
3. Visit a patent attorney.
4. Have a patent search done ($300 to $700).
5. Transfer money from savings to your checking account.
6. Apply for a patent ($5,000 to $10,000).
7. Produce a high-quality prototype ($3,000 to $6,000).
8. Find a manufacturer to make a mold.
9. Use credit cards for a $20,000 cash advance.
10. Produce the first mold and 50 units ($10,000).
11. Discover a small flaw in the product design.
12. Redesign the mold ($3,000).
13. Place an initial order for 1,000 units ($6,000).
14. Take out a second mortgage ($25,000).
15. Order packaging artwork and materials ($7,000).
16. Design and order ten mail-order ads ($15,000).
17. Release the ads and wait for money to roll in.
18. Quit full-time job.
19. Wonder where the orders are. Check with the post office to see if mail is being delivered.
20. Borrow $15,000 from spouse's credit cards.
21. Place new ads ($15,000) for more exposure.
22. Wonder where the orders are.
23. Get a part-time job to feed the family.
24. Surrender to defeat and beg spouse for forgiveness.

process is that it conserves your cash, allowing you to move as far as possible with your investment.

This book is organized by topics such as financing, the initial sales period, and the initial go/no-go decisions, and it doesn't necessarily follow each step sequentially. When you are taking your idea to market, refer to Figure 1-2 anytime you are not sure what step you should take next.

One of the most important points to notice in Figure 1-2 is the number of times you should approach investors. This is true for both underfinanced and well-financed entrepreneurs. Your best investor strategy is to get investors involved in the project early, for small amounts of money. It is easier to attract investors with a graduated investment strategy. It can be difficult to find investors if you wait till you need $50,000 to $100,000.

Figure 1-2   The Product-to-Market Approach

1. Sketch idea on paper.
2. Write down thoughts of how the idea will work and what the product's benefits are.
3. Send $10 and the document disclosure form to the U.S. Patent Office.
4. Find comparable products that provide similar benefits.
5. Prepare a benefit grid of comparable products.
6. Verify premise that the product is needed by consulting both consumers and sellers in the market.
7. Produce sample ads and a package.
8. Have people compare the ads and package to ads and packages for similar products.
9. Adjust the product based on consumer input.
10. Check out distribution channels.
11. Determine which channels are easy to sell through, and reconfigure the product to fit the distribution channel.
12. Do another ad layout if needed, and then ask people in the channel for input.
13. Adjust the product if needed to fill industry needs.
14. Determine the targeted customer and price.
15. Produce a rough model or prototype.
16. Find products with similar technology.
17. Get a rough cost from manufacturing.
18. Determine if the product can sell for four times its cost.
19. Find industry people to help with the product introduction.
20. If needed, approach potential investors for a small start-up investment.
21. Make an initial go/no-go decision.
22. Finalize the prototype and ad layouts. Make product changes as needed.
23. Check on the manufacturing cost again to be sure it is still in line with the initial estimates.
24. Try and obtain orders through the distribution channel.
25. Go to the investors for a small investment to make products for a market test.
26. Find a manufacturer that will help or participate in a joint venture.   *(Continued)*

Figure 1-2 *Continued*

27. Produce a small quantity of products with minimal tooling expense.
28. Sell the small quantity of products through the distribution channel.
29. Make a go/no-go decision based on test-market results. Adjust the product if necessary.
30. Target a small market for an initial sales period. Prepare a transitional operating plan.
31. Offer a proposal to a manufacturing company.
32. Ask the investors for more money based on successful test results and the manufacturing agreement.
33. Apply for a patent if appropriate.
34. Begin small-scale production for the target market.
35. Prove the product is a winner through sales success.
36. With the manufacturer, determine start-up costs for full production.
37. Establish additional contacts in the distribution channel.
38. Prepare a business plan.
39. Obtain additional investments and financing.
40. Watch as product sales grow.

WHAT ARE THE ODDS?

I always hesitate to talk about odds because I believe that product entrepreneurs are their own biggest enemies. Their own mistakes are the reasons most of them fail. On the other hand, many inventors look at all the steps involved in the product-to-market approach and say, "I don't have to worry about all those steps; I have a great idea." The harsh reality is that very few product entrepreneurs succeed. Based on income tax reports, patent applications, and business start-up reports, there are about 250,000 people each year trying to introduce new ideas. From my experience and research, I believe that no more than between 250 and 500 individuals successfully market products each year. That means that out of every 500 to 1,000 people who try to introduce a new product, only one succeeds.

Why do so few product creators succeed? It's not because people don't have good ideas. Well over 75 percent of the people I talk to, who are serious about introducing a new product, have ideas that are just as marketable as the products manufacturers are introducing. I'm willing to venture that even 20 to 30 percent of the people who just have ideas, with no intent of marketing them, have potentially successful ideas. People fail primarily because of their own mistakes. They don't modify their ideas to the market needs, pick the wrong products, run out of money, or just give up too soon.

Another important reason more inventors don't succeed is that just 10,000 consumer products have significant introductions each year, and they include products from consumer giants such as 3M, Sony, Procter & Gamble, and Mattel. The market for products is limited. Retailers have only a certain amount of shelf space, only so many TV commercials and space advertisements can be run, and only so many sales calls and direct mailings can be made. Product creators have to be prepared to compete not just with each other, but also with established companies that are trying to introduce new products.

It takes hard work to introduce a product, but individuals are still introducing their ideas every year. Bruce Ohman was a utility worker who saw a need to develop a better way to thaw the ground around a buried utility line in the winter. Bruce and his crew used to bore three-inch holes around the line and then thaw the ground with propane torches. This could take two or three days, because just as much heat escaped to the atmosphere as went into the ground. Bruce created a four-foot by six-foot thermal blanket, full of propane-produced hot air, that could defrost the ground in 24 hours. Bruce started Frost Belt Utilities, a company that has sold 60 units in its first few months, and he expects sales of $200,000 in the first year of business.

DROPPING IDEAS

The product-to-market approach that I advocate will give you much better odds of success. For your best chance, you also need to learn when to drop an idea and start to look for a new one. In many cases, you can keep modifying an idea and make it right for the market, but that's not always possible. There is no point in pursuing a difficult-to-introduce idea for too long; you are better off dropping the idea and moving on to a better one.

Any discussion of the odds for a product creator's succeeding contains a number of negative statistics. Books about how to market product ideas should be positive, but I decided to include this information because I don't believe that an individual can introduce a product idea unless it meets all the criteria for successful marketing. When you start a project, it won't always be apparent whether a product can be introduced. As you move through the introduction cycle, you will get a better idea of your product's profit potential. If you learn, even after a year or two of work, that your product falls short of meeting the criteria, drop it and move on to another product. Dropping a product can be very painful, but it needs to be done if you want to increase your odds of success to over 50 percent.

I had a painful experience with a tire cutter that I once worked on. The tire cutter was designed to cut the tire along the line where the side-walls meet the tread. This product was originally created by Ron R., a tire dealer. He never had enough room for his waste tires, which became a breeding ground for mosquitoes. Ron wanted to cut his waste tires up quickly, at a minimal cost. He saw that cutting the tires at the junction of the sidewall and the tread would greatly reduce space requirements. The sidewalls would lie flat, like a stack of plates, and the tread, without the sidewall support, would form a flat strip on the ground. He would eliminate the mosquito problem by eliminating the open space inside the tire.

Ron made cutting the tires easy and inexpensive by designing an attachment for the hydraulic machine he used to mount tires onto wheel rims. When Ron was over 70 years old and had given up on his idea, he gave it to me and my partner.

We tested the product with several tire dealers, all of whom liked the product. We had several positive meetings with a tire equip-ment dealer who sold tire-mounting equipment throughout the Upper Midwest. These contacts helped us, as we modified the product to give it an acceptable price/value relationship. The contacts also helped us realize that the tire cutter would cut tires only when they were still on the rim. Most waste tires were already off the rim and therefore couldn't be cut on tire mounters. We developed a second product, a tire expander, which could be placed in a tire in about 15 seconds and would then act as a wheel rim.

All of our market intelligence was positive, but we had a prob-lem: Waste tires from large tire dealers don't go from the dealers to a landfill or tire shredder. Instead, a junk-tire dealer picks up the tires. The junk dealer picks out the best of the discards and then sells the rest to a tire retreader. Any tire that still has a respectable amount of rubber gets a new tread, and only the remaining tires go to a tire shredder or landfill. The junk-tire dealers did not like our product, which had the potential to put them out of business. The large tire dealers would use our product only if free tire pickup was part of the package. The retreaders didn't seem to care one way or the other about our product, because they could get used tires from companies that owned fleets of cars. Only the small tire dealers, who stored tires for a long time, were eager to use the cutter.

Changing the tire industry would take too much time, money, and effort, and I dropped the idea after working on it for eight months and spending $1,000. There was no point in fighting an uphill battle. I felt I was much better off looking for a new product with more potential.

THE STEP-BY-STEP APPROACH

One purpose of telling the tale of the tire cutter is to show how you must be willing to drop ideas whenever new information becomes available. The story demonstrates another point: Product creators have to take a slow, step-by-step approach. If they don't, they might spend all their money before they discover complications that will prevent them from introducing a product.

Many product creators have told me: "I can see why developing the tire cutter was complicated. After all, it is a somewhat complex mechanical part. But my product is real simple. It will be a snap to introduce." The tire cutter did have more mechanical features than most products, but most of the complications came from the junk tire dealers, retreaders, and tire-shredding companies, none of which were directly related to our product. Five to ten problems have surfaced unexpectedly during the introduction of every product I've worked on. Some inevitable problems can be overcome, if entrepreneurs have spent their money sparingly.

TIME MANAGEMENT

Most projects require at least five to ten hours per week for a successful launch. This is a significant commitment, especially for someone who needs to keep a full-time job in order to meet current bills. The task gets even tougher when a product creator has to make the most of his or her important contacts during regular work hours.

To keep a product moving, I recommend establishing goals, with a specific timetable, for each month. My April timetable for introducing the tire cutter (Figure 1-3) can serve as an example, and my comments on each goal will explain the sequence and time frames that were assigned.

You're headed for trouble if you don't prepare and follow a timetable. Roy L., for example, created a soda can holder that attached to the handle of a bike—a well-designed product that was easy to manufacture and had a manufacturing cost of less than 15 cents per unit. Roy developed a prototype and then tried to obtain large orders from soft drink distributors and from a chain of convenience stores. Roy had a very strong response from one chain of convenience stores. The buyer

Figure 1-3 One-Month Timetable for Introduction of Tire Cutter

---

Goal 1. Finalize contract manufacturing arrangements.
Actions:

- Visit the final three contract manufacturing choices on April 9 and 12.
- Choose the final contract manufacturer by April 18.

Time Required:

- Half-day on April 9.
- All of April 12.

Comments: We had three considerations guiding our choice of a contract manufacturer. (1) We needed design help. The original product was put together with a variety of parts purchased from a farm implement store. Although the product worked well, it didn't look finished. We needed a manufacturer that would redesign the product, at its expense, using commonly available, inexpensive materials. (2) We had to have product liability insurance. The tire cutter, which cut through a tire in about 15 seconds, was capable of injuring someone. If we could find a manufacturer that had other products with similar safety problems, we could obtain a rider on the manufacturer's already existing insurance policy. The alternative was a $2,500 to $5,000 insurance deposit from our own funds. (3) We wanted the product's manufacturing costs to stay low, to allow us to make money on the project. All in all, we had quite a few points to negotiate, especially since we were willing to pay only $250 to $300 for our initial prototypes.

Goal 2. Obtain an insurance company's preliminary approval for a new product design.
Action:

- Present the design from the contract manufacturer to the insurance company on April 23.

Time Required:

- Four hours on April 23.

Comments: The original product design didn't have some safety features required by the insurance company. Before moving ahead, we wanted to be sure the tire cutter's new design was acceptable.

(Continued)

Figure 1-3   *Continued*

Goal 3.   Prepare a preliminary product flyer to be shown during market tests.
Actions:

- Develop preliminary ideas for the flyer, April 1–10.
- Work out the final flyer layout, April 11–20.
- Have artwork completed by a high school art student by April 30.

Time Required:

- Two to three hours every Tuesday night and Friday night in April.

Comments: When you are showing a new product, prepare a sample product sales brochure to help people quickly understand what you believe are the benefits of your product. Response to your flyer will help you determine which product features are important to potential customers. You don't need to spend a lot of money on a flyer. Photographs, headings prepared with stencils or press type, and simple artwork are usually enough to capture the benefits of a product.

---

told Roy in January to come back with an actual production model and appropriate proof that Roy could deliver a large order. The buyer was prepared to issue an order if the product was as good as the prototype and if Roy could hold his price to 22¢ per unit or less.

Because Roy had to start working overtime at his regular job, he couldn't give the buyer a response until June, when the spring buying period was over. The buyer he had contacted had left the convenience store chain, and a new buyer had not yet been hired. Roy's other contacts all asked how his product was doing. When they heard Roy had failed to sell any units during the spring, they lost whatever enthusiasm they had had for the product.

Your continual progress on a project is crucial to its success. Distributors, retailers, buyers, and virtually every other contact will judge a product's merits at least partially by how well it is doing at other locations or by how much progress you've been able to make between visits. You must commit enough time to your project and you must stay on your original schedule to maintain the momentum you need to succeed.

2

FINANCING: FORGET THE MYTHS—HERE'S THE TRUTH

I get phone calls every month from people who state, in effect: "I've got a sensational idea. Where do I go to get financing?" My answer to almost every underfinanced entrepreneur is: "Look in the mirror, because you're going to have to come up with the money yourself—from savings, borrowing against personal assets, or recruiting investors among family and friends."

The truth of financing is that virtually no one will lend money to an unproven entrepreneur for an untested idea. According to Jerry Christenson, an assistant district director of the Small Business Administration, 90 percent of start-up money comes from private sources. Most of the other 10 percent goes to people who have proven business backgrounds.

What about venture capitalists? Most believe a start-up is a company with $500,000 in sales. Only a very small percentage of venture capital money goes to people with just an idea. Getting money is difficult and time consuming, and it is a source of constant worry for product creators.

Am I saying that underfinanced entrepreneurs shouldn't try to start businesses? Not at all. People with very little money start them all the time. Every year *Inc.* magazine rates the fastest-growing small companies in America. Typically, 20 to 25 percent of these companies are started with less than $5,000.

Keith Kendall designed a line of expensive fashion clothing. He wanted to market his product, but he had only $1,000. Keith didn't even have a sewing machine, but he borrowed one and started sewing his product in his basement. After receiving positive responses from a few stores, Keith went on to sew $10,000 worth of clothes in his "factory." Keith has 13 employees now and sells $400,000 worth of product a year.

My point is that you won't be able to count on borrowing money from outside sources. You need two strategies to overcome this problem:

1. Conserve your money, spending as little as possible on each introductory step.
2. Court potential investors during your initial development steps.

The best people to court are insiders, people who work in the market in which you want to sell your product. Distributors, retailers, and marketing people for other manufacturers in the industry are all insiders. They won't look at a product as a profit-and-loss statement, but instead they'll look at the idea for its sales potential.

SOME HARD FINANCIAL FACTS

When you start a project, all you'll have is an idea—and trouble borrowing money from anyone, at this point. As you start to work on the project, you'll have models, prototypes, market research, and, eventually, a small number of actual sales. My goal is to get you to that point for $1,000 to $5,000—and in some cases much less.

The traditional approach to getting financing is full of obstacles for all inventors, and underfinanced product creators have even more than an average number of problems. This section will cover some of the traditional hurdles product creators will encounter. The next section will deal with how to overcome these obstacles if you are underfinanced. Don't let the hard financial facts discourage you; think of them instead as the rules of the game that you need to learn to live with.

You Always Need Your Own Money

Investors and bankers don't care how much money you've spent on a product; all that matters is how much money you have left to invest.

For example, Tony G. and three partners created a product called Pizza Stick. The product resembled a corn dog but had cheese and sausage or cheese and pepperoni on the inside and a pizza crust on the outside. Tony and his partners sold the product for three or four years at the Minnesota State Fair, the Minneapolis Aquatennial parade, and a host of other outdoor events. Pizza Stick was always popular.

Tony and his partners thought Pizza Stick would be a great supermarket product. A frozen Pizza Stick could be heated up and eaten as a snack or as a dinner for one. Tony and his partners invested $175,000 in developing the product and its packaging, and then they spent two years trying to put it on the market. They weren't successful, primarily because Pizza Stick couldn't be heated in a microwave oven. Supermarkets and convenience stores believed the product had to be microwavable.

Pizza Stick's creators went back to their kitchens, developed a product that could be heated in a microwave, and prepared to reattack the market. By now, they were broke, and they needed some investors. They couldn't find any, and their product died. Their problem was that investors looking at Pizza Stick saw a company without any assets. The investors wanted Tony's group to put up at least 20 percent of the money before they would participate.

Equity Ratios Are All-Important

Paul Santille started Pasta Mama's, a company that sells 32 flavors of pasta, in 1987. Sales grew by 175 percent in 1988 and were projected to hit $2 million in 1989. Paul needed to borrow $400,000 for a new building in order to expand. Banks wouldn't lend him the money, because Paul couldn't come up with $50,000 as his share of the equity.

Banks always require an entrepreneur to have some equity in a venture before they will lend money for it. The amount of equity depends on the stage a business is in. Most banks require a new venture to have a one-to-one equity basis, which means that, in order to borrow $15,000, an entrepreneur must invest $15,000 of his or her own money.

For an ongoing, successful business, banks and investors usually want a four-to-one loan ratio: They will lend $4 for every $1 the business has in cash. A profitable product and a strong business plan are still needed, but the necessary ratios must be met if you are to have even a chance of raising money.

You Must Have Business Experience on Your Management Team

Every potential investor or lender is going to evaluate your ability to run a business. If you don't have substantial business experience, you'll find it difficult to borrow money. Some banks and investors believe that the skill of a company's management team is more important than the merit of a company's product.

This might sound like an insurmountable obstacle if you have little business experience and are marketing a product for the first time. The obstacle will shrink if you can get industry insiders to invest in your idea and help you market it. Chapter 9 discusses how to line up experienced insiders and create a strong management team.

To confirm the importance of a management team (usually yourself and one or two part-time partners), watch the local papers for stories of new businesses that receive start-up financing. You'll find that almost all of these companies are headed by three or four people who have significant business experience.

Self-Employed People Are Bad Credit Risks

A self-employed person needs at least a year or two of proven earnings before he or she is considered a good credit risk. Because entrepreneurs marketing a new product may not make money for a year or two, they may have to wait three or four years before they can take out a personal loan to support their business.

Employed people, on the other hand, are usually granted both personal loans and a high limit on their credit cards. If you decide to fund part of your venture with personal loans, be sure to set your lines of credit before you quit your job. Because you may have to wait 12 to 18 months, or longer, for income, keep your regular job as long as possible and pay off all your personal debts. I'd also recommend that you save money by driving an old, reliable car, having garage sales, and selling anything else of value that you won't be using.

Overhead Costs Hurt Your Chances of Borrowing Money

Another name for overhead costs is *fixed expenses:* rent, utilities, property taxes, or lease costs. Some product creators think that by leasing small plants with manufacturing equipment, they become better credit risks. Just the opposite is true. Fixed expenses represent bills that you have to pay every month, no matter what your sales volume is. You become a bad credit risk because you can be forced out of business by a few months of poor sales.

The 1990s buzzwords for entrepreneurs are *virtual company.* This is a company that outsources manufacturing, R&D, accounting, and almost every other function and has very low fixed expenses. A virtual company is considered the best strategy for inventors and product creators introducing a new product because of its low overhead structure.

One traditional technique is to work out of your basement or garage. A better tactic is to find a small manufacturer and then rent out its space and equipment as you need it. If necessary, you might also be able to rent, by the hour, an experienced employee who can help you set up production runs.

To find a small manufacturer that might rent you space and equipment, check for business start-ups in your area. Owners have to file (usually with the office of the secretary of state in their home state) their assumed name prior to starting a business. These filings are typically announced in small community newspapers. At your state's capital, you can review all the filings processed over the past year or two. A second method is to watch for businesses filing for Chapter 11 bankruptcy protection. These companies are still operating, and they are usually willing to do almost anything to bring in extra money. Bankruptcies are filed by county and can be researched at your county courthouse.

A final method is to check with salespeople who call on the type of companies you are looking for. For instance, if you need a company with machining capability, check with companies that sell cutting tools or machining equipment. If you need a plastic part, check with manufacturers or distributors of injection molds or plastic. They'll know most of the companies in the area and often can recommend likely partner manufacturers to you. A last approach is simply to look in your state's industrial directory for the type of manufacturers you need and then contact them to see if they will talk to you about helping with prototype development.

DEVELOPMENT FINANCING

During the development period, a product goes from its initial conception through its beginning sales period. Most product creators obtain development financing from personal savings, family or friends, credit card cash advances, and personal loans.

Jan Dutton started Paper White with $10,000 of personal savings. Susan Anderson started her company, which sells antistatic kits for computers, with a $20,000 personal loan. Other entrepreneurs I've talked to started out with $25,000 to $75,000 drawn from their personal savings or invested by friends.

Does it sound as though some pretty hefty financial reserves are needed in order to introduce a product? Yes, it does sound that way, but underfinanced entrepreneurs without any wealthy relatives or friends can also take products to market. They just have to be sure to choose ideas that can be developed in their basements or garages and introduced for $1,000 to $2,000. Of the products I've seen that an entrepreneur could introduce, I'd say that 40 to 50 percent could go through the development stage for $2,000 or less.

That $2,000 still has to be raised, but almost anyone committed to an idea can raise that much money. Many entrepreneurs get second, and possibly third, jobs; they cut their expenses as much as possible, and they save their money until they have the amounts they need.

Some product entrepreneurs elect to rely heavily on credit card advances for development financing. Credit cards are certainly an option, but you risk running up your debts to the point where you can't repay them. The risk affects you personally, because you might go bankrupt, and bad personal credit will hurt your chances of borrowing money later on, when the product has started to sell.

Some readers will be able to easily put up $20,000 to $40,000 for development financing. Your good financial position does not mean that you can afford to spend money freely in the development phase. Of the products that initially pass the go/no-go decision point, I'd estimate that 70 percent become unmarketable for unanticipated reasons. Many of these reasons aren't discovered until the last phase of development—the first sales period—when the product entrepreneur tries to prove the product will sell (see Chapter 11). You won't be able to start over if you've spent most of your money finding out that a product won't sell.

Having extra money set aside is helpful in any circumstances. After you prove a product will sell, you'll enter the transitional sales period, a time when extra money is extremely useful.

RUNNING OUT OF CASH

Most product entrepreneurs keep spending their own money until they run out. Then they try to get investors. The rationale behind this is that the longer an inventor waits for investors, the larger the share of the company he or she will end up owning. The first problem with this tactic is that you don't have any negotiating power when you don't have any money. The second problem is that you are passing up your best possibility for the ongoing financial support most projects need to overcome all the little obstacles that come up.

Tom C. had a chance to buy the Dish-Net, a product that holds down small plastic lids, small cups, and other small items in the top of a dishwasher. He wanted to take on the product, and he thought he could afford the $15,000 he expected it would take to introduce the product. But rather than do that, he took on three other partners for $5,000 each. Tom held 40 percent of the company, and the other investors held 20 percent each.

The key feature to the Dish-Net was the netting material. It would stretch to accommodate different-size dishwashers, could tolerate the high heat of dishwashers, and wouldn't fatigue with constant stretching. Tom ran into the following problems:

1. *The original netting vendor went out of business.*
2. *The product as originally designed was not wide enough and a redesign was needed.*
3. *An order for 3,000 pieces had to be canceled until a new supplier could be found.*
4. *The new vendor had difficulty making the netting correctly.*
5. *Product packaging needed to be redesigned to better fit supermarket shelf space.*
6. *The benefits of a $10,000 product launch were lost when the product couldn't be shipped.*
7. *Several sales agents had to be replaced once the product was ready.*

Now Tom did get his product on the market. But he had to go back to his investors six times for more money—$25,000 from each in total. Tom succeeded for only one reason: He had a network of investors to go back to time after time.

One of the traps of new-product introductions is that you never know for sure where the end of the road is. A product creator who has spent $25,000 on a product may discover that he or she needs to spend an additional $3,000 for a product change. What can the inventor do? Spend $3,000, which might be lost, or not spend it and be guaranteed to lose $25,000. Most product creators spend the $3,000. Faced with the same situation, the investors will spend the $3,000, too. They don't want to lose their initial investments any more than the entrepreneur does. Every project ends up costing much more than entrepreneurs anticipate. Getting investors involved early, with a small investment, can give you the money you need to keep moving forward.

STAGING THE INVESTMENT PROCESS

Refer to Figure 2-1.

Craig Z. came into my office and told me he had a great gift-wrapping product, and he just needed $75,000 to put the product on the market. Now $75,000 is a lot of money, and Craig didn't have any of his own money to put into the project. Craig also didn't have the business experience needed to show that he could handle the product introduction. Craig didn't have much chance to raise the $75,000.

Figure 2-1   The Financing Process for Underfinanced
Product Entrepreneurs

---

1. Pull together as much money as you can to pay for a rough ad, prototype, or model.
2. Find potential investors among friends, industry insiders, or fellow workers.
3. Ask several people for small amounts of money to help pay for models for market research.
4. Find a manufacturer willing to help with prototypes and small production runs.
5. Work out a low-cost arrangement for further prototype work.
6. Ask investors for another small sum of money for an initial market sales test.
7. Based on sales results in the market test, ask the manufacturer to pay up front for tooling costs and charge instead an extra tooling fee for each unit supplied.
8. Ask all suppliers for 60- to 90-day terms.
9. Go to investors and either request that they co-sign for a loan or invest additional money for the transitional sales period.
10. Use creative cash flow strategies, such as using orders to borrow money, selling receivables, or getting large down payments to help fund a transitional sales period.
11. Request additional investments from investors and your manufacturer for a large-scale product launch.
12. Raise the additional money needed from traditional sources, such as other private investors, banks, venture capitalists, or public stock offerings.

I asked Craig how much money he would need to sell the product in five to eight stores as a market test. That sum of money was $2,500. I suggested to Craig that he get five investors to invest $500 each for a market test. If his product was as good as he said (I never did learn what the idea actually was), Craig should be able to get $500 investments from independent sales agents in the industry, store owners, family or friends, or work associates. The manufacturer might also be willing to participate with an investment if the idea had merit.

Craig's immediate response was that this was not a good approach because he couldn't possibly make money on this small volume. I explained that a market test isn't designed to make money, it is meant to show that a product will sell so that an inventor can raise the money needed. Consider all the benefits of the small, staged investment for Craig:

1. He would be able to demonstrate that his product would sell in a store.
2. He would have an easy, low-cost entry point for investors.
3. He would improve his negotiating position with his manufacturer.
4. He could show his managerial competence.
5. He would generate momentum for his product.
6. He could overcome the fact that he didn't have money to invest.

The last point is very important. Investors at later stages will look at how much money early investors, including the company founder, have placed into the company. Even if you haven't placed much money into the project, but others have, you will still have an acceptable structure to get more investors.

Staging your money needs—asking for money only when you need it for a specific purpose—will greatly increase your odds of getting money. Asking for a large lump sum, though ideal for the product creator, typically doesn't work. The biggest benefit of finding small investors is that they may be able to help you with your project. Having a sales agent investor will help you introduce the product. Small investors will continue to invest with you to overcome a particular problem. Store owner investors may offer you a chance for a prominent display space that you can use in a photo for a press release.

Plenty of People Are Willing to Be Investors

"I can't get anyone to invest in my idea." Every year thousands of inventors and product creators repeat this same refrain. Is it true? I don't think so. There are thousands of people who want to be part of the next red-hot product. Your job is to make it easy to start investing by offering a low-cost investment option and to convince investors that your venture could be successful. Figure 2-2 details the seven key points you need to demonstrate in order to get investors.

Selling Stock in a Staged Process

The mechanics of selling investments in a staged manner are pretty simple, though you should get a lawyer to help you draft the proper documents. The steps you should follow are:

Figure 2-2   Seven Keys to Getting Investors

1. Look like a winner. Investors have to believe in you and in your partners' capabilities. Be upbeat, don't complain, and present yourself in a professional manner.

2. Show you are investing. If you can't invest, be sure to have some investors who have invested small amounts in your project before asking for a large sum of money.

3. Never show your product or drawings in a rough, unprofessional form. If you have only a rough working model, prepare a nice brochure for presentations or show a good-looking picture.

4. Demonstrate that a product will make money. A product must cost less than 25 percent of the product's selling price. Get price quotes on similar products to show that your product will have a high profit ratio.

5. Prove the product can sell. The best way to do that is to actually get orders for the product. If your product isn't ready to sell, get letters of endorsement—or better yet, investments—from people in the industry. Experienced marketers or retailers are the best choices.

6. Contact a distribution network that will sell your product. You need to show exactly how your product will get to market and that the distribution network will handle the product.

7. Show that investors can get ten times their money back within three to five years. Risks are high and investors need a big potential return.

---

1. Decide to have either one million or two million shares of stock available.

2. Issue 100,000 to 200,000 shares in your name. This does not mean you own 5 to 10 percent of the company. Your share is based on the actual number of shares owned or issued and not the shares available. Investors often prefer the entrepreneur to have a low number of shares compared to the shares available. The low number seems to tell people you are not trying to hog all the profits, but instead are willing to share the company's fortunes with investors. You can raise your stock share later by simply taking stock in lieu of salary or in return for taking a partial salary during the company's first and second years. Granting yourself 20,000 to 25,000 shares per year of stock is not unreasonable if you are not drawing a salary.

3. Offer shares to initial investors at 25¢ to 50¢ a share. You should tell these investors that you plan to charge the next group of investors $1 per share. Constantly raising the price per share demonstrates that your product has momentum, plus it helps investors believe they are getting a good deal.

4. Use the money to achieve some progress with your new product.

5. Approach your original investors, along with new investors, to buy shares at $1 per share. Two points are important at this step. First, you already have people investing with you. That is a big incentive to new investors. Second, the price is up to $1, and your next sale will be at $1.50 per share. This step encourages people to buy while they can get the best price.

You can continue with this process until you are through the transitional sales period, when you'll be able to use more conventional tactics.

If you plan your strategy carefully, you will still keep control of the company. As an example, let's say you start with 100,000 shares and add 25,000 shares per year for your efforts to introduce the product. Your sale of shares would look like this:

	Time Period	Share Activity
1st investment	6 months	100,000 shares issued to founder 10,000 shares sold at 25¢ per share **Total shares 110,000**

Note: Once you take on your first investors you should incorporate, typically as a Subchapter S corporation. You can then list the total number of shares the corporation has (one million) and the number owned by each party. Open a business checking account at this time if you haven't already done so.

2d investment	9 months	20,000 shares sold at 50¢ per share **Total Shares 130,000**
3d investment	12 months	25,000 shares to founder for 1st-year efforts 30,000 shares sold at 75¢ per share **Total shares 185,000** **Founders' shares 125,000**

You can continue in year two in a similar fashion, raising money with stock offerings at increasingly higher prices—for example, at $1.25 and $1.75 per share. Be sure to take another 25,000 in shares in year two for your unpaid efforts. Your only limitation with this financing method is that you can have only ten new nonaccredited investors (an investor who makes less than $200,000 per year or has less than $1 million in assets) per year and fewer than 35 nonaccredited investors in total.

Paul Sullivan of PumpWorks created a seamless pump powered by magnetic pistons. He raised $175,000 using tactics similar to the ones described above to get his product through the transitional sales period, at which point he could use more traditional financing methods. Over a two-and-a-half year period his price rose from 50¢ per share to $3.75 per share. His investors were typically family, friends, and coworkers, most of whom put up $5,000 or less. The momentum of the increasing prices was a big incentive, and the investments of a large group of investors encouraged others to invest.

One often overlooked method of raising money is to use investors as co-signers on a loan. For example, Jim S. received an $80,000 loan from a bank, based on personal guarantees of three of his investors. In return, the company gave the investors 10,000 shares each for making the loan possible, plus the company made the payments for the loan. Jim used this strategy because his investors couldn't afford to put up the $80,000, but their credit was good enough to guarantee the loan.

TRANSITIONAL PERIOD FUNDING

The transitional period is the time during which a product entrepreneur develops a base of sales in a limited geographic area or in a small niche market. At the end of the development period, a product creator has established only that a product *can be* sold. The creator may have sold the product in six or seven stores. Those few sales don't mean that the product can support a viable business; the distribution network is too small.

In your transitional period, you have to develop a minibusiness in a small part of the market. You will be setting up a distribution network, running a small manufacturing operation, and actually making sales in a competitive market. Your minibusiness is not likely to generate enough sales to support you financially, but it will allow you to prove that your product has merit and can support an ongoing business. That proof should enable you to obtain outside financing.

The transitional period is very difficult to finance. You don't have enough sales proof to borrow money. Yet you have to set up the manufacturing, marketing, and sales functions of a small operating company. Throughout the book, I'll explain how to minimize these expenses, but you'll still need $10,000 or more to enter the transitional period.

When you have trouble getting the money you need to start the transition period, there are other tactics for raising money. These tactics include:

- Receiving extended credit from a manufacturer
- Using actual orders to borrow money or find investors
- Selling products for cash
- Selling receivables
- Getting extended terms from suppliers

Each method is described in the following sections.

Receiving Extended Credit from a Manufacturer

Your best chance of getting financing help is receiving what I call *aid-in-kind*, which is when a manufacturer provides services for free or at discounted price that you would otherwise have to pay for.

Dwayne Szot started Arts for All, which manufactures inclusive art products that attach to wheelchairs. Dwayne's products let people with disabilities create large paintings and chalk drawings. They attach to wheelchairs and are mechanically complicated. Dwayne started his project with limited funding and no business experience. Virtually any standard evaluation method would have said Dwayne had little to no chance of introducing his products.

But Dwayne did successfully put his products on the market, and he did it with just one small investor, a modest grant from the Rockefeller Foundation, and plenty of help from manufacturers. When Dwayne started, he struck a deal with a one-man machine shop to rent equipment for a low hourly rate. With this assist, Dwayne was able to make a few early prototypes that he used in art classes for disabled children and adults at the Gillette Hospital for Children in St. Paul. These classes generated interest at Gillette in Dwayne's products. Dwayne was able to sign an agreement that let him use Gillette's model building shop to produce his products in limited production runs. In return, Dwayne promised to do volunteer work at the hospital. This support allowed Dwayne to get through an initial sales and marketing period, during which Dwayne was able to get orders and deliver his products.

But Dwayne was still a long way from being able to enter the transitional sales period and set up an ongoing company. Once Dwayne demonstrated that his products would sell, he was able to convince a manufacturer to sign an exclusive manufacturing agreement in return for $140,000 of in-kind services, including:

- *Free rent for a 2,000-square-foot space*
- *Free manufacturing fixtures and product documentation*

- *An arrangement whereby the manufacturer agreed to buy all raw materials and not bill Dwayne until 30 days after products were built*
- *90-day payment terms*
- *A $60,000 credit line*

These services were just as good as a large investment and allowed Dwayne to keep up his product momentum. Figure 2-3 explains the benefits of in-kind manufacturing assistance.

Using Your Orders to Borrow Money

Ralph Q. created an elaborate plant stand that sold for about $30. Ralph sold about 80 units at various craft fairs, but he couldn't afford to start producing the stand in enough volume to enter the transitional period. Because of his shaky work history, Ralph was unable to borrow money from anyone. Ralph went to another fair and took a $10 deposit on each of 50 orders. He showed the orders to a retailer friend, who then not only lent Ralph enough money to produce the 50 orders, but started to carry Ralph's product.

Your chances of getting a loan from family, friends, or insiders will be greatly enhanced when you have actual orders in hand. Orders seem to make everyone believe that this might be a chance to get in on the ground floor of a winning company.

Sharon DeCarlo received an order from QVC and Mary Ellen's Products for a combined total of 4,000 units with just prototypes. Once she had the orders she was able to get financing help from her brother and friends, and she was able to line up a manufacturer to help her.

If you plan to use this tactic, try to bunch together as many orders as possible, even if you have to hold shipments for two or three weeks. Every additional order will improve your chances of raising money.

Selling Your Product for Cash

One of the biggest investments you will make is for operating cash, which covers the time between when you pay for materials to make your prod-

Figure 2-3 In-Kind Financing from Manufacturers

Why are manufacturers willing to offer product creators such good deals? Primarily because this is also a good deal for them. Some of the benefits to manufacturers include:

1. A per-unit profit is made on every product they manufacture for you.

2. Profits on their own products are increased by reducing their per-unit overhead costs. Manufacturers divide their overhead (or fixed costs) among all their products. For example, a company with $25,000 in overhead that produces 250,000 products per year might place a 10¢-per-unit overhead cost onto each product. If you help the manufacturer raise its volume to 300,000 units, you've lowered the overhead cost on every unit in the manufacturer's plant.

3. New products are provided for the manufacturer. Companies have to keep coming up with new product ideas or they will go out of business. Your product helps keep the manufacturing cycle going.

4. A company's new product risks are decreased. New products are risky ventures no matter who introduces them. When a manufacturer works with an inventor, its costs are lower, because it has someone else doing the work it would otherwise need to do or pay for on its own.

5. Free marketing assistance is provided. Small manufacturers often have no marketing staff and little marketing experience, and, as a result, they aren't able to effectively introduce new products. You can help bridge this gap.

Small manufacturers might have four or five failures for every success. They understand the risks of new products and need you to prove only that you have a good plan and a good chance of success in order to help you out.

uct and when you get paid for the product. You can greatly reduce your operating cash requirements by getting cash at the time you sell the product, rather than using the more common method of accepting payment in 30 or 60 days. You can get cash through down payments and by selling on a cash-on-delivery (COD) basis.

In the previous example, Ralph was able to get $10 down payments. You can also get down payments or COD terms from small retailers (especially on initial orders) and industrial companies. Some small businesses, such as convenience stores, pay for a significant number of products with cash. You can often get a down payment anytime you are selling to small companies or anytime there is a large number of small vendors in a market. When I worked in the semiconductor industry, for example, about 15 to 20 percent of small suppliers requested a 25 to 50 percent down payment.

You also might be able to trade off an exclusive distribution agreement for an up-front payment. Steve K. created a unique patio swing for two. Steve sold about 40 units at fairs and home shows, but he didn't have the money to move ahead until he struck a deal with a small chain of patio stores to give him a 25 percent down payment in return for exclusive distribution in its market.

Another option is to concentrate on selling product for cash to consumers. For example, Victor Toso and Stuart Spector sell annually about 75,000 of their $35 Nada chairs to consumers, primarily at trade shows. Victor and Stuart developed their product while they were learning to meditate. Meditation relaxed them mentally, but sitting on the floor in the lotus position gave them very sore backs. They created a sling that goes around the legs and back when a person is seated. The support from the legs prevents slouching and, consequently, reduces the problem of backaches. Victor and Stuart decided to market their product after they learned that it was effective for secretaries, computer operators, and anyone else who sat in a straightbacked chair.

Their product has a very unusual appearance, and it was difficult to get investors. Victor and Stuart got started by setting up booths at trade shows and demonstrating the product. The demonstration helped sell it, and the cash sales helped keep the business operating.

Selling Your Receivables

When you sell a product for terms, the customer doesn't have to pay you until the end of the period specified by the terms. For example, if you sell a product with 30-day terms, the customer won't have to pay you for 30 days. When a customer has taken delivery but hasn't yet paid for the product, you have a receivable: an amount of money you expect to receive in the near future. You can sell a receivable to a commercial finance company for 88 to 95 percent of the receivable's value. If a company owes you $100 for a shipment you've made, you can sell the receivable for $88 to $95. The advantage of selling receivables is that you can get a fast cash turnaround. The disadvantage is that you are relinquishing a significant portion of your profits.

You can find commercial finance companies in the Yellow Pages of your phone book or by looking for ads in local business newspapers or magazines. You can also find them at trade shows geared toward small companies.

Another variation of selling receivables is to offer a discount for prompt payment. You could offer a 7.5 percent discount for payment on delivery or 5 percent 10/net 30 terms, which means a buyer will receive a 5 percent discount for payment within 10 days or pay the full amount within 30 days.

Clyde and Jamie Leach and their company, C. J. Leacho, supply an example of how a product survives through the transition period. Clyde and Jamie's product was the Wiggle Wrap, a cloth restraint with a Velcro closing, originally designed to keep their baby son safely seated in a high chair.

The development phase of a product like the Wiggle Wrap is inexpensive because early models, prototypes, and even the first production runs can be made at home. The Leaches were able to fund the initial product testing with their personal savings. Then they sold 8 percent of their company to get enough money to buy materials for larger production runs. The Leaches also arranged a deal with a contract manufacturer, which kept down their costs for manufacturing and packaging equipment.

However, the Leaches didn't have enough operating cash to support their business during its beginning transition period, when sales were $1,100 per month. They sold their receivables to a commercial finance company at a 5 percent discount. This allowed them to keep cash coming into the business, and it helped Wiggle Wrap's sales to grow, in only two years, to $25,000 per month.

Note that the Leaches had to give up a part of the company to obtain investors. Many entrepreneurs get greedy and don't want to sell off parts of their companies. They're making a big mistake. In the transition period, a new product creator can't survive without enough money. Being able to line up investors may determine whether a product can be taken to market. Owning a share of an ongoing business is better than owning all of a business that can't get off the ground.

Getting Credit from Suppliers

Another tactic for cutting operating cash requirements is to receive credit, or terms, from suppliers. Before you choose a supplier, explain how you are starting to increase sales. Then tell the supplier that you need 90-day payment terms to fund your growth. Not every supplier will grant you extended terms, and most will probably offer only 30 days (rather than requiring cash on delivery), but every bit of extended terms will help. Suppliers might also become investors, if you can show them how your sales growth will help their businesses.

FINANCING THE GROWTH STAGES

Once you survive the transition period and have established a solid minibusiness, you'll be able to grow your company into a full-scale production company. Chapter 17 covers all the different financing approaches you can use to support a business's rapid growth cycle.

3

DROP YOUR PARANOIA: TALK ABOUT YOUR PRODUCT IDEA!

Susan B. and Linda R. thought they had a million-dollar idea. As workers in retail stores, they noticed that the stores had a haphazard way of shipping merchandise between branch locations. Linda and Susan (an MBA in market research) set out to see whether their idea had potential. After interviewing every major retail chain in their area, they decided that a service business that delivered merchandise between branch stores had tremendous potential.

After only six weeks and expenditures of $35,000, the women were out of business. Why? When they did their market research, the women were afraid to explain their idea thoroughly; they were sure someone would try to steal it. They never asked potential customers whether they would buy their service. Instead, they asked whether they transferred merchandise. Linda and Susan found out too late that stores do transfer merchandise but weren't willing to pay to have it done.

One out of 500 product entrepreneurs successfully markets his or her product. One out of 3,000 product ideas becomes commercialized. These odds underline the two main reasons I caution against being overly concerned about secrecy:

1. Manufacturers, sales representatives, and distributors all know the odds of success are long, and they are rarely motivated to steal an unproven idea.

2. Product creators must thoroughly test their products, which means they have to show them to people who will either sell or buy their ideas.

WILL YOUR IDEA BE STOLEN?

Ideas occasionally are stolen, but the time to worry about theft is after you've started to sell the product, not when the idea is in the concept or prototype stage. Someone who steals an idea in the concept stage won't be sure the idea will sell and will have to do all the work necessary to introduce the product.

By waiting, a thief will save money on product testing and will more than likely be able to steal the idea legally. To steal most product ideas, all that's necessary is to change a few features. For example, Mr. Coffee was the first coffeemaker on the market, and it was introduced with several patents. Now, five to ten different but similar products are available. Many product entrepreneurs would say that Mr. Coffee's competitors stole the original idea. Most businesspeople would say that Mr. Coffee encountered some competition. The company that introduced Mr. Coffee took all the risks of a product introduction. After the product started to take off, competitors entered the market. There is nothing illegal about competing against a patented product, as long as enough modifications are made to avoid infringing on the product's patents.

There are three reasons why your idea probably won't be stolen:

1. Nobody knows what products will sell. Ninety percent of companies' introductions fail, and those products were chosen by experienced marketing people. A potential thief won't be able to look at your idea and know for sure that it's worth stealing.

2. People who know how to promote products have plenty to choose from. They don't have to steal ideas. A marketer who is looking for products to promote can easily find 50 to 60 every year, and many of those products can be bought cheaply from down-and-out product creators.

3. A large initial investment isn't required to buy a product idea. Ideas are usually not bought outright. Instead, they are purchased under an arrangement that pays the product creator a royalty in a range of 2 to 15 percent of the net sales of a product. A person who has a 5 percent royalty agreement would receive $5,000 for every $100,000 of sales. If the product doesn't sell, then the idea's buyer

loses only the advance to the product creator, which is usually only $1,000 to $10,000. If the product is a big seller, then everyone makes money.

There isn't much motivation for a person or company to steal an idea.

WHY YOU SHOULD SHOW YOUR IDEA

There is plenty of motivation for a product creator to show an idea. The first advantage is that essential input can be gathered from the people who will buy, sell, or make the product. These people know whether similar products were previously introduced and the market's reaction to those products. They can provide key information about how your new product could be marketed.

I worked as a marketer for a dental company for seven years, taking potential new products to dentists, dealers, and the company's sales force. I never felt that I knew everything there was to know about a product or its market, and I never failed to uncover a key piece of new information while showing a new product idea.

Another advantage to showing your idea is that it gives you a way to make vital contacts. Many key people will offer helpful input when you tell them you're doing market research. Those same people may not even agree to see you when you say you are trying to sell a product.

When I was in the dental business, Dr. James Pride created a new concept for placing equipment in a dental office in a way that increased a dentist's efficiency. Dr. Pride was offering seminars around the country and had become quite influential. When we were designing a new piece of dental cabinetry, we asked Dr. Pride to come to our plant and evaluate how well our cabinets would work for his office concept. We told Dr. Pride that we would welcome any product changes he might suggest. Dr. Pride benefited because he had the opportunity to influence products that would actually be sold on the market. We benefited because Dr. Pride was a valuable contact. I seriously doubt that we could have made much progress with Dr. Pride if we had been trying to sell him equipment that we had designed.

PATENTS

Most product creators, as well as the media, tend to worship the power of the almighty patent. Unfortunately, the patent system, as it relates to individual inventors, provides much less benefit than most inventors expect. As a result, people are probably wasting over $100 million every year in needless patent applications and litigation.

The original purpose of the patent system was to discourage secrecy. The intent was for inventors to disclose their inventions so that other people could use the new technology in other products. For example, a new development in rifle-sight technology could, through information disclosed in the patent, eventually be incorporated into microscope equipment. In return for helping other inventors, a patent was awarded to the original inventor. He could then sue anyone who, without permission, tried to market or manufacture the original product. The goal of the patent system was to share technology—an admirable goal, and one that still exists to some degree in high-technology fields.

How could such a system hurt product entrepreneurs? The problem arises from the word *novel*; to receive a patent, one is supposed to have a product that is novel or unique. I believe that the authors of the U.S. Constitution (particularly Article I, Section 8) thought *novel* meant a significant technological breakthrough. I'm not sure what *novel* means today. Virtually any product seems to be able to receive a patent, if the claims are written cleverly enough.

The disposable kitty-litter box provides an example of how far the patent system has sunk. Between February 28, 1989, and October 3, 1989, a period of just over seven months, patents were issued for nine disposable kitty-litter boxes. Each of these boxes had some differences from the others, but I'd hardly call them novel, especially since there were already several disposable kitty-litter boxes on the market.

Most product creators don't understand what patents do for them. They believe that a patent on a disposable kitty-litter box, for example, gives them the right to be the sole manufacturers and sellers of disposable kitty-litter boxes. That's not what patent holders receive at all! They receive the right to sue anyone who makes or sells their *specific* product designs. There may be hundreds of patentable designs for any given product. You can prove this point by going to any large store and looking at competitive products in each section. All of them may have patent numbers listed, even though consumers identify all the products as one category.

I once got an irate letter from a patent examiner who didn't like an attack I had published on the patent system and the word *novel*, which he interprets as just "different." In fact, Webster's dictionary defines *novel* as "strikingly different." And what does the patent examiner think of that definition? I will let him tell you in his own words:

> Do you think for one minute that a government agency could possibly run less "amok," if we were to require some holier-than-thou government official to sit in judgment of the relative significance of every invention, as you have on these nine? That's an absurd proposition.

The Patent Office doesn't decide if you get a patent on how novel or advanced or beneficial your idea is. It only has to be different. According to William Kovensky, a Washington, D.C., patent attorney, even in cases where a broad patent is not available, he is able to obtain a patent for a certain aspect of the invention—the way a hook is configured, for example, or the way a hinge is used. Next time you encounter someone who thinks getting a patent means you have a significant invention, show the person this section. And, whatever you do, don't walk up to an experienced new-product marketer and say that you have three patents. Marketers might treat you nicely, but they are probably writing you off as just another naive inventor.

PATENTS DO HAVE THEIR PLACE

There are cases in which patents are valuable and you should pursue them. As a reference, I've included Figure 3-1, which explains how to determine if a patent has a strong business value.

Strong patents are those in which claims are very broad or detail the most effective or only way an invention can work. Patents have other benefits, such as delaying competitive product introductions. In many cases, patents can also help you raise money or license your idea.

Delaying Competitive Product Introductions

For complex products, patents slow up competitors because they need to redesign products to avoid infringing on the patents. This can give a company a head start of a year or two in the market.

When I worked for a dental supply company, dental handpieces, the tools dentists use to drill teeth, were one of our products. A competitor introduced a patented fiber-optic handpiece that had a small light next to the drill bit, a feature that gave dentists better visibility. It took our company nine months to perfect a new design, nine more months to complete the tooling, and another three months to introduce our version of the fiber-optic handpiece. In effect, the patent gave our competitor extra time as a sole supplier of an innovative product.

Manufacturers take this strategy one step further when they use patent-pending status. A patent is a public document, in which competitors can see what your claims are. When a patent is pending, all details about it are secret. Companies like to wait to finalize their patent applications until just before the products are introduced. Thus, competitors first

Figure 3-1   Determining the Business Value of a Patent

The value of a patent is totally dependent on its claims. You need to be able to evaluate those claims. Follow these simple steps to gauge a patent's true worth.

> **Step 1.** Don't worry about the legalese in a patent's description. The claims are the only part of a patent you really need to read, and that section is usually not that long. The claims are the only part of the patent that offers protection.

> **Step 2.** Follow the patent until you come to a line that states "What is claimed is," or "We claim," or a similar statement. This statement will be listed in the "Detailed Description" of the invention, but it won't be called out by a major heading of any sort.

> **Step 3.** Call out the key words and phrases in the first (and main) product claim. For instance, the key product words in the claim on the next page are: "hook," "support plate," "strap," "loop on strap and aperture," and "individual, spaced apart raised ribs." The number of key product phrases in a claim is important, because to violate your patent someone has to include in the invention every one of the features represented by the key words. Patents with claims that have a large number of key phrases are weak. A strong patent is one with a straightforward, simple claim with one or two key words or phrases. For example, a claim stating "the use of subzero temperatures to improve the compressive strength of metal products" has just one key product phrase—"subzero temperatures"—and is a broad, strong claim.

> **Step 4.** Decide if there is any way to make the product without substituting an alternative feature for any of the features listed in the claim. For example, one of the features listed as a key phrase in the patent claim is a strap. Could you substitute another feature for the strap—such as a snap-on holder? If you can, you then are able to get around the patent claim. At one seminar I conducted, people came up with over 20 ways to get around the patent claim that follows. If a patent doesn't stop competition, it doesn't have much value.

PATENT CLAIMS—PATENT #4,969,580

What is claimed is:

1. A hanger support apparatus for use in a shower with a bottle having a neck at one end thereof, said one end having an end wall

(Continued)

Figure 3-1 *Continued*

that extends laterally of the neck to a side wall of such bottle (*so far, this is just a hanging device for a shampoo bottle*), said hanger comprising a frame, said frame being elongated along a longitudinal axis and having a *hook* (*anything other than a hook would not infringe on this patent*), means for supporting the frame at one end thereof, and a *support plate* at the opposite end thereof, said *support plate* extending generally at right angles to the longitudinal axis of the frame (*the invention calls for a plate at a right angle to the frame; there are dozens of other ways to hold a shampoo bottle*) . . . the means for retaining a bottle on said frame comprising a *strap* that surrounds the frame with a method of adjustably securing said strap comprising a *loop at one end* of said strap having an aperture there through that is a selected dimension measured in direction along the length of such strap and the opposite end portion of said strap having a *plurality of individual raised ribs . . .*

This is a patent for a product that holds a shampoo bottle. Now go into your closet and get a hanger. Push the sides of the hanger together so you have the hanger hook on top and the rest of the hanger hanging straight down. Put your hand on the bottom of the hanger and bend it up. You now have a shampoo holder. You have a hook, but none of the other features of this claim, and therefore you should be able to introduce this shampoo holder without infringing on this original patent.

have to wait for the patents to be issued, see what the claims are, and then redesign the products.

Your Design Is the Only One That Will Work

A patent offers protection for your specific product design. The patent doesn't offer much value if your idea can be easily produced with another design. But it offers a great deal of value if your design is the only one that actually works. A wind surfboard needs a mast that swivels and flops over at a 90-degree angle. For several years only one mechanism let the mast work properly. That mechanism's patents were potentially very valuable.

You can run into many problems, even when you have a strong patent. Figure 3-2 outlines some of the potential pitfalls patent holders face.

RECENT CHANGES IN PATENT LAW

In 1995 the U.S. patent laws were changed, much to the detriment of inventors. Prior to 1995, a patent could be applied for only by the original

Figure 3-2   Problems with Patents

1. Patents are expensive. A utility patent can cost anywhere from $5,000 to $15,000 and sometimes even more.

2. You have to be careful that you patent the right product. If you patent an idea early and then need to make product modifications, you may find that your patent no longer applies to your actual product.

3. The U.S. Patent Office does not guarantee the validity of a patent. You could go to court on an infringement suit and have your patent overturned.

4. The only person who enforces a patent is the patent holder. If you find someone infringing on your patent, it is up to you to take action. Infringing on a patent is not a criminal offense. Your only recourse is civil action.

5. Defending a patent can be very expensive. Typical lawsuits start at $20,000 and can go into the millions. Ken Hakuta invented the Wacky Wall Walker and he has had to spend much of his $10 million in earnings on legal fees to defend his patent.

6. Patent suits can take a very long time before being finalized. Jerome Lemelson sued Mattel, claiming Mattel's Hot Wheel Track that features 360-degree loops infringed on one of his patents. Jerome filed his suit in 1977 and finally won it in 1989.

inventor, and the inventor had a one-year grace period in which to apply for a patent after a product was placed in the public domain, which means the product, or information about the product, was made available to the public in some way. Selling the product, sending out press releases, and displaying the product at a trade show would all be putting a product into the public domain. This "first-to-invent" patent process and one-year grace period in place prior to 1995 allowed inventors to test their ideas, finalize product design, and prove their products would sell before applying for patents.

In 1995 the patent process changed to a "first-to-file" process, which means whoever files first is awarded the patent. The U.S. Patent Office has come out with a provisional patent, which allows you to have a one-year delay in filing a formal patent application. Unfortunately, the provisional patent application requires the same written description of the invention as a regular patent application. Since the written description includes the claims, it should be prepared by a patent attorney. The net result is that the provisional patent will cost you almost as much as a regular patent application. Technically, a provisional patent doesn't need to include claims, but without them it doesn't offer much protection against potential patents filed by other inventors.

Today an inventor taking a year's delay in introducing a product runs the risk of someone else filing first. In some cases, this risk is unacceptable and the inventor should get a patent first, especially if he or she plans on licensing the idea.

One good feature did come out of the new patent laws. You can now file a Patent Cooperation Treaty (PCT) application, which costs from $2,500 to $3,500, but gives you 18 months to apply for foreign patents after you apply for a U.S. patent. This is a big advantage over the old system, in which you had to apply for all the foreign patents at the same time as you applied for a U.S. patent. Since the cost of foreign patents can easily exceed $100,000, foreign patents formerly were out of reach for most inventors and small companies. The new laws also make international patent rights more affordable, as you can now apply for all European patents through the European Patent Office for just one fee.

STEPS TO TAKE

Deciding how to handle your patent invention is much more difficult with the new patent laws. But it still can be done. The key fact to remember is that you can't afford to spend $5,000 to $10,000 on a patent unless it provides you significant economic benefits. You don't need a patent to introduce a product; in fact, many products on the market don't have patents. So don't spend the money unless the patent can pay for itself.

Step 1: Keep a Notebook

For each project you start, buy a bound notebook—preferably one with numbered pages. If the pages are not numbered, number them yourself. The engineering notebooks or accountants' ledgers sold in office supply stores are ideal. As evidence of your activity, everything you do should be entered into the notebook, in sequence, and dated. This includes drawings, ideas you consider, and discussions with vendors or customers. Include the date and time of each event and note if the interaction was in person or on the telephone. Every week or so, have someone read each page and then sign and date the bottom with the notation, "I have read and understood this page." This notebook documents your progress and can be useful with potential partners and investors. It can also be useful in case you need to demonstrate that you invented the idea and didn't just take it from someone else.

Step 2: Keep Your Idea Confidential

Ask a contact to sign a confidential statement anytime you show your idea before it is ready to introduce. The appendix to this book has a sample confidential form, or you can get one from a book of legal forms or your attorney. In some cases, people will not sign a form. If you are just asking someone for market feedback or an investment, I'd recommend that you ask the person to keep the idea confidential and then send a letter reminding the person to keep your idea secret. If you are trying to license your idea, you might want to get a patent first. A confidential statement is not a patent, and it can be difficult, if not impossible, to enforce. Fortunately, most people will honor the agreement.

Step 3: Make the Go/No-Go Decisions

The go/no-go decisions (Chapters 6 through 10) provide a preliminary analysis to decide if an idea is worth pursuing at all. Many ideas fail this analysis or need substantial modifications before they pass.

Step 4: Determine the Product's Potential Life

If your product is a fad and likely to be on the market just for a year or two, I wouldn't worry too much about a patent. Competitors won't have time to duplicate your product before the fad is over. If your product could be on the market for an extended period of time, you should consider getting a patent.

Step 5: Determine if a Patent Will Produce an Additional $100,000 to $200,000 in Sales

That's the approximate dollar amount in sales necessary to generate enough profit to pay for the patent. If you are in a small, limited market with little competition, having a patent may not produce any more sales.

Step 6: Decide if a Broad Patent Claim Is Possible

In most cases, you don't actually patent a product idea, you patent your specific product design. In some instances, however, you may be able to get broad patent protection. For example, the first wind surfboard may have had a broad patent claim that would say, in effect, "a board-type device with a mast attached in the center with said mast having a horizontal bar and with said mast and bar being capable of accepting a sail with said board able to have a person stand on the board and move the mast and sail component to direct travel of the device." This is considered a broad claim because certain features, such as how the mast is attached or how the sail-mast combination moves, are not listed.

Patents with broad claims are strong, because a wide variety of specific designs may infringe on that patent. If you have a chance for a broad claim, you should see a patent attorney. Before seeing an attorney, do a computer patent search on the Internet or at a patent depository library (see the section on patent searches at the end of this chapter). If other patents have been issued on your type of product—for instance, in the case of the wind surfboard, a previous patent on any board-sail combination—it may prevent you from obtaining a broad patent claim. You still may be able to get a patent with a narrower claim, but they are much less valuable. If you think there is a chance of getting a broad claim, visit a patent attorney and get his or her opinion in writing. That will help you get an investor if you need one to apply for your patent. You could be forgoing a substantial business asset if you bypass a product that can receive broad patent protection.

Step 7: Decide on the Potential Value of Your Specific Claims

You may have specific design claims that still offer good protection, if your design allows a product feature that would be hard to duplicate. For example, at the dental company I worked for, we designed a vibratory root canal cleaner. We utilized a standard air turbine used in dental drills to drive our product. Our patent called for the use of air turbines. A competitor would have had to design a completely new driving mechanism. This would have been expensive and difficult to do, and, as a result, our patent prevented competition.

To decide if your product design could have a significant feature, list all the components of your invention. In the patent discussed in Figure 3-1, the features were a strap, a support plate, a hook, a loop on the strap with an aperture (opening), and individual spaced-apart ribs. Next, decide if you could produce the same result with another design. For example, you might use a strap with a loop or a solid circle, or you might just have an open frame that could go over the showerhead. If other designs could easily be substituted for yours, your patent will have limited business value.

Figure 3-3   Questions to Ask Patent Attorneys

1. *Is my product eligible for a broad claim? Note:* Do a computer patent search or a low-cost patent search prior to seeing the attorney. He or she will need to see that data before offering an opinion.

2. *Will you be able to have a single-feature claim?* To return to the example of the shampoo holder, a single-feature claim would be the use of a strap to hold the shampoo bottle. Single-feature claims are better than multifeature claims because another product has to avoid only one of many features listed to get around the patent. Multifeature claims typically don't offer much competitive advantage.

3. *To what degree would a competitor have to change your product to avoid your potential patent?*

4. *Which of your features would a patent protect?* List your features by priority before you go into the attorney's office, then ask which features are going to be claimed in the patent. Make sure your important features can be claimed. If you can cover only minor features, your patent will be of limited value.

5. *Will any of the patents you've uncovered prevent you from selling your product?* Just because you can't patent your product doesn't necessarily mean you can't sell it. But be sure to check with the attorney first.

6. *If you do get a patent, would the attorney be willing to take a patent infringement case on a contingency basis?* If not, you could be looking at a minimum cost of $20,000 just to get a suit started.

7. *What parts of the product can't be changed without losing protection, once you've applied for the patent?* This will tell you what changes will require additional expensive patent work. Be sure you are confident that your features are right for the market before applying for a patent.

If you believe that any of your features could have significant value, see a patent attorney to get an informed opinion. Figure 3-3 lists questions you should ask a patent attorney to determine whether any specific feature will provide strong protection against competition. Again, get this opinion in writing if it's positive, so you can show it to an investor.

If you can't get an investor and can't afford the patent yourself, still proceed with your idea. You run the risk of losing the idea, but the risk is probably less than 10 percent. Make some money on this idea, and then be in a position to patent your next idea.

Step 8: Consider a Copyright

Copyrights cost only $20 and they can be useful on some products. You can get a copyright on something you publish—a book, a song, game rules, or instructions—but you can also get a copyright on a graphic design, a game board, a T-shirt design, a doll, or a product's appearance. Request an information booklet from:

Registrar of Copyrights
Copyright Office
Library of Congress
Washington, DC 20059

The hot line for forms is 202-707-0700.

Step 9: Apply for a Patent Yourself

If it turns out that you won't get significant patent protection, you can apply for a patent yourself. You should apply for significant patents through an attorney, but if that is not possible, I don't think it matters much if you have a well-written or poorly written patent.

The advantages of filing for a patent yourself are, first, that it costs you only $365 to apply for a utility patent yourself. Through an attorney, the cost will be $3,000 or more for a utility patent. A design patent costs only $150. The second reason is that there are benefits to having a product in the patent-pending phase. It delays competition, looks good to investors, and is helpful if you are trying to license your idea. It will cost you about $600 to $700 to have the patent issued. But you don't need to do that; you can just let your application expire.

An excellent book to read if you want to patent your own idea is *Patent It Yourself* by David Pressman (Berkeley, Calif.: Nolo Press, 1992).

PATENT SEARCHES

There are many ways to do a patent search on your own, especially now that the Internet is becoming readily available at small business development centers and even copy centers such as Kinko's. You should learn how to do a preliminary search yourself, because it can save you $300 to $800.

Find Out Your Patent Classification Number

One of the more difficult tasks with a patent search can be determining the correct classification. Some products fit neatly into a classification, but others don't. You can get the correct classification from the Patent Search Room at the U.S. Patent Office. Prepare a one- or two-page report containing:

- Features of your idea, including how it is or will be constructed
- How the product idea will work
- Intended uses or purposes of the idea
- Rough sketch of the idea, viewed from all sides, with each part of the idea labeled in a fashion similar to the patent drawing in the appendix of this book

Send these documents to the patent office and request that they tell you the correct classification number. There is no fee for this service. Just send the information to:

Branch Chief
Patent Search Room
U.S. Patent and Trademark Office
Crystal Plaza 3—Room 1AO1
Washington, DC 20231
Fax 703-305-5491

You'll get a response in two to six weeks. You can start your search without this information, but still send for it. That way if you did search in the wrong classification you can come back and do another search.

Doing Your Search

The best place to do a patent search is at a patent depository library. These are public libraries throughout the country that contain microfiche copies of patent office records. Call up your local public library and ask if it is a patent depository library. If it is not, ask where the closest one is. These libraries typically have classes once or twice a month on doing your own patent search.

If you don't have access to a patent depository library, you can do a patent search on the Internet. These searches generally rely on matching key words, and, as a rule, they are not as effective as a direct search at a library, because a competing patent may not use any of your key words. For example, the key words "shampoo holder" may miss many patents that don't use that term. A shampoo bottle may be referred to as a "1- to 2-inch cylindrical bottle," and the holder might be referred to as a "vertical holder with hook."

Another way to do a patent search is to go directly to the U.S. Patent Office's Internet home page at *http://www.uspto.gov/*. Click on the category

General Patent and Trademark Information, and you'll go into another directory where you can click onto Patents. Follow the screen's instructions, and you can do a patent search that will turn up prior patents on your idea.

The Patent Office gives you only an abstract of the patent on the Internet, so if you want more information about the patent you'll need to send $3, along with the patent number, to the U.S. Patent Office in order to receive complete patent documentation. The address is:

U.S. Department of Commerce
Patent and Trademark Office
Washington, DC 20231

You can also get patent documents through the Yahoo index at *http://www.yahoo.com,* which is a topical index of the World Wide Web, showing complete patents. However, it is somewhat limited because it is arranged by topics, and patents don't always follow topics. A second index that's helpful is the Lycos index at *http://lycos.cs.cmu.edu/,* which is a key-word index on the Web. Lycos has the additional advantage of calling up magazine articles and press releases about new products, which will help you develop a profile of competitive companies.

If you don't have access to the Internet, find a friend who does or check in your Yellow Pages. In almost every big city there are companies that sell time on the Internet. You can also call your state's small business development center or commerce department to find an Internet location.

Locating Low-Cost Patent Searches

If you don't think you can do a patent search yourself, there are several low-cost sources for patent searches. Look in the classified ad section in magazines such as *Popular Mechanics* and you'll see ads for patent searches from patent agents. You can also check the Yellow Pages of your phone book under "patent attorneys" or "patent searches." Often you'll see patent agents from Washington, D.C., or Virginia, who will offer much lower prices.

4

PROFESSIONALISM: KNOW WHAT YOU'RE DOING

Leo S. created a product that removed cracked oil filters from the standard oil filter clamp. Over 95 percent of the time, an oil filter clamp, which fits over the outside of an oil filter, will twist off, leaving the filter intact. Sometimes, however, the filter is stuck on so tightly that the clamp cracks the filter's housing, leaving a big mess—and the filter still won't come out. Leo's product fit into the broken housing and removed the filter.

Leo had market-tested the product and felt it could sell at retail for no more than $45. Leo's initial production run yielded a manufacturing cost of $28. A distributor approached Leo about carrying the product. Leo said yes, but only if the distributor would agree to buy the product at $40 and then sell it for no more than $45. Needless to say, the deal fell through. The distributor needed at least a 50 percent markup before the product would be carried. Leo should have sold the distributor the product at $30, a tactic that would have developed a sales base to grow from, and then worked toward cutting his manufacturing cost.

Product entrepreneurs have to realize that, before they can sell an idea, they first have to sell themselves. They must convince people that they are persons who will be reliable business partners. Only then will they get an interested audience for a marketable idea.

What should Leo have done? First, he should have leveled with the distributor, telling his contact that he'd love to sell through him but he had a problem. His cost was $28 and his research found that the market price should be only $45. There just wasn't enough margin to sell through a distributor. Leo could state that he wasn't sure how to proceed, though he'd like to work with the distributor if at all possible. Several results could have come out of the conversations. The distributor might have:

- Wanted to try selling the product at a higher price
- Tried a test run at $45 anyway, as long as Leo would work long term toward a lower price
- Helped Leo get a better production price from another manufacturer
- Agreed to try Leo's product later once he could offer better pricing

Unfortunately, examples like Leo's aren't isolated. In fact, they are common. Not only do you hurt yourself by not knowing what you're doing, you hurt every other inventor. Leo's distributor contact never came back to Leo, and the contact is probably soured on inventors forever. One of the reasons I stress professionalism so much is that most inventors start out being perceived negatively, and that perception is an obstacle you need to overcome.

ATTITUDE

You must project four attitude characteristics to every contact, if you want to receive maximum cooperation and have the best possible chance of turning a contact into an investor. Your attitude must say, in effect:

I am appreciative.
I have perseverance.
I am open to suggestions.
I can cope when things go wrong.

By projecting your attitude in each conversation or letter, you'll be able to establish solid, ongoing relationships with all of your contacts.

Being Appreciative

Throughout the introduction process, you will be dealing with people who have seen many products come and go. They'll know that your chances of success are slim, but they'll also know that some products do make money. Most people will help you, provided you make their experience with you enjoyable.

Be sure to thank people for the time they spend working on a project with you. Explain to them how you need their help and expertise. After the meeting, send a thank-you note.

Persevering

You've probably read that entrepreneurs need pluck and luck to succeed. Pluck is another word for perseverance. The line between perseverance and recklessness can be quite thin. A product entrepreneur who spends $50,000 on an idea, against progress that is worth only $2,000, is not showing perseverance.

You can use several methods to convince people that you won't be discouraged by obstacles that you might encounter.

1. Take the time to research the idea (or hire a professional research service). If you can show that you've taken the time needed to really look into an idea, you'll start to convince people that you're serious about getting it onto the market.
2. Develop three or four models or prototypes. This effort will show you are willing to devote time and energy to the quality of the idea or product.
3. Put together a team of three or four people, each with different skills, to work on the project. This approach will show that you know hard work lies ahead and you have taken steps to be sure the work gets done right.
4. Discuss freely other difficult projects you brought to completion.

Perseverance is an intangible quality that is difficult to prove in advance. Still, people will see that you are dedicated to your project and that you know the difficulties of introducing it.

Welcoming Suggestions

The goal in a project's early stages is to obtain input so that you can understand how people are likely to react to an idea. Most people won't give accurate input unless they believe a product entrepreneur is open to suggestions. To receive valid input, you must learn to listen closely to people's comments, take notes, and ask clarifying questions.

This sounds like simple advice, but eight out of ten product creators I talk to don't listen at all. They spend their time telling people how great their ideas are, and they argue with anyone who is bold enough to mention any of the products' shortcomings.

Listening to people's criticisms can be very difficult. I remember the first time I did a product brochure. I spent a month on the preliminary layout before I sent it out for evaluation. I was devastated when the brochure came back with suggested changes. We all feel vulnerable when our work is evaluated by someone else.

When you're interviewing people to get feedback, use clarifying questions to determine exactly what the people are telling you. For example, if someone mentions that a product doesn't look like it's worth $20, follow up that comment with: "What makes the product look like it's not worth $20?" or "Why do you say that?" Asking clarifying questions will give you valuable information and will show that you're open to suggestion.

Not asking enough questions can cost you a lot of money. Cameron E. created a little piece of tape that wrapped around the spokes of a bike. The tape was flashy and appealed to kids, and it had the potential of being an outstanding promotional item for a chain of convenience stores or a soda manufacturer. A buyer told Cameron: "This is the type of product we like. Last year, we bought 20,000 units of a similar item. Be sure to stop back when your product is ready." Cameron interpreted that to mean the buyer would buy 20,000 units once the product was on the market.

In reality, the buyer was only telling him to come back when the product was available. Cameron missed the following key points by not asking enough clarifying questions:

- *The product purchased last year had its price discounted 70 percent. Cameron couldn't afford that large a discount.*
- *The buyer's boss approves all large orders. The buyer couldn't project what his boss would think of the idea.*
- *The chain ran only one big promotion per year. Typically, as many as ten products were considered for each promotion.*

Being open to suggestion does not mean that you must consider making all the changes people propose. Keep a clear vision of what the final product should be, but gather reactions to know whether an idea will sell.

Coping

Contacts will be wondering how well you will cope with the inevitable problems encountered by product entrepreneurs. Coping with problems is another intangible trait that's hard to prove in advance. A tactic for showing how you can cope is to offer contacts a short explanation of your activities every time you call them. Some examples of short explanations are:

> I've narrowed down my list of potential contract manufacturers to three.
>
> I've completed the initial phase of my product research.
>
> I've completed field-testing of the product at six different sites.
>
> I've finalized the layout for the package.
>
> I've started my initial contract negotiations with several key distributors.

Your summaries should be extremely brief; omit details of the obstacles you had to overcome. The message is that you expected problems and you solved them in a businesslike manner. Giving a short summary shows that you are in control of your project and that it is moving along.

Maintaining Ongoing Relationships

You should keep in touch with all your contacts. Calling them periodically shows that they're important to you and establishes a pattern in which you call on a routine basis. Contacts will then feel that they're part of your project and that you don't call only when you need help.

Whenever you start a project, start a contact file. Include a person's name, address, phone number, and capacity for possible future help. Record the date, time, and agenda each time you talk. If a contact tells you to call "my Uncle Fred," by all means make up a contact card and call him. You never know when someone might be a key contact in helping you to put your idea on the market. *Making these initial contacts during the development phase of a project is critical.* Rapport with key people has to be established *before* you need their help in manufacturing or selling a product.

WHAT YOU NEED TO KNOW

I believe the two most important ingredients for a product creator's success are having the right product and having the help of people in the market. Knowing a market offers two big advantages:

- Your contacts are much more likely to talk freely with someone who understands their business.
- Your questions about your idea and its potential will be more concise and detailed; you'll know enough to be able to gather more valuable responses.

You're not going to be able to learn everything about a market, nor can you totally overcome any lack of experience you might have. But you can certainly gain a working knowledge about how a market or industry operates. Knowledge by itself doesn't make an idea succeed, but it provides a road map for the introduction cycle and it makes contacts confident about your business capabilities.

Before starting to introduce a product, entrepreneurs should know the market aspects that are described in this section. The next section tells where you can find sources and data.

Industry Margins

Most people think businesses that stay in business are raking in sky-high profits. Actually, the vast majority of businesses make less than 5¢ for every $1 of sales.

An industry margin is an important indicator of how many sales are needed before an entrepreneur makes back an investment. For example, if the expected margin in your industry is 10 percent and you've invested $10,000 in a project, you'll need $100,000 in sales ($10,000 divided by 10 percent) to break even.

You can find the margins in the *Almanac of Business and Financial Ratios* (published by Prentice-Hall) at larger public libraries. Look for the line titled "Net profit before taxes as a percent of sales." In most categories, you'll find the average margin is either very low or negative. Find the highest margin in the column and make that your projected margin.

Note particularly the column titled "Other expenses"; these generally run anywhere from 12 to 20 percent of sales. These are the miscellaneous expenses that hurt most new businesses, primarily because entrepreneurs don't anticipate them. Office supplies, insurance, interest expense, postage, freight on incoming shipments, utilities, and so on, are "other" expenses.

Cash Flow-Through Chart

Figure 4-1 analyzes where the money goes when a $100 sale takes place in the hardware industry. (Every industry has a slightly different pattern.)

A small manufacturer in the hardware industry receives only $51 from a $100 sale: $40 goes to the retailer's discount and $9 to the distributor's discount. A $5 profit, which most readers will think is tiny, is actually a very normal 10 percent profit margin ($5 profit/$51 sale). Most manufacturers would gladly settle for $5 profit on a $100 retail sale.

Note how closely you have to watch sales, marketing, and administrative expenses. Overspending in these areas could eat up all of a product's profit.

Figure 4-1   Typical Cost Flow-Through Chart for Hardware Products

Item	Cost	Comments
Retail price	$100	
Less: Retailer discount	40	Can go as high as 50% in some industries.
Distributor discount	9	10–15% discounts to manufacturers' reps or distributors are common.
	51	
Less: Manufacturing cost	25	Includes packaging and shipping.
Sales cost	6	Salespeople, telemarketers, and order entry.
Marketing cost	6	Advertising, literature, promotional materials, and so on.
Product support	3	Regulatory approvals, warranty returns, product modifications.
Administrative cost	6	Interest charges, accounting, executive salaries, and miscellaneous charges.
Profit	$5	Most companies are lucky to have this much profit.

Manufacturing Techniques

A product entrepreneur once boasted to me that his product had a six-cavity mold. I asked the significance of the mold, and he replied that it indicated how sophisticated his product was. In reality, the number of cavities indicates how many units are made at once; it has nothing to do with a product's sophistication. A six-cavity mold produces six units at the same time.

At first glance, the entrepreneur's not knowing the real value of having six cavities doesn't seem like a serious oversight. But a knowledgeable businessperson, hearing about a six-cavity mold in use for a product that has no proven sales history, would know that the entrepreneur is wasting money. If the first cavity for a part costs $3,000 to $5,000, each additional cavity will cost about 60 percent of that initial amount—in this case, $2,000 to $3,000, for a total cost of about $15,000. The tooling for the initial production run could have been completed, using a one- or two-cavity mold, for less than $5,000; or, the initial parts could have been machined for $1,000 to $2,000.

Ernie S. had designed a $5,000 piece of equipment that could inexpensively make concrete blocks. The product was intended for underdeveloped countries, to allow small villages to make their own homes or

buildings. Ernie's product called for some heavy metal parts. These parts could have been made from high-quality steel permanent castings, which are expensive, or they could have been from a sand casting, which is a mold made out of sand and a bonding agent. Sand castings are inexpensive, but they last for only one or two parts, and they require more labor. Ernie stopped his project because he thought he couldn't continue without $25,000 worth of permanent castings. I asked Ernie why he didn't use a sand casting; the costs would have been minimal. Ernie could even have made the model for the casting himself. Unfortunately, Ernie wasn't aware that sand castings could be used.

Manufacturing is the area about which product creators know the least. Their lack of knowledge is a tremendous handicap. They make a poor impression on their contacts, and they often end up paying too much for prototypes and initial product runs.

Another factor causing product creators to make poor manufacturing decisions is the conflicting information they receive from various manufacturers, who almost always recommend their own manufacturing processes exclusively. For example, if a plastics manufacturer has equipment for vacuum-forming parts, its reps will sometimes recommend a vacuum process, even if another process might be more effective. The result to the product creator may be an ill-designed part that costs too much.

Joe L. and Chris P. created a plastic tool-storage compartment that bolted to the underside of a workbench. The part was 6 inches wide, 9 inches long, and 3½ inches deep—too big for economical injection molding, but a candidate for vacuum forming or rotational molding. An engineer from a rotational molding manufacturer told Joe and Chris that the company's process would produce parts with a better finish and would use less material than a vacuum-forming process. Joe and Chris decided to make their parts with rotational molding equipment.

In my opinion, this was a bad decision. The rotational mold cost $3,500, and the manufacturer suggested four molds to speed production. Joe and Chris could have made the vacuum-formed mold out of wood, in a basement, for under $200. The rotational mold would produce parts with a slightly better appearance, but the part wouldn't be visible under a workbench and a vacuum-formed part would have been fine. As for plastic usage, vacuum-formed parts do use more, but wastage could have been minimized.

The net result was that Joe and Chris, before selling even one product, invested $13,000 in tooling. A small production run of vacuum-formed parts would have cost less than $500.

To succeed, an undercapitalized product entrepreneur needs a close relationship with a contract manufacturer. That relationship can happen only if the entrepreneur knows enough to evaluate a manufacturer's advice.

You're going to need to spend time researching techniques for manufacturing your particular product. No easy-to-use reference source is available. Manufacturing issues are discussed in Chapter 8, but this book can't address all of the different types of products. Use the sources described in the next section and dig diligently to get the information you need.

Comparative Products

A comparative product isn't identical to yours, but it has characteristics that are similar. For example, suppose you have created an electronic golf aid that you hope to retail for $19.95. Your creation would have two types of comparative products: golf products, with a retail price range of $15 to $25, and other electronic products with similar circuitry.

By finding comparative products in your target market, you can generate valuable marketing information. When you talk to contacts, you can ask them to evaluate your product against that information. A comparison will help you to project potential sales volume and will answer questions such as:

Which product has a more important benefit?

Which product is unique?

Which product has a better price/value relationship?

You can also ask contacts about the promotional programs and distribution networks used by the marketers of successful comparative products.

Manufacturing Cost

The one area where inventors consistently show their inexperience is that of manufacturing cost. I hear comments such as "the product shouldn't cost much to make—parts are only $3 and labor should amount to less than 20 minutes." This shows a total lack of knowledge, which will scare off any insider, investors, or manufacturer.

There are three major components to manufacturing cost: labor, material, and overhead. Typically, overhead makes up 30 to 40 percent, and sometimes an even higher percentage, of a product's total cost. Overhead includes all the items directly related to production, such as energy bills, liability insurance, quality control, testing, product engineers, and plant managers. Companies take the total overhead and divide it on some basis, such as machine-hours, labor-hours, or sales volume among their products. This accounting practice ensures that all manufacturing costs, both variable and fixed, are allocated to a product.

For example, take Sun Flower Plastic, a company that manufactures plastic containers for holding tools and other products in the back of vans or four-wheel-drive vehicles. Its monthly overhead costs might look like this:

Rent of manufacturing space:	$ 700
Product liability insurance:	350
Quality control—⅓ person's time	700
Shipping—¼ person's time	500
Machine depreciation	300
Utilities (electricity, etc.)	150
½ management time	1,500
Scrap and rework costs	300
Purchasing—¼ person's time	500
Total	**$5,000**

The overhead cost must be allocated among the products. Sometimes it's done by machine-hour. Sun Flower may need to run its one machine 100 hours per month to make production volume, so it would allocate cost by machine-hour, making the cost $100 per hour. Under this system, if a product takes 15 minutes to make, a $25 overhead charge would be added to the product. Sun Flower Plastics could cost $15 for materials, $10 for labor, and $25 for overhead, for a $50 total. Overhead could also be allocated by labor-hours, which would mean, if the company averaged 320 hours per month, the overhead charge could be $5,000/320 or $15.62 per labor-hour.

When asked about overhead, most inventors will say it's small. In reality, it's almost never a small percentage of costs if it is calculated correctly. Inventors also tend to overlook many material costs such as packaging, incoming freight, operation and maintenance, and preparing and printing manuals.

Unless you have a strong manufacturing background, most people won't believe your estimated costs. You should get quotes from other manufacturers in order to substantiate your estimates.

If you need to get investors early in your introduction cycle, you might not have enough information to get an accurate quote. One way to get around this is to find comparative products built similarly to how you expect your product to be built. Try to get at least three or four similar products, and then you can say that the retail price will be close to yours. Chapter 8 includes more information on estimating your manufacturing cost.

Typical Packaging

A product's package often determines how effectively its benefits can be communicated, which, in turn, may affect how well an idea will sell. The package can impact on a product's perceived value. High-priced perfumes, cosmetics, and jewelry are examples of items that concentrate on packaging more than low-priced items do. Toys are another example. When sold in cardboard boxes, with 100 or so units per box, toys are priced at 50¢ to $1. The *same toys* will sell in blister packs for about $2.

Marketing Data

Target markets, market size, and distribution outlets are a few of the marketing components that you need to learn about. The marketing lingo is another; vocabulary can be different from one industry to another. For instance, the computer industry calls a company a *direct response marketer* if it sells products at a discount through magazine ads or catalogs. In the dental industry, the same type of company is a *mail-order discounter.* You'll be able to learn an industry's language by reading the trade magazines discussed in this chapter's next section.

You can really impress people if you know specific information about a local or niche market: the big three distributors, or the last major product introduction, or which retailers control sales promotions, and so on. Every time you talk to a contact, try to find out at least one or two pieces of specific market information.

Regulatory and Other Approvals

Many product areas have a wide variety of requirements, such as liability insurance, bar codes, and U.L. (Underwriters' Laboratories) or government approvals. You should learn not only what approvals are required, but their cost and how long it takes to get them. U.L. approval, which is needed for virtually any electrical item, might cost over $5,000 and take up to a year to obtain. Even a simple bar-code number, which is required on products sold in most retail outlets, costs a minimum of $300. Four to six weeks are needed to obtain a new company bar code. Product liability insurance may require $2,500 up front. I'll explain in later chapters how you can minimize your approval problems by working with a contract manufacturer.

WHERE TO FIND INFORMATION

The Library

At larger libraries, you can find trade magazines, which are the best source of information about a particular industry. *Plastics Technology, Potentials in Marketing, Tire Wholesalers, The Home Shop Machinist,* and *Modern Castings* are just a few examples of trade or specialty magazines that can provide you with data that usually can't be found anywhere else. Try to read at least a year's worth of back issues. Look for competitive products, specialty mail-order catalogs that might sell needed supplies, and information about upcoming trade shows.

If your nearby library doesn't have a wide assortment of trade magazines, look at *Gale's Source of Publications,* a reference book that lists almost every magazine and newspaper published in the United States. Publications are listed both by the state in which they are published and by industry category. Look up the trade magazines for your category, including those directed toward retailers, wholesalers, and manufacturers. Many of the magazines will send you a free back issue if you express an interest in subscribing.

Most libraries keep files of sales catalogs from mail-order houses. These catalogs are an excellent source of competitive information and examples of comparative products.

The *Thomas Register of American Manufacturers* is the leader among industrial catalogs. It lists manufacturers for virtually every conceivable type of product and publishes a separate catalog in which companies can purchase space for their sales brochures. Look up specialty material suppliers that you might need to make your product. I've always preferred trade magazines to the industrial directories, primarily because magazines have more current information. If you can't find the right trade magazine, then the directories can be helpful.

Another place to look is in the index for your local newspaper. A number of press releases and small stories about developing businesses will appear in almost every edition. Sales volume and market-share statistics may be revealed in these news items. The *Reader's Guide to Periodical Literature, The New York Times Index,* and other business and scientific indexes offer similar help.

Try to get annual reports from companies in a target market. Your library might have some of these reports on file for local companies. If you can't find the reports you need, look in the *Million Dollar Directory* for addresses of companies whose reports you want to request.

Your library will have books on manufacturing techniques and model building. The "Helpful Sources" section at the end of this book lists some of my favorite how-to books for making models, prototypes, and initial production runs. Your library may have others that are just as helpful.

Salespeople and Manufacturers' Representatives

These individuals are selling products similar to yours in your targeted market. They generally know a great deal about an industry and can provide a considerable amount of background information.

Your best contact will usually be either a friend or a referral from a friend. You can often find a contact just by asking people whether they know anyone who sells products in the market to which you're hoping to sell. If that doesn't work, request product information from the market's suppliers and manufacturers. You can locate these companies through trade magazines or industrial catalogs. The information will usually come from a company's local salesperson or its manufacturers' representative. You can call this person, explain what you're doing, and then ask whether he or she would mind answering a few questions.

If you have a consumer product, you typically can't find salespeople or manufacturers' representatives by requesting product information. Instead, have some business cards printed to display your name and the name of your company, and apply for a sales tax number from your state's Department of Revenue. Having these proofs that your company exists will allow you to visit wholesale merchandise marts and trade shows directed toward retailers, which will give you an idea of how the industry works and a chance to meet helpful salespeople, distributors, and wholesalers.

I prefer to work with manufacturers' representatives rather than salespeople. Because they sell products for, on average, four to ten manufacturers, they have a better knowledge of the industry—and they will usually tell you more of what they know. A salesperson working for just one company is more likely to look at you as a competitor and, consequently, will be more secretive of what he or she might feel is proprietary information.

Retail Stores

Keep track of how similar products are displayed to the final consumer. Check local stores to see how products are packaged, how much of each product the stores carry, what the typical price range is, and what other similar products are originating from small companies.

Utilize any contact you might have, from family or friends, who owns or works in a retail store. This person can explain what a retail store wants to see in a product and provide names of manufacturers' representatives or distributors that serve the local market.

Packaging Suppliers

A package is important to a product's success. You need to know what your options are, and the benefits and cost of each option. Packaging suppliers seem to know a great deal about how other new products are doing. For example, I wanted to put a small jewelry item in a point-of-purchase display. The packaging supplier's salesman, who wanted my business, told me about four other novelty items he worked with, described how they were packaged, and gave me a rough idea of each product's unit volume.

You can find packaging suppliers in the Yellow Pages or in the local business-to-business phone directory at the library. Other sources for suppliers are trade magazines and trade shows. An alternative is to contact a buyer at a local manufacturer of similar products, tell the buyer that you're looking for a packaging supplier, and ask which ones the manufacturer uses.

Small Business Assistance Groups

Local chambers of commerce are usually excellent referral sources. If they can't help you, they can at least direct you to a member who can. "The chamber of commerce suggested I call you" is a great way to start a conversation. Because chamber members run successful businesses, they know the problems entrepreneurs encounter and how they can overcome them.

I've never had much luck when I approached state or federal small business groups; their information tends to be too general. The one area in which they can be helpful is regulatory approvals. For example, the Small Business Administration or a state agency is the best place to call if you need to know how to get a bar-code number or where you can find out details about U.L. approvals.

Your city or town may also have inventors' groups, entrepreneurs' groups, or small business networking groups. You should attend at least one meeting of each group, as some of these people might be able to help you. Also check out any sales and marketing groups of manufacturers' associations in your town. A good way to find these groups is to call the managing editor or business editor of your local paper and ask when it publishes meeting notices. Usually the paper will list all upcoming meetings once a week. You might find several helpful groups if you track meeting notices.

HOW TO PACKAGE AN IDEA

When I worked for the dental manufacturer, I used to receive, free, more than ten new product ideas a month. These ideas were submitted by people who weren't hoping for profit from an idea but wanted to be able to buy the product. All of your contacts are exposed to people who give their ideas away and to others who spend only a week or two on their ideas before giving up on them. You must do something to immediately prove to contacts that you're serious about putting an idea on the market.

The best way I can recommend to make a strong impression is to package your idea well. When a consumer looks at a product that is properly packaged, he or she immediately knows what the product is and what its benefits are. Marketers know that a first impression is all-important. The same principle applies when someone is conducting market research.

There are two components to packaging an idea before a product is in its final form: the initial materials and the backup materials (those used after someone expresses interest in an idea).

Initial materials have four parts:

1. A drawing of what the product will eventually look like
2. A drawing of how the product will be used (try to get both drawings on one sheet of paper)
3. An ad layout, which consists of a drawing or sketch, with graphics
4. A model, prototype, or drawing of the package, if you have a consumer product

You don't need to have professional drawings on ad layouts. Instead, use appropriate pictures from magazines. If you can, find an art student, or drawings done by high school art students, or friends with artistic talent, or, as a last resort, a freelance professional artist. You should be able to prepare the initial materials for under $100.

The second part of packaging the idea is to have the backup materials, which contain thorough marketing information, ready to discuss with a contact. You should prepare the following information:

- Projected retail price
- Target market
- Market size
- Key benefits
- Product description
- Market trends
- Competitive products
- Similar successful products
- Other pertinent data

If possible, compile this information in a booklet. You won't have to use the information with everyone, but when contacts are interested in knowing more about your idea, having these data will be essential.

OFF AND RUNNING

Professionalism will help you to succeed; you'll also find it makes your project a lot more fun. Instead of stumbling along, you'll be in control. As an added benefit, people who are successful will offer you helpful advice. Most important, you'll enjoy the project because your money won't be running away from you. There is nothing more disheartening to a product entrepreneur than to spend $10,000 without making any meaningful progress. The steps I've listed in this chapter will take time to complete, but they will eventually save you time, money, and aggravation.

5

LICENSING: THE PRELIMINARY WORK

In 1986, Lonnie Johnson, a spacecraft systems engineer for Jet Propulsion Laboratories, formed a joint venture with LIN Toy Company (a subsidiary of MCA records) to manufacture and market a toy water gun. Due to production difficulties, LIN folded in 1989, and in 1990 Lonnie went on to license his water gun to Laramie Corporation, which manufactured the product under the name Super Soaker. During 1991 and 1992, the Super Soaker was the hottest-selling toy in American history, breaking records set by Nintendo and the Ninja Turtles.

Tomima Edmark, a marketing representative for IBM, was in a movie theater where she saw a woman with a ponytail with an unusual twist. After experimenting with numerous prototypes, Tomima came up with a winning design and, to date, her company, Topsy Tail, has sold over $80 million worth of this simple hair care product. She ran her own two-minute TV commercials and sold 3.6 million units, and her product is now available in a wide variety of retail outlets.

Who is better off—Lonnie with the license or Tomima with her own product? The fact is that they both did well, and they both made the choices that were best for their respective products. Licensing is a viable option anytime you have a product that possesses compelling characteristics—or, as I prefer to call them, *driving forces*—that give your licensing partner an important market entry.

A driver could be a very innovative product, like the Super Soaker, or a product that:

- Has very large sales potential
- Allows a company to knock out its major competitor's top product
- Provides a strong entry into an emerging market
- Allows a company to expand its distribution network
- Has a significant, obvious product benefit
- Solves a large industry problem
- Solidifies a company's product line

Did the Topsy Tail have a strong business driver? Not when it was in the stage to be licensed. Its benefit was nice, but I wouldn't say it was a breakthrough. Did the Topsy Tail have tremendous market potential? No industry professional would have predicted the product's incredible sales. If Tomima had tried to license her idea, most marketers would have reviewed it as a nice idea, with a limited market potential, which would require extensive advertising. A product without a large potential or big driver will get lost in the shuffle in a big company, but it can still do very well for an inventor in a smaller market.

LICENSING ISN'T THAT EASY

I recently talked to an industrial designer who had worked for Tonka Toys, a company that has since been sold to a larger corporation but that had introduced products such as the Nerf toys, Transformers, and Pound Puppies. He told me that in his eight years with Tonka it had licensed only three products from outside inventors. And toy companies are generally considered to "frequently" license ideas.

People do license ideas every day, but the number of those who do is small—probably only 300 to 500 per year—and many of those licenses don't produce any significant royalty revenue. There are four reasons that licensing inventions can be difficult:

- Companies have trouble identifying marketable ideas until they are in a finished form.
- Most small companies have trouble introducing any product and are reluctant to take on outside new products.

- Companies that know how to market products usually have plenty of their own product ideas to introduce and will take on only truly novel, innovative products.
- It is difficult to reconfigure products to make them easier to license.

Identifying Marketable Ideas

I once heard Woody Allen talk about how he never views his own movies. He starts a movie project with an image in his mind of what the movie will be like, but the actual movie never lives up to his original image. So he never sees his own movies in order to avoid being disappointed.

New products suffer from the same high expectations. It is rare that a product can be brought to market in the exact form the inventor originally envisioned. Compromises are made, mechanical features never work quite as planned, and the product's aesthetics don't have the novelty originally hoped for. Most companies deal with this problem by working on 10, 20, and sometimes many more products until they see which products will end up being marketable. Until a product design is finalized, companies won't know if it is marketable.

Most inventors I talk to believe that a company can recognize the worth of its idea from a drawing, and that drawing, along with maybe a patent, is all the company needs to get a license. But experienced business people have usually had their own product failures, and they have had many "great" ideas that never made it to a product launch. To have a strong chance at a license, an inventor needs to take a product all the way to completion. Inventors will raise their odds of success even more if they actually sell a few products before attempting to get licenses.

Small Companies Typically Aren't Good Marketers

The state of Minnesota recently did a study to see how many companies of 250 employees or fewer had marketing plans. Only 37 percent had them. I've discovered that I can walk into most small companies and find anywhere from 5 to 25 product ideas that the company has never been able to get off the ground. Such a company might have one or two strong products but is unable to introduce any additional ones.

With a company that doesn't believe it can introduce a product, offering a finished product isn't enough to get a license. You need to develop a marketing strategy, a distribution plan, and even a distribution network before you have a chance to get a license. Small companies without marketing direction make up a major share of the companies in any town. This is why I personally prefer to work on a contract-manufacturing or joint-venture basis with manufacturers. They need more business, they want your marketing help, and there are a lot of manufacturers to choose from. It is much easier to set up a joint venture with a small manufacturer than it is to license a product to it.

The Product Needs to Have a Big Motivator

Companies that actively introduce new products look for new products all the time. Salespeople, marketing staff, customers, and the R&D department all come up with new product ideas. So when you contact a company, your idea has to stand out as superior to any of the company's own product ideas, even if you have already finished and sold your product.

There are two reasons companies are reluctant to take on a new product from an inventor. The first is the "not-invented-here" syndrome, whereby some people in any company—particularly R&D people—don't like to think someone else could come up with better ideas than they do. The second is that a royalty can cut pretty deeply into a company's product-line profits. Most companies make approximately a 10 percent profit on sales. If a company pays an inventor a 5 percent royalty, the company doesn't have a lot of allowance for its own profit.

I met a woman at a housewares show who sold a magnet device for dishwashers, which had a slide that revealed either the word *clean* or the word *dirty*—a nice, simple product that let people know if dishes in the dishwasher were clean or dirty. The woman claimed she had sold over $3 million worth of this product in five years. While this was a profitable product for the inventor, it would be very hard to license. The product just didn't have enough sales potential for a company to consider.

Reconfiguring a Product for Licensing

When an inventor is having trouble marketing a product, the easiest tactic for regaining momentum is to target a smaller market.

As an example, Ted G. originally tried to sell a back brace with a microwavable warming device to sporting goods stores. Ted had trouble penetrating this market, so he narrowed his target market to health clubs. He added a chilling device that could be activated just by cracking the package. His product was ideal for someone who had just sprained an ankle or wrist.

This tactic doesn't work at all for licensing. Companies want a product they can license to appeal to the broadest possible market. They want huge potential. Unfortunately, the hardest products of all to develop are ones that appeal to everyone.

I don't want to discourage you from trying to license an idea. It certainly is done all the time. But you should realize that licensing an idea can be as much work as marketing an idea yourself, and it calls for the same careful approach.

A WINNING LICENSING APPROACH

Figure 5-1 details the 12 key steps to licensing an idea. This chapter will cover the first eight steps. Step 9, proving your product will sell, is covered in Chapters 6 through 11. These steps are the same whether you are licensing the idea or marketing the product on your own. It doesn't matter what your strategy is, people won't buy into your idea unless you can prove it is marketable. Steps 10 through 12 are covered in Chapter 13 on licensing.*

This licensing strategy is created to address the four major points any licensing strategy should consider:

1. Companies that are ineffective at marketing license only products that have complete marketing and distribution plans.

2. Companies that are effective at marketing require that a product have a *compelling* reason to be marketed, or they need absolute proof that the product will sell.

3. Companies are approached by many inventors, and personal connections are almost essential in getting an idea considered.

4. Most business executives believe inventors generally have poor research, marketing, and business skills. Inventors need to take great care to appear professional in every contact with a prospective licensee company.

STEP 1: CREATING AN IDEA

I don't like to dwell too much on creating an idea, because I think people come up with great ideas all the time. The problem they have is knowing

---

* It may seem odd that licensing information is spread throughout the book, especially if you view licensing and marketing a product as two distinct activities. I believe the two are closely related because both require the inventor to prove that a product will sell. A first-time inventor's chances of licensing a product are very slim unless he or she completes most of the steps through the first sales period. Placing the final licensing chapter near the end of the book is deliberate, as I hope it will encourage you first to do all you can to prove your product's potential.

Figure 5-1   Key Steps to Licensing an Idea

1. Create the idea.
2. Research the market.
3. Decide on the type of company you want to approach.
4. Determine your basic positioning statement and marketing strategy.
5. Pick out the companies you want to approach.
6. Start making personal contacts with sales representatives and marketing personnel.
7. Decide when you need to get a patent.
8. Finish developing your idea—if necessary, start working to get an investor or partner and also apply for your patent, if appropriate.
9. Develop proof that your product is marketable.
10. Prepare your presentation materials.
11. Make your presentations to the appropriate companies.
12. Negotiate the contracts.

how to market their ideas. The most important point to worry about with any new product is what I call the "wow" factor. You need people to look at your idea and say, "Wow, that's really great!"

Most invention and marketing books use a formula for creating an idea that includes finding a problem, developing a solution, and then finalizing the invention. This may sound like an intelligent approach, but I don't think it will get you too far. Did anyone need a VCR? A camcorder? A Corvette? A dishwasher? A 25-inch TV? A power screwdriver? No. These products are responses to the question, "Wouldn't it be great?" Since, to succeed, inventors have to have better products than those offered by companies, I think they are better off looking at products that will be amazing to the people who buy them.

Instead of looking for problems, look at a situation and think about what would be a really great addition or modification to it. The product doesn't have to be cheap, or practical, or even the best solution. It just needs to be a solution that people will smile at. Try writing down something that would be amazing every day for 60 days. At the end of that time, go through your list and select the five best ideas—not from a practical point of view, but the ideas you'd most like to see carried out. Then follow the same procedure for another 60 days. If you continue this procedure, sooner or later you'll find an idea that will really get you excited.

STEP 2: RESEARCHING THE MARKET

Chapters 6 through 9, which cover the go/no-go decisions for product entrepreneurs, explain most of the market research you need to license a product, including questions on distribution, marketing, and manufacturing.

One of the differences between marketing a product yourself and licensing the product to a company is your market-targeting approach. When you market a product yourself, you look for a small market niche in which you can establish a product, while in licensing you try to sell to as broad a market as possible. For example, if you create a new power scissors and clipper system for dogs and want to market the product yourself, you might modify the product so it is ideal for trimming dogs at shows. That market is small and easy to reach, but still big enough to establish a market foothold. If you were trying to license this same idea, you would want the market to appeal to as many people as possible, which would include dog groomers, people who show dogs, and all the little dog boutiques and cutting salons in the market.

There is a subtle but very important difference between these two approaches. When you go for a narrow market definition, your emphasis is on immediate results. If you were trying to market the dog trimmer, for example, you'd want to offer all the little features that potential users of the product want right now. When your goal is a broad market definition, you are actually selling greater opportunities, which means that what you really need to sell is how a product can help a company over the next few years.

When you are going to try to license a product, you need to look at market trends and the way the industry is moving. You need to understand how your product fits into the trend and then use it in your sales approach.

I worked for a dental company whose most successful product was a vibratory scaler licensed from an inventor. A scaler is a product that is used to clean the calculus, or tartar, off your teeth and it is used on almost every dental patient. At the time, the only scaler on the market was geared for gross removal of calculus. The scaler was messy and expensive. The vibratory scaler was lightweight, clean, and easy to use, but it also worked best on light tartar, as opposed to the heavy cases of tartar for which the competitor's product was designed.

The main licensing points of this product were:

- *People were visiting dental offices more often and they had less tartar buildup. The new scaler would fit right into this market trend.*
- *Toothpaste companies were all working to develop tartar-control toothpastes (now on the market), which also lessen tartar buildup. Again, this point emphasized a market trend.*

- *The product would allow us to move out of a rather narrow market area and open the door for us to expand into new market areas (opportunity).*
- *The product worked well.*

To find the important trends in your target market, first read the trade magazines I discussed in Chapter 4. Another good source of information about trends is speeches presented at conventions or local association meetings. The trade shows usually are listed in trade magazines, but at larger libraries you can also find reference sources listing each industry's shows. Call the organization responsible for the show and ask if it has reprints of the speeches. If not, ask for a list of the key speakers, which will be available on the show's promotional material. Then you can contact the speaker and request a copy of the speech.

The Internet also has a wide range of literature search sites where you use key words to search for any published articles. Once you have some idea of what the market trends are, I recommend that you contact the editors of trade magazines, ask them what they believe to be the major industry trends, and see if they agree with you.

STEP 3: DECIDING ON THE TYPE OF COMPANY TO APPROACH

Your best chance of licensing an idea is to approach a company where your idea can make an impact. If you have a nice idea, such as the Junk Drawer Organizer for kitchen drawers, to whom will you be able to license the idea? The product has appeal and is certainly capable of selling $1 million to $5 million per year. But it's not really a product with enough potential to be of interest to a big company.

Many company executives think it is a nuisance to deal with product entrepreneurs. They need to spend extra time negotiating with inventors, then they have to listen to the inventors critique the company's business strategy. For the most part, executives have to learn to live with the inventor's desire to know why the company isn't doing more to promote his or her idea. To the executive, inventor contacts represent aggravation. So the idea has to be truly innovative and have the potential to make a significant impact on the company.

The Right-Size Company

I believe you should try to license ideas only to companies at which your product would represent at least 40 to 50 percent of the current sales volume. If your product has $3 million to $5 million in sales volume, you should look to license the product to companies with $5 million to $10 million in annual sales. The only exception to this rule is if you have a product that will fill in a company's product line so it can compete more effectively. For example, the dental business I worked with had every item a dentist needed except a dental light. That gave us a competitive disadvantage that we solved by buying and reselling dental lights from an inventor in England.

Inventors consistently make one major mistake in projecting volumes. They project the volume for all possible sales, instead of projecting the volume just for markets in which the product entrepreneur has proven that a product has potential.

For example, earlier in the chapter I mentioned Ted G., who created a healing wrap for sprains that could be sold in health clubs. The market Ted knows is sales through health clubs. He doesn't know for sure that the product will sell through drugstore chains, sporting goods stores, and mass-merchandise retailers such as Wal-Mart, Target, and Kmart.

But chances are that Ted G. would try to sell his idea by projecting volume in all the possible markets. These other markets are only upside potential. The only markets that companies would typically include in a projection for this product would be health clubs. Ted G. faces three obstacles if he overstates the market:

- *He will look naive to the company.*
- *His product idea will be too small for the companies that he will approach.*
- *He will miss out on opportunities to approach companies to which his idea will appeal.*

Finding the Right Companies

You need to be careful in choosing companies to target. Companies don't like to take products that have been shopped around to a lot of other companies. They reason that, after all, there must be something wrong with the idea if no one has taken it before. There are three major ways to find companies to approach: trade magazines, trade shows, and directories.

Product press releases in the *trade magazines* discussed in Chapter 4 are the best places to locate small to midsize companies. A product press release typically appears in a new-products section, and it generally lists brief information about the products, along with pictures. A product press release would read something like the following:

Dish-Net Keeps Small Plastic Dishes in Place

A new product promises relief if you're tired of having small plastic cup lids, bottle nipples, and other small dishes accidentally forced out of your dishwasher rack. The new Dish-Net product from Jet USA in Denver, Colorado, has a stretched net that covers a portion of the dishwasher rack, preventing items from being dislodged by the dishwasher's water pressure. The Dish-Net is universally sized and fits on all dishwashers. For more information, contact Jet USA.

Product press releases are written by the company selling the product. I think it pays to track these companies, because they are actively introducing products and will be easier to sell to than companies selling only established products. You should contact the company and request information anytime you see a product that is sold to the same market as yours and that is priced similarly to your product.

Once you get information from a company that indicates it is a good match for your product, go to your main public library and look in state industrial guides or the *Million Dollar Directory* to see how big the company is. If your library doesn't have either of these sources, ask the reference librarian for assistance in looking up the information. Another tactic is simply to call the library in the company's hometown and ask for information about the company. The library will often know the company's size, plus they might have newspaper articles on the company that they will send you.

Industry trade shows are another good source for company names. The shows will be listed in the trade magazines, but you can also find them in reference sources at your library or on the Internet. An excellent reference source is the *Directory of Conventions,* published by Successful Meetings, 633 Third Ave., New York, NY 10017. Call the organization responsible for the show and request a copy of last year's directory. This should list the companies' names and their products. You should call for information on products selling to similar markets and then follow up to see how large the company is, in the same manner that you did for trade magazines.

One last method for finding companies is to look at industry directories or association membership listings. The best directories are usually published annually by the trade magazines, and they are usually willing to send you copies of their most recent ones.

STEP 4: DETERMINING A POSITIONING STATEMENT AND MARKETING STRATEGY

A company doesn't really decide to buy a product on its own merits. It buys the product to fit into its business strategy. I've found it will help your presentations if you show that you understand what a company's goals are and then show how your product will help to meet them. For example, I mentioned earlier a dental scaler that a company licensed from an inventor. The company wanted the product because it broadened its product line into a new application area and because the product was a good match for its manufacturing capability. The company wasn't sure the product would sell, but it gave the company a low-risk opportunity to implement its strategy.

A company generally is pursuing one of five strategies that can help an inventor: (1) protecting a market position, (2) upgrading a market position, (3) expanding into new markets or applications, (4) improving the distribution network, or (5) specializing for an industry or application. Once you understand these strategies you'll be able to customize your presentation for every company you approach.

Protecting a Market Position

Typically, a company is interested in three items to protect its market position:

- Keeping its lead (most important) product strong
- Having a product line breadth equal to or better than that of its competitors
- Developing new products to meet new trends or changes in the industry

A company's *lead product* is generally the product that the company is most associated with. Lead product strategy is usually much more prevalent in industrial companies than in consumer products companies, but it does apply to both. Fisher Instrument might have as its lead product nondestructive coating measurement systems for gold platings. Trek USA would probably consider its high-end racing bike as its lead product, because that is the bike that determines the company's market reputation. I'd say the Big Mac is McDonald's lead product, the Taurus is Ford's lead product, and the riding lawn mower is Toro's lead product.

Companies do everything they can to protect lead products. Unfortunately, this is also the most difficult concept to sell. Companies like to think they know virtually all there is to know about their lead products, and they aren't open to ideas from outside inventors.

Product line breadth relates to customer needs. When a company can supply all or most of a customer's needs in a certain area, the company is said to have a broad product line.

As an example, I recently helped an inventor-led company sign a mul-timillion-dollar distribution agreement with an $800 million com-pany. The inventor's company manufactures industrial pipe couplings that connect 2-inch to 18-inch mining and industrial polypropyl-ene pipes.

The inventor's product was a coupling that did not have to be press-fitted or heat-fused onto the pipe. The company to which we sold the product didn't have a product like this, but its major competitor did. The $800 million company agreed to distribute the product just so it could have the same breadth as its competitors. With a full prod-uct line, the company felt it could knock its competitors out of several distributors.

Companies are receptive to products that can fill in their product lines. But it calls for careful research on your part. You need to know who the major players in a market are and what products they are missing. The best way to do that is to keep reading trade magazines and attending industry trade shows. I've met several inventors over the years who actu-ally use this approach to determine what ideas they'll work on. They con-centrate on industries where major competitors have sales in the $30 million to $80 million range, find several companies that do not have pres-ences in their particular product lines, and then go out and create better products than those already on the market.

Products for *new market trends* is another area where companies will listen to new ideas. Companies want to protect their market shares, and they know they need to adjust to new trends in the market to stay com-petitive. Many small to midsize companies have limited R&D resources, so they aren't always able to keep up with the market changes. For exam-ple, a few years ago it was obvious that CD-ROMs, faster telecommuni-cation lines, and videoconferencing were all new trends. One of the problems with computers at the time was that it took several seconds to put a completely new image on the screen (referred to as a *screen refresh*). An inventor who concentrated on products that resulted in quick screen refreshes would have a salable idea.

Another example is lawn mowers. A few years ago there was talk in the industry of a move toward mulching mowers. An inventor who developed a product to attach to current mowers to add mulching capa-bility would have had a good chance of licensing the idea. The best ways to stay on top of what the industry sees as new trends are to be a member of the industry association and attend keynote speeches at trade shows.

Incidentally, some inventors and engineers work almost in reverse of the typical invention process. These inventors look for openings in the market, either due to product-line shortages or new trends. Then they work at developing products to fill those voids.

Upgrading a Market Position

Major competitors in the market are usually tough to license to unless you have a very innovative product. Other, smaller companies that are actively introducing new products typically have a difficult time keeping up with the engineering work of their own introductions. That leaves a third type of company, one that is not overly active in introducing new ideas, but which may be receptive to them.

A company raises its image when it *advertises a new product* that the market finds exciting. People in the market stereotype companies as innovative, solid, middle of the road, or stodgy. Companies that fall into the last three groups are usually looking to enhance their images and they represent viable licensing candidates.

Three approaches a company can take to upgrade its image are: (1) offer an innovative product that advertises well; (2) offer a product to compete with one supplied by a single company; (3) offer a product that can generate expert or university research support.

A product needs immediate appeal to generate the positive response companies are seeking. If people look at your ad and say "wow" in less than two seconds, you have a product with advertising appeal. These products are hard to come by, and they need to have benefits that everyone recognizes immediately. Examples of products like this are tartar-control toothpaste, L'egg's panty hose (the appeal of which is primarily from its package), the first drip coffeemakers, Slim-Fast, CDs, mulching mowers, and string edge trimmers (such as the Weed Whacker). These products make sense to consumers, who recognize the benefits in seconds.

As a rule, a product that is *supplied by only one company* is not well received by the market. The perception follows that the company overcharges and is arrogant, simply because customers have no other place to go for the product. Sole-source companies often have strong patent positions on their designs. Since most companies create new products by modifying other people's products, the patent protection may stop competitors. Companies are usually leery of attempting to create new technologies, and, as a result, a company with a strong patent position can be a sole supplier for a long time. But that doesn't mean other companies wouldn't like to compete. They just need inventors to give them new products.

I think that a new product, going up against a sole supplier, has one of the best chances of being licensed, provided it gets around the original product's patents. The dental scaler I mentioned earlier was a good example of a license against a sole supplier. The competitor had a product that sold $5 million to $10 million per year at 80 percent profit margins. The product we licensed had only marginal advantages, but it was different, and that's all we needed to compete in a very profitable market.

Some products also *appeal to researchers.* If you have a product for treating a new or high-profile disease or a new technology that will appeal to university or industry researchers, you'll find that companies that pride themselves as high-technology organizations make good licensing prospects.

Expanding into New Markets

Companies are either market or product oriented. A market-oriented company tries to provide more products and better service to a specific market. For example, a paint company might want to provide every product it could for a retail paint center. A product-oriented company concentrates on its product or technology, such as a special paint formula, which it tries to sell into as many applications as possible.

Market-oriented companies like products that broaden their lines into markets or applications, while product-oriented companies like products that allow them to expand into new applications. For example, Devee Philpot created the Junk Drawer Organizer, which was a nice little housewares product. She struck up a joint-venture arrangement with a manufacturer that sold similar plastic products to hardware stores. The owner of the company wanted access to the housewares market, but he needed a strong lead product to break into it. When licensing a product to break into a new application, it is especially helpful if you have already sold some products or have established a distribution network.

Improving the Distribution System

Every company wants to expand its distribution network. You can help a company do that in two ways: (1) by having an exciting new product that stores will try, and (2) by offering a product that might have small volume sales, but which the distributor nevertheless wants to carry. An example of a hot new product was the Super Soaker; it was carried in every store and enhanced Laramie's whole product line. Companies are frequently leery of licensing this type of product until they are positive it will take off.

The other type of product that will expand distribution is one that a distribution channel believes it must sell. For example, drugstores believe they must sell nail care products. These products haven't changed much over the years, and no one is making much money from them. If an inventor were to take a familiar product like this and rejuvenate it, companies would be interested in licensing it because it would give them access to a wide retail distribution network.

Specializing for an Industry or Application

Specializing in an industry or application is called *niche marketing,* and it is a strategy followed by many companies. The thinking behind the strategy is that a company will maintain a stable sales base by fulfilling the needs of one market better than anyone else. Niche marketing is a popular strategy and one to which companies will respond. The key to licensing a product with this strategy is to have a product for which the market niche has a strong desire and that will fit into another company's product line.

Strategy Summary

Using business or marketing strategy to sell an idea calls for research on your part. You need to check carefully to find the right strategy for the companies you've chosen. You may even decide to take a different approach for each company.

I know that figuring out a positioning strategy is a lot of work, and I know that you probably want to just move in and explain your idea. But before you decide to skip this step, let me explain your visit from the viewpoint of the marketing people at the potential licensee. They've had a busy day, and more likely than not they don't really feel they have the time to see you. They are going to pop in for a few minutes just to see what you have, but their expectations are very low, because most ideas from inventors don't turn into successful products. This is the audience you have to expect. So you need an introduction to get the people to sit down and get in the mood to listen to you. Then you can present your product idea.

On the checklist in Figure 5-2, indicate for your records the positioning statements that you think belong to your product. The right-hand column rates the effectiveness of each strategy when approaching a potential licensee.

STEP 5: SELECTING THE COMPANIES TO APPROACH

Most inventors who want to try and license products will run out to the first two or three companies they think of or that they find in the *Thomas Register* and try to license their products. Typically, they fail in these attempts, and often they give up on their ideas. This is a big mistake. First of all, only one of five or ten companies is really a good licensing prospect. Second, most inventors don't research how far they need to take products toward commercialization before they talk to companies. Frequently, they just don't have the products finalized to the point where companies will take them.

Figure 5-2 Effectiveness of Positioning Strategy

Positioning Strategy		*Effectiveness*
Protecting a market position		
• Keeping a lead product strong	_____	Low
• Adding product line breadth	_____	Medium
• Providing products for new market trends	_____	High
Upgrading a market position		
• Offering products that can be effectively advertised	_____	Medium
• Competing with a sole supplier	_____	High
• Offering products that can generate university research	_____	Medium to low
Expanding into new markets		
• Using product-oriented manufacturers	_____	High
Improving the distribution network		
• Introducing an exciting new product	_____	Low to medium
• Filling product distribution channel needs	_____	Medium
Specializing for an industry or application		
• For an industry	_____	High
• For an application	_____	Medium

You need to find companies in the industry, get copies of their literature, find out how big their R&D departments are, and decide if your product is a good fit for their strategies. Following is a priority list of characteristics that you want a company to have:

1. They should have licensed successful products in the past.
2. They should have strong marketing but weak or nonexistent R&D departments.
3. They should have neglected to introduce a product for some time.
4. They should have a product line that is missing key products.

5. They should be concentrating on supplying the needs of a specific market.
6. They should be product oriented and need to expand into new markets.

You can find companies by looking in the *Thomas Register*, reading trade magazines (especially issues containing listings of companies in the industry), attending trade shows, and getting trade show directories from recent years. You can also find potential licensees by looking for products in retail stores, though that method will overlook many potential licensees. If you live in a larger town, your public library may carry the trade magazines you need. Otherwise, you'll have to order them from the publisher (see Chapter 4).

Your next step is to order literature from each company and find out the size of each, as well as who their presidents and marketing directors are. You can simply call companies to get brochures of their full product lines. Your library will have resources to help you determine company sizes, including state industrial directories, the *Million Dollar Directory* and the *Middle Market Directory* (both published by Dun & Bradstreet), *Standard and Poor's Register of Corporations, Directors and Executives,* and *Dun & Bradstreet's Reference Book of Corporate Management.* If your library doesn't have these resources, be sure to ask your reference librarian for help. They probably have an on-line computer service that can give you this information.

A key fact you can sometimes get from corporate management books is the relative importance of the R&D department. A company is a good licensing candidate if it doesn't list an R&D vice president but *does* list a marketing vice president. Another tactic is to look at the background of the president. The company will be a better licensing candidate if the president has a marketing background rather than one in engineering or finance.

You should be able to generate a priority list of between five and ten potential licensees and a second priority list of another five to ten companies based upon these three criteria:

1. The annual sales volume of the company is one to two times your product's potential.
2. Your positioning strategy fits into the company's business strategy.
3. The company has one or more of the six desirable licensing characteristics.

You're not ready to start approaching companies yet—first, because you don't have your product finished and, second, because you can benefit greatly if you can get an inside contact within a company. But you should have a firm grasp of what companies you will approach, why you will approach them, and what tactics you'll use in your sales presentation.

STEP 6: MAKING PERSONAL CONTACTS WITH COMPANIES

Your odds of licensing a product rise dramatically if you can get a personal contact within a target company early on. This contact can help you in three ways:

1. By adding or modifying features that will help sell your idea
2. By providing a person who will champion your idea within the company
3. By getting you in the door to make the presentation

The two best ways to make these contacts are by following up with the sales representatives that send you literature and by attending trade shows. I believe it's essential to attend at least one industry trade show. You'll learn more about the market by seeing companies' actual products, plus you'll get a chance to see how aggressive companies are by the size of their booths and staffing levels. Avoid talking to potential contacts during busy periods at trade shows. Instead, talk to them just as the show opens or in the last hour or two in the evenings when booth activity is low.

Before you make any contact, you should work out a two- or three-paragraph statement that explains what you're doing and why you're doing it, as well as the reason you think you should be talking to this contact's particular company. You must look very professional in your first contact if you want to be taken seriously. Your statement should follow a sequence similar to the following:

1. Greeting. "Hi, I'm (*your name*). I'm developing a product for the (*list market or application's name*). Can I ask you a couple of questions?"

   Comment: Don't say you're an inventor looking to license an idea, which will often immediately turn off businesspeople.

2. "Let me explain something about my background."

   Comment: Tell the person why you are interested or involved in the industry and why you should be able to develop a product that will sell. You might be in sales and marketing, or be an industry engineer or an end user of industry products.

3. "I believe there has been a need in the industry for a product that (*whatever your product idea will do*). Do you also see a need for this type of product?"

Comment: You should verify that the person sees the same need as you do; otherwise, he or she won't end up being that helpful. The person might also explain why the industry doesn't have the need you've identified, which would be important market research information.

4. "I believe the most important feature of this type of product needs to be (*state here what you believe to be your product's most important benefit*). Do you see other benefits as being equally or more important?"

   Comment: Again, you're collecting information. Asking for and respecting the contact's input will encourage the contact to support you.

5. "Once the product is through its market-testing phase, I'm considering having it distributed by another company. I believe your company would be ideal for this because my product would help it (*list the reason you developed from your positioning strategy*). Do you think your company would be interested in selling the product?"

   Comment: Licensing a product after complete market-testing is the best-case scenario from a company's point of view. If a company isn't interested in taking on products at this stage, it won't be interested in taking them on earlier in the development cycle. You may not be able to take a product this far, but at least you know the company is a licensing candidate if its representative says yes to this question.

6. "Has your company ever sold another company's product or licensed a product before?"

   Comment: Just more market intelligence to help you select the best company target? If the company isn't interested in distributing another company's product, ask if the person knows other companies in the industry that have sold or licensed products from other companies.

7. "Can I call you and ask you questions as I proceed on the project?"

   Comment: Half the time people will say yes and they can be ongoing contacts for you.

8. "Is there anyone else at your company I should contact?"

   Comment: Get as many names as you can for future follow-up. You can then call them and mention that your contact suggested you call.

You should be able to develop a list of three to five contacts, and hopefully more, at companies you've targeted as ideal licensing candidates.

STEP 7: DECIDING WHEN TO GET A PATENT

While in many cases a patent may provide uncertain or negligible bene-fits, it may be difficult to license an idea without a patent unless it has just a small potential market. I believe most companies will see your not hav-ing a patent as a sign that you don't have confidence in your idea. You don't want to have to tiptoe around the question, "If your idea is so great, why weren't you willing to patent it?" However, you need to decide *when* to get a patent when pursuing a licensing strategy. The times you could apply for a patent include:

- Prior to developing industry contacts in Step 6 of the licensing strategy
- After developing a network of industry contacts
- After developing information regarding the go/no-go decisions (see Chapters 6 through 9)
- After a prototype or preproduction model is built
- After an initial sales period (see Chapters 9 and 10)

Prior to Developing Industry Contacts

I don't recommend getting a patent until you know that the industry regards the need you've addressed as important and at least a few compa-nies have expressed interest in the concept of selling or licensing another person's product. Before that point, too many things can go wrong. You might find that other similar products have been introduced and have failed or the industry is moving in another direction to solve the problem. You could also discover that companies in the business won't license ideas. Any or all of these circumstances are indications that your product will be difficult, if not impossible, to license.

After Developing Industry Contacts

I rarely recommend getting a patent immediately after acquiring an industry contact. The only time I think this is possible is when a company has expressed a high degree of interest and might be willing to fund the rest of the product development. When evaluating a license, a company will be concerned with the following:

- Will the product sell?
- Can the product be made as designed?
- How much time, effort, and money will it take to produce and commercialize the idea?

- Can the product be manufactured at a price low enough to produce profits?
- How much protection does the idea have in terms of patents or trademarks to stop competition?

You've addressed only the first and last of these concerns after you've made industry contacts. That is simply not enough information for most companies to accept a licensing arrangement. You don't have an answer at all for the remaining concerns. The only situation that lends itself to successful licensing at this time is if a company has already decided to develop a product similar to yours.

After Researching the Go/No-Go Decisions

The go/no-go decisions discussed in Chapters 6 through 9 address the concerns of marketability, manufacturing technology and cost, distribution channels, and inside help. After you complete the go/no-go decisions, you can usually answer every question. The only exception is if your product is complicated or has difficult mechanical features, so that you can't answer the question of whether you can produce the product as designed.

This is a good time to go for a patent if you have the money. It allows you to use a tactic that I refer to as a "get-acquainted" offer. This tactic addresses one of the factors I've found to be consistent in the invention business: Few people decide on the spot to invest in, distribute, or license an idea. It seems to take several contacts to sell an idea. This works against the inventor when he or she makes an all-or-nothing licensing proposal.

A get-acquainted offer shows a company a product in drawing form after the go/no-go decision period. You can make a strong presentation for the product, but a company is unlikely to license it until a prototype has been built and some proof of sales exists. Instead of offering to just license the idea, the inventor can offer three options:

1. License the idea immediately.
2. Pay a sum of money (say, $15,000) to have a prototype developed, or pay a larger sum (say, $45,000) to have a prototype developed, tested, engineered, and sourced for production.
3. Pay a still larger sum (say, $75,000) to have the product tested in several markets.

In return for advancing you the money, the company would have the right of first refusal for a licensing contract. Chances are the company will say that it's not interested in any of those options, but it would like you to come back when the product is further developed. This reaction is exactly what you are looking for. A positive response like this will help you get an investor, plus it puts you in a much stronger position for your next visit. But this is a dangerous strategy to pursue without a patent.

After a Prototype Is Built

The danger of applying for a patent before you build a prototype is that you may not be able to make your product exactly as planned. Any changes you end up having to make may result in your product not having any patent protection.

The term *prototype* implies different concepts to inventors and companies. Inventors see a prototype as a last stage before beginning production. A company will look at a prototype as a first step in the industrial design process that might cost anywhere from an additional $20,000 to $50,000—even for a simple product. Typically, what a company wants to see before licensing is a preproduction model, which is a high-quality product that will look just like production units.

For some products, such as tools or simple plastic parts, an inventor can put together a preproduction model, but for other products that are more complicated, inventors just don't have the experience or equipment to make a polished-looking product. When this happens, product entrepreneurs looking for licenses need to get help from industrial designers.

Inventors unable to produce preproduction models are in a difficult spot. Even though they pay for patents, they still might have trouble getting licenses without preproduction models. If the inventors do pay for preproduction models, there is still no guarantee that the products will be licensed. I believe that inventors should get their patents, if the products have passed all the go/no-go decisions discussed in Chapters 6 through 9, and then try to leverage the situation to their advantage, using the following steps:

1. Apply for a patent. If you can't afford to apply for a patent, approach a friend or family member for an investment. Explain that you need a $3,000 or $5,000 investment to patent an idea before you approach a manufacturer.

2. Talk to industrial designers and see if you can find one who will work on your invention at a reduced rate, provided you get a positive response from a manufacturer, in return for a percentage of the profit from the invention. For example, instead of paying $20,000, you might pay $5,000 and give up 20 percent of the invention's profits to the designer. (*Note:* You will need to make a presentation to the designer about the merits of your idea for this agreement.) Don't sign an agreement yet; just get a commitment.

3. Approach the targeted manufacturers and offer to either license your idea to them or develop a preproduction model for just $5,000. Explain that you have a designer who has agreed to work for a reduced rate in return for a share of the product. The manufacturer may say no, but, again, you are exposing the idea to the manufacturer and raising your chances of eventually getting a license.

4. Go back to the designer and investor and explain that you've had a positive response but you need the designer to work at a reduced rate and the investor to help with expenses. Once you have a request from a manufacturer, people typically have trouble saying no.

This approach won't always work, but sometimes it will, providing you can convincingly show that your idea has a chance to succeed.

After an Initial Sales Period

You may be able to produce and sell products with simple mechanical mechanisms. Under the former first-to-invent patent laws this was a low-risk strategy; however, it is much riskier under the current first-to-file patent laws. If you can afford a patent, I recommend that you apply for one once you've finished a prototype. If you can't afford a patent, I would recommend that you first do a small initial sales period (covered in Chapters 11 and 12). If your sales period is successful, you will increase your chances of getting a license, which should increase your chances of getting an investor who will pay for the patent.

STEP 8: FINISHING THE DEVELOPMENT OF YOUR IDEA

In Steps 1 through 7 you've been involved in a planning process, determining who your target customer is (the companies you'll approach for a licensing agreement), and what concept or positioning statement you are going to sell them. Your job now is to develop a product that appeals to the customers of those companies. The next three chapters cover distribution, product appeal, and manufacturing. After you finish those chapters, you will be ready to put together a licensing presentation that you can use for guiding your product development, investor and industrial designer meetings, and eventual licensing meetings (see Figure 5-3).

I've learned over the years that one of the safest steps an inventor can take is to prepare his or her licensing presentation first, before completely developing the idea. This approach offers four major benefits:

Figure 5-3 Sample Presentation Information Based on a Pillow Pad Device That Attaches to the Bottom of a Baby Walker

---

The Licensing Presentation—Key Elements

1. Provide a short overview
   a. Product description: *A new product that protects furniture from a baby walker.* (A great name will add considerably to the presentation.)
   b. Target market: *The 20 million parents per year who have children six to 12 months old.*
   c. Market size: *Four million baby walkers are sold each year.*
   d. Yearly profit and sales potential: *The product has an annual sales potential of $4 million per year, with an expected net annual profit of $600,000.*
2. State why you developed this product (which should be a personalized story): *I was tired of my baby ramming into the dining room furniture.*
3. Verify that the market sees the same need as you do: *I did a search through 12 months of trade magazines without finding any similar products, and I talked to six people in the industry who all agreed that a baby bumper product is one that should be available.*
4. State your objectives in designing the product: *You wanted the product to:*
   - *Meet new industry trends*
   - *Help the company licensing the product to solidify its product line so that it can expand its distribution network*
   - *Stand out and sell itself on a retailer's shelf*
   - *Be easy and safe to use*
   - *Meet the safety requirements of children advocacy groups*
   - *Be inexpensive to the manufacturer*
   - *Be eligible for significant protection from a utility patent*
5. Demonstrate and show the product. During the demonstration, list the two or three major product highlights:
   - *Ease of installation*
   - *Rugged protection*
   - *Appealing design*
6. List and show the major selling features of the product:
   - *Velcro straps*
   - *Adjustable to a variety of walkers*
   - *Easy-to-manufacture construction*
   - *Dirt-resistant fabric* (Continued)

Figure 5-3 *Continued*

- *Soft, high-impact-resistant foam*
- *Product looks great in a low-cost package*

7. Show projected retail price and manufacturing cost. Be sure to show how you determined these.

   a. *Suggested retail price is $14.95. We determined this price by having 15 consumers compare the product to six other products* (list the other products on an overhead or display board) *and then having the consumers rank the products in order of their value.*

   b. *The listed cost is an average of three manufacturing quotes.*

8. Tell the manufacturer why you decided it would be the ideal licensing candidate: *The company's competitors have broader product lines, your product is a perfect match for another product in its line, the company's competitors have recently introduced new products, or another reason you've identified.*

9. State your goal: *I want to license my idea to you.* Then, depending on the company's resources, list additional help you can offer:

   - *Arrange for a pilot plant production run.*
   - *Initiate agreements with distributors or manufacturers' sales agents.*
   - *Arrange for final industrial design and engineering documentation.*

---

1. You'll have a clear vision of the product you want to develop. Most products require at least two or three modifications from your original vision. You'll make better decisions about how to execute those changes if you know exactly what you want to end up licensing.

2. You'll get feedback about what the market needs or wants, which should help you create a more salable idea.

3. You'll have information to present to people who might invest in your idea.

4. You'll be fairly confident that you have an idea with potential before you start spending money for prototypes and models.

Once you have finished a first draft of the licensing presentation, you are ready to move on to making a model or prototype, generating market research, and then, if necessary, producing a preproduction model. Chapters 7 and 8, on distribution and product appeal, will help you research the important features for your idea and then proceed to finalize your idea.

THE NEXT STEP

Step 9 is to develop proof that your product will sell (see Chapters 6 through 11). That's the very same step product entrepreneurs need to complete in order to get investments. I don't like to treat licensing as a totally different approach from introducing an idea on your own. Every step you take to demonstrate that your idea will sell dramatically increases your odds of getting a license. Most inventors don't think this way at all. They believe they can just build prototypes—or maybe even just get by with drawings—in order to get licenses. While some inventors do get licenses with just drawings or prototypes, most don't.

A year ago, I worked with four men who had developed a tow bar that attached to the front of a car. The tow bar had two applications: one for cars being pulled by RVs and the second for farmers who could pull their cars behind trailers when they switched fields. Farmers needed this product because they often leave their tractors in the fields and then drive back and forth to their homes. They are then in a jam when they want to move their tractors to other fields.

The product competed against a standard tow bar that would attach to the back of an RV or tractor. While the RV and agricultural markets are large and the product innovative, companies weren't interested in licensing the product when they weren't certain how well the design could be executed or how well the product would sell. The group finalized the design of the product and came up with a solid invention, then proceeded to get a patent. But they still couldn't prove the product would sell.

The group's next step was to build a limited inventory and start to sell the product at RV shows and through limited advertising in trade shows. One thing the group learned was that it didn't have the right design. So the group redesigned the product and started to sell it again, with limited success.

This is where I came into the project. The group had run out of money and didn't know which way to go. I put together an aggressive PR program, and we managed to get more than ten press releases published in trade magazines. Then we stopped selling to people directly from the PR leads and, instead, used those orders to entice distributors to sign up with the company. Once the company started adding distribution locations, one of the market's major players approached the company to buy it out on a royalty basis. The group worked for four years to license the idea. It took this long because they started out thinking that licensing was an easy approach that wouldn't take much time.

––––––––––––––––

Chapter 13, following the chapters on selling your product, will discuss Steps 9 through 12, which cover preparing your final presentation, approaching exactly the right companies, and negotiating a licensing agreement.

PART TWO

THE GO/NO-GO DECISIONS

A product creator's decision-making process should be based, at least in part, on an evaluation of risk/reward ratios. At every moment in a project's introduction cycle, a product entrepreneur has to know how much money he or she is willing to risk on the project. I believe that no more than 40 percent of a product's projected yearly income should be invested. The risks involved in taking a product to market are too great to justify a higher percentage.

For example, if you have a product that you can reasonably project will have annual sales of $1 million per year, and your industry's breakout chart (from Chapter 4) lists a profit percentage of 10 percent, you will have a yearly profit potential of $100,000 before taxes, or roughly $70,000 after taxes. You shouldn't invest any more than $30,000 in the project.

The key phrase in the previous paragraph is *reasonably project*. This isn't just what you think can be sold or what you'd like to sell. Chapter 6 discusses how to reasonably project a product's potential sales.

The risk/reward ratios are guides throughout an entire project. I once looked at an interesting dental product that could possibly produce a yearly income of $250,000. But I couldn't be sure. Was the product feasible? Could it be produced at a low enough price? What would the development costs be? For a $300 fee, an engineering group looked at the product and gave me its opinion on my three questions. I thought that the $300 expenditure was worthwhile, because it represented only a small percentage of the $50,000 to $100,000 the project was worth. The study, I knew, would also help in finding investors and/or partners. Would I have been willing to pay $5,000 for the study (which some companies wanted to charge me)? No; it wouldn't have left enough money to cover all the other introduction costs.

Part 2 covers the go/no-go decisions you'll need to make on your project. Some decisions will have absolute guidelines, such as: Don't try to sell a product when its benefit isn't obvious. Other criteria aren't absolute. On some projects, a certain dollar risk is acceptable, because the project has strong sales potential. On others, the risk would be too high.

For example, suppose you have a product that makes painting corners and edges easier. When you survey the market, you find that most painting products are sold through chains of paint stores, hardware stores, or discount stores. Now assume that none of these firms has a headquarters near you and that a minimum of $1,500 for travel would be needed to get essential inside help for promoting the product. Is it worth going ahead? I'd say yes, if the product is unique, and no, if the product is only an improvement over an existing project.

The risk and rewards of your product can be a guide to the best way to proceed on your project. As the creator of the painting product described above, you might see that getting an industry person to help on the project is worth only $1,000. Instead of trying to visit home offices, you might team up with another entrepreneur and buy a booth at a local or national trade show. This tactic would hold costs down to an acceptable level.

Remember, as you read Part 2, that there is not a clearly defined time when you make go/no-go decisions. You make them all the time, over and over again, checking whether to continue. Make it a point to check your go/no-go decisions at least every month or two, and before incurring any major expense.

6

DISTRIBUTION: NOTHING IS MORE IMPORTANT

Jan Dutton loved lacy things: aprons, doilies, tabletop items, decorative bedroom ensembles. About ten years ago, Jan noticed that there weren't many handmade lace items on the market. Jan formed her own company, Paper White, and started selling a line of lace products, at retail prices of $90 and up, to a few expensive New York stores.

Mike Murphy, a 23-year-old hospital orderly, noticed how some patients had trouble moving in bed and consequently developed painful bedsores. Mike thought bedsores could be eliminated if he could make various parts of the mattress removable. He designed the DeCube Health Care Mattress, a 7-inch foam mattress that contains removable cubes in the areas where the patient using the mattress is likely to develop bedsores. Mike then started to sell the product to hospitals and nursing homes through medical distributors.

These ventures have a common feature: The products created were made to sell in markets that are small, easy to identify, and simple to reach. In this type of market, inventors have the best chance of setting up a distribution network.

The market for Jan Dutton's line of lace products is upper-middle-class and wealthy women who like handmade lace. This small market is an advantage to Jan: She won't encounter much competition, and she'll be able to charge a higher price. Because handmade lace products are sold through a limited number of stores, the market is easy to identify and simple to reach.

The market for hospital and nursing home mattresses may seem, at first glance, a fragmented one. However, medical products are sold through well-established distributors who are happy to handle a new and unique product. The market is simple to reach.

Distribution is the marketing term for the method or process by which a product moves from the manufacturer to the consumer. For example, for clothing, the chain of selling may begin with a manufacturer and continue on to a wholesaler, a distributor, a clothing store, and finally, a consumer. This whole process is called a *distribution network*. Some manufacturers have a much shorter network; they may, for example, send out mail-order catalogs and then receive orders on an incoming 800 number.

Why do most inventors overlook distribution, when the go/no-go decisions regarding distribution are critically important? Distribution is an activity that most consumers are never aware of. They see only the product on the market, and they take its presence there for granted. Most product creators have no idea of the distribution considerations that are involved in introducing a product. Many potential entrepreneurs have worked at companies that have distribution networks in place. These people don't realize the work their company went through to establish its network.

I'm not saying that you shouldn't go ahead with a product that has distribution problems; there is always room in the market for a truly novel product. But be forewarned about the difficulties you'll face before you develop an introduction strategy.

WHY YOU MUST EVALUATE DISTRIBUTION

In one word, the reason is *money*. Each distribution network has four concerns that involve money:

1. How much product support is needed?
2. How big is the market?
3. How long will it take to collect receivables?
4. How should the product be designed?

How Much Product Support Is Needed?

Joan P. created a kit of directions for 50 to 60 projects that parents and young children could do together. What made the kit outstanding was

that every activity could be done using common household materials.
Joan had created her kit because she got tired of always having to run
to the store for materials when she wanted to do a parent/child activity.

Joan's product was exceptionally good, but she wasn't selling many units. Her problem was that her market was fragmented. Because most educational toy stores are individually owned, she couldn't reach them by calling on a few buyers for large chains. Educational toy stores are a relatively new segment, and there are no established distributors or manufacturers' sales agents. Joan had to have her own sales force call on each store. Maintaining a sales force creates high product-support expense.

Joan's other options were to sell her product to mail-order catalogs, to send a sales flyer to the names on a purchased mailing list of parents of young children, or to advertise in magazines. Joan didn't think mail-order catalogs would generate enough sales, and she couldn't afford a large mailing or magazine advertising. There was no inexpensive way for Joan to put her product on the market.

Every market has a variety of distribution networks. You need to choose a network that you can afford and can penetrate. As an example, let's look at exercise equipment. The potential distribution networks include mail-order catalogs, health clubs, medical equipment (for physical therapy) distributors, order blanks in magazine ads, sporting goods stores, discount or department stores, and other manufacturers.

Let's take a quick look at the promotional cost for each network.

- *Mail-order catalogs.* If you sell to a mail-order catalog company, your only promotional expense may be the cost of providing a color picture and a short explanation of the product. The problem with mail-order catalogs is that a product can be overlooked in the middle of name-brand, low-priced, and discounted items. A mail-order catalog might work well for an inexpensive consumer item, but high-priced equipment from an unknown manufacturer probably won't sell in a catalog unless it's endorsed by an athlete or famous personality. Celebrities don't endorse products for free. They usually charge a minimum of $10,000, or they require a percentage of the product's profit.
- *Health clubs.* Promotional costs will be high. At a minimum, you will need to demonstrate a product before health clubs will consider it. You may be required to leave it at the clubs for a free trial period. To demonstrate health equipment, you'll need either a salesperson or a sales agent. Product creators typically prefer a sales agent working on a 15 to 20 percent commission, but very few sales agents handle health club exercise equipment. The market is dominated by just a few large companies, such as Nautilus, that carry a wide variety of products. The advantage of selling to

health clubs is that products established in the clubs will sell more easily in other markets. Word-of-mouth advertising works well in a small market like that of health clubs because many of the buyers know each other.

- *Medical equipment distributors.* Like health clubs, these distributors will have service and demonstration requirements. An endorsement from a medical expert may also be needed. An advantage of this market is that there are established distributors and sales agents for medical products. Sales agents usually won't sell a product that has extensive service and demonstration requirements, unless they get a minimum $300 to $500 commission per sale.

- *Order blanks in magazine ads.* NordicTrack (exercise equipment) is an example of a manufacturer that sells many of its products through magazine ads. Placing ads in magazines has several advantages. A key benefit is that you can have more control of your business. Retailers and distributors may decide to stop carrying a product, but magazines always take ads. If sales fall off, you can run more ads. Another plus is that, as the manufacturer, you receive the total retail price. The big disadvantages of magazine ads are that they take a huge up-front investment and they are rarely effective until people see them at least three or four times. Some ads don't produce a positive return for six to nine months. Over that time period, an investment in ads could approach $50,000, with no guarantees of success. An ad campaign can flop completely, no matter how many times the ads are run.

- *Sporting goods stores.* Chains such as Sportmart and numerous independent sporting goods stores are found in virtually every medium-size and large city in America. Sports product creators will run into stiff competition from major manufacturers, especially at large chains. The chains will request an advertising campaign to support the product's sales. Independent stores can be a better outlet for a product creator. When counted together, independent stores make up a good share of the market, but each store's small size prevents it from getting a large discount. By offering a large discount, a product creator can give a retailer a chance to make more money per unit sold. The network of distributors and manufacturers' sales agents that already serves this market can be contacted by attending regional trade shows for sporting goods retailers.

- *Discount or department stores.* Selling to Kmart, Wal-Mart, or Target is the dream of every new entrepreneur. The lure of the potentially large orders is irresistible, but these orders can be difficult for an entrepreneur to obtain. Most discount stores prefer products with well-known brand names, an ad campaign, or a huge promotional discount. Another problem for budding entrepreneurs is that most large stores don't look favorably upon small, one-line companies. Too often, the companies quickly go out of business.

- *Other manufacturers.* In this network, an inventor sells to another company, which then packages and sells the product under its own name. When I worked for the dental supply manufacturer, we sold a dental light that carried the company's name. The product was made for us by a tiny manufacturer in England. When the product was first created, the inventor didn't have a marketing department or a sales force, so he offered the product to us. We had no dental light in our line, so we were happy to carry the product. Selling to another company is the quickest way for an entrepreneur to achieve a significant sales volume with minimal product support costs. A disadvantage of selling to another company is that profits can be hard to come by. Manufacturing companies typically have sales and marketing costs totaling 20 to 30 percent of their sales dollars. When another company, in effect, becomes your sales and marketing department, you need to offer a discount of 40 to 50 percent, which is the same as almost doubling your marketing and sales costs. Only products that can be sold for six to seven times their manufacturing cost can afford this discount.

Based on these evaluations, a poorly financed entrepreneur has only three viable options: mail-order catalogs, independent sporting goods stores, and other manufacturers (also referred to as *private labeling*).

If you're unsure about the promotional costs of a distribution network, find a manufacturer in the same market but with a product that won't compete with yours. For example, if an exercise equipment manufacturer makes a cross-country ski machine, then a noncompeting product could be a stationary bike. Call up one of the manufacturer's salespeople or a manufacturers' representative (or sales agent) and ask what types of promotion the manufacturer uses and what expenses you can expect when you introduce a product.

How does a hopeful entrepreneur come up with the various ways to distribute a product? By following the guidelines on professionalism, given in Chapter 4. I can't emphasize enough how important it is to know the basic information about a market.

How Big Is the Market?

"The market" is not the total of all potential customers. The market is the customers that can be reached by the distribution networks you can afford. For example, for the exercise equipment market, an estimate of the size of each distribution network can usually be found in trade magazines. A typical statistic would indicate that about $20 million worth of equipment is sold through health clubs. If you can't find information in trade magazines, locate the industry's trade association in *The Book of Associations*, available in the reference section of most large libraries. Most associations will provide market size data directly, if requested. Another way of estimating the market is to research companies' annual reports to see whether they list a product line's sales dollars and market share. The sales number can be divided by the market share to calculate how big the market is. Independent statistics give the best profiles of market size. If necessary, fall back on the information from industry insiders or salespeople.

To calculate a risk/reward ratio, you need to be able to estimate your potential sales volume. Entrepreneurs like to say that they should be able to capture a certain percentage of the market. One inventor told me that he had such a superior product that he would be able to capture at least 25 percent of the market. That's a totally wrong approach. Markets are not that predictable.

A much better way to estimate sales potential is to gather data on the market shares of companies in the market. Most markets have three types of competitors:

1. *The market leaders.* Usually one or two companies dominate a market. Their name recognition and promotional muscle make them tough to dislodge.

2. *The second-tier companies.* Three or four companies will usually have a market share that is about 25 to 50 percent of that of the market leaders.

3. *The small companies.* Several companies in a market will have small market shares.

Your highest potential market share can be expected to lie somewhere between the share of the top small company and that of the lowest second-tier company. As a rule, you'll find that this market share ranges from 5 to 8 percent.

If you have a completely new product, you can estimate your potential sales by gathering data on another product in the same industry.

Terry P. created 18-inch-high posts that could be placed in a garden in such a way that gardeners could run a soaker hose through them. The benefit of Terry's product was that, by preventing plants from blocking the hose's spray, it allowed more even watering.

When Terry couldn't find any products like his on the market, he consulted The Great American Catalog Guide *at his library. Terry found the address for the Gardener's Supply catalog, which had the slogan "Innovative Gardening Solutions." Terry ordered the catalog and found in it a product called Hose Guides—little wheel-tracks atop 10½-inch steel spikes, for routing a hose around the outside of a garden. This simple guide eliminates the problem of gardeners crushing flowers after accidentally pulling a hose into the garden. Terry's next steps were to order the Hose Guides, see who the manufacturer was, and call that company for more information on potential sales volume. Most manufacturers will share a considerable amount of information provided you send them a drawing or product sample to reassure them that your product does not compete with theirs.*

Product creators are disappointed when they find that a similar product has a relatively low sales base. Market share is based on more than how good a product is: A company's promotional muscle and distribution network are key factors, and most inventors don't have them.

Entrepreneurs are not wrong in looking at the total size of a potential market; that large market could make an idea worth a million dollars. However, to penetrate an entire market takes five to ten years. Dollar volume and risk/reward ratios should be predicted only for the market size served by the distribution network selected for initial sales efforts.

How Long Will It Take to Collect Receivables?

Manufacturers would like to think that once they ship a product, payment immediately follows. Sales don't work that way. Payment in 30 days (net 30) is common, but, in some markets, distributors or stores pay only after 60 days. A one-product company that is not a regular supplier is always paid last. Because you won't have much cash, how long it takes to get paid is a big consideration. You might receive money immediately from someone ordering from a magazine ad, but you might not be paid until after 90 days if you sell to sporting goods stores through manufacturers' representatives.

Operating cash is an inventor's responsibility. Six months may go by between the time supplies are purchased and the time payment is received. Calculate carefully how much operating cash you will need to make your projected shipments. As a safety precaution, add an extra 30 to 60 days' operating cash to your projections.

Lack of operating cash causes many inventors to fail. They line up some distributors, their products are placed on store shelves, and then, because of cash problems, they are unable to ship additional orders. The distributors then lose interest in the products.

I had operating cash considerations when I introduced a lottery pen, a novelty item for picking lottery numbers for Lotto America. The pen's top compartment held 48 white and 6 blue balls. On the side of the pen were 2 long slots. To pick lottery numbers, the user tipped the pen upside down to bring all the balls into the top compartment, and then tipped the pen down so that the balls would run down into the slots. Next to where each ball stopped was a number from 1 to 54. A lottery player would use the numbers next to the blue balls for his or her lottery ticket.

I introduced the pen in October. My two partners and I thought that timing was ideal. Before starting sales, we had to figure out our operating requirements. Our key target market was convenience stores that were lottery locations. About three-fourths of the convenience stores were chain stores; the rest were independents. To sell to the chains, we had to go through rack jobbers. We could sell directly to the independent stores through salespeople.

Rack jobbers are important in many distribution networks. In addition to convenience stores, they sell to drugstores, variety stores, and some large department stores such as Target. A *rack jobber* obtains a verbal or written agreement to supply all of a certain type of product to a store. For example, a drugstore might use a hair products jobber as the supplier of all of its brushes, barrettes, ponytail holders, and so on. A convenience store might have all its stationery products and toys furnished by a jobber. Typically, the jobber provides the initial merchandise at no charge to the retailer and invoices the store for only the merchandise the jobber replaces. This is a great service for the retailer, who receives an inventory loan, a weekly or biweekly restocking of merchandise, and an ability to stock small quantities of products at a reasonable cost.

Jobbers are difficult for an entrepreneur to deal with. They are an extra step in the distribution process, and they usually require a 30 to 45 percent discount. More important for our lottery pen, jobbers are almost always low on cash because they have to put merchandise in stores without charging for it. The jobbers don't get paid for 60 to 90 days, and it's very tough for a new entrepreneur, with just one product, to have to wait 120 days to be paid.

Sales to independent stores, through a salesperson, could be made directly for cash on delivery. Our problem was recruiting salespeople for a three- to six-month job when a box of pens sold for $34 and we paid only a $9 commission.

There were roughly 1,500 locations in our area that sold Lotto America tickets. About 1,000 of them were convenience stores. On our supply side, we had a $1,500 line of credit from the manufacturer and 30-day terms. Our price was $18 per box. The manufacturer would not ship us product if we were over the credit limit. Figure 6-1 shows our operating cash analysis. An important point to note is that we didn't want to have more than 60 boxes in inventory at any one time, to minimize our risk if the product didn't meet expectations.

Figure 6-1 Operating Cash Analysis—Lottery Pen Sales

Sales Goals: **Sell 250 boxes of pens between October and December, and 300 boxes between January and March, with 25 percent of the sales being cash sales.**

Comments: You need a sales goal to determine how much operating cash is needed. Otherwise, you won't know how many units to buy. Set your goals modestly. If your goals are too high, you might not be able to come up with enough money. If sales are much higher than you expect, you should be able to use those orders to borrow money from a bank. Our goal was based on selling 2 boxes each to 125 stores; we were expecting to sell to about 12 percent of the lottery locations.

Cash Flow Analysis

	Sept.	*Oct.*	*Nov.*	*Dec.*	*Jan.*	*Feb.*	*Mar.*
Units ordered	18	126	54	54	130	85	85
Cash outlay ($)	—	(324)	(2,266)	(972)	(972)	(2,340)	(1,530)
Cash sales (units)	—	20	20	20	30	30	30
Cash received ($)	—	500	500	500	750	750	750
Credit sales (boxes)	—	90	35	30	72	72	72
Cash received ($)	—	—	—	—	—	2,250	875
Total cash received	—	500	500	500	750	3,000	1,525
Change in cash position	—	176	(1,766)	(472)	(222)	660	(5)
Ending cash position	—	176	(1,590)	(2,062)	(2,284)	(1,624)	(1,629)
Ending inventory (units)	18	34	33	37	60	43	26

Notes:

1. We expected payment on credit sales in 120 days. Our actual terms were 60 days, but we anticipated late payments.

2. We paid for the products received from our supplier in 30 to 45 days. Most new entrepreneurs will have to pay cash on delivery to their suppliers.

3. We could afford to make only one big (90-unit) sale to a convenience store, in order to hold our operating cash requirements to less than $3,000. Notice how we projected another big sale in January, one month before we expected payment on the first big order. Most entrepreneurs have to watch carefully how they take big orders, to avoid a cash crunch.

4. Chapter 4 has an operating cash statement for an entrepreneur/manufacturer of a product.

Some people take a shortcut to calculate their operating cash. They take the average units ordered per month (in this case, 100 boxes) and multiply it by the difference in time between when the customers pay and when supplies have to be paid for (in this case, 4 months minus 1 month, or 3 months). The operating cash is then that number (300) times the cost from the manufacturer ($18). Using this method, our operating cash requirement was $5,400 plus a contingency of $900, or $6,300. I prefer the more detailed method, which provides a more accurate amount. A thorough approach helps you to set sales goals and sales patterns based on their impact on operating cash.

We sold the lottery pen for only 3 months. We put about 300 boxes on the market, but each box took 30 to 60 days to sell out in a convenience store. That turnover wasn't fast enough to generate the repeat sales we needed to have a profitable product. We made money on the project, but not enough to justify our time and effort.

How Should the Product Be Designed?

Most products can be made in a variety of ways. For instance, exercise equipment can be made from chrome-plated steel and sold for a premium price, or it can be made from painted plastic parts and sold for a low price. Each distribution network sells a slightly different type of product. A health club, for example, wants a sturdy, premium-priced unit. A sporting goods store looks for midpriced products. Discount stores want to buy only low-priced products.

Suppose you are manufacturing toys and you decide to sell them through distributors, then rack jobbers, and then convenience stores. You know from your market research that rack jobbers won't handle a product with a retail price over $10. You also know that the required discounts are 40 to 50 percent for convenience stores and another 30 to 40 percent for rack jobbers. That means the rack jobbers will buy the product from you for about $3.00, and the convenience stores will buy it from the rack jobbers for about $5.00. You have to make the product for $1.50 if you want to make any money. As an example of how the discounts affect a manufacturer, our lottery pen sold for a retail price of $2.99. The retailer paid $1.55 per pen and the rack jobber paid $1.05.

What your product needs to be like is not a distribution go/no-go decision. But the cost of the product will be important when you decide on how to manufacture it. (Manufacturing issues are discussed in Chapter 8.)

Your first three go/no-go decisions revolve around the costs of doing business within a distribution network:

1. Does a network exist in which you can afford the product support required?

2. Is the market size of that network large enough to justify your initial investment for developing the product as you envision it?
3. Can you afford the operating cash requirements for your chosen method of distribution?

WHEN IS A PRODUCT EASY TO DISTRIBUTE?

I have four criteria to help me determine whether a product will be easy to place on the market:

1. Is the market small?
2. Are consumers easy to target?
3. Is the distribution network concentrated?
4. Is the market open?

If you can't answer yes to at least three of the four criteria, you'll have trouble and you'll need a lot of money to introduce your new product idea.

Is the Market Small?

I consider any market of less than $5 million to be small. I believe the ideal market size for a product creator is $3 million to $5 million. Some of you are probably surprised to see this limited recommendation because a big market is where you can really make money. However, an inventor has several advantages when approaching a small market.

1. *Better market information.* Insiders in a small market will be able to predict fairly accurately whether a product will succeed. They will also be able to offer you a detailed introduction plan. These insiders are knowledgeable because there aren't many companies in the market.

In big markets, companies with new products come and go quickly. A wide variety of consumers support big markets, for different and sometimes changing reasons. Product creators will always have trouble predicting how their products will do in big markets.

2. *Larger profit margins.* A profit margin is calculated by dividing profit, after all expenses, by total sales dollars. If a company had a $10,000 profit on total sales of $100,000, its profit margin would be 10 percent. Large markets are crowded with competitors and generally have lower profit margins than small markets. The margins can be especially low for entrepreneurs who don't have a low-cost manufacturing method.

In a small market, usually none of the manufacturers has a low production cost. Most small-market companies are saddled with high overhead, which allows inventors to enter the market in a favorable cost position. As a result, inventors can often make a 20 percent (or higher) margin in a small market.

3. *Minimum competition.*   Large companies don't like small markets. A company's costs for maintaining product support, which includes manufacturing documentation, engineering time, quality control, and purchasing, are almost the same for a low-volume product as for a high-volume one. This fact discourages large companies from entering small markets.

4. *Stability of small markets.*   The same products can sell for years in a small market. The primary reason for the inertia is that the market size is too small to justify the expense of a steady stream of new products. This is a tremendous advantage for product creators. With a market that is slow to change, entrepreneurs may keep market positions for a long time.

5. *Diversity of small markets.*   Many industrial products have small markets. Semiconductor wafer handling equipment and a device that simplifies the installation of fire sprinklers are examples. Some consumer markets are also small. A device that alerts homeowners when their external water pipes are about to freeze, and an auto blizzard-survival kit have specialized and quite different markets. Actually, the total potential market for the blizzard-survival kit is fairly large, but the product is sold exclusively through automobile clubs—another reminder that a market's size is determined, in part, by the size of the distribution network.

Are Consumers Easy to Target?

Fred J. created a product that allowed a motorcycle to be towed without a trailer. All a motorcyclist had to do was take off the front tire, lock the wheel so it wouldn't turn, and then attach the wheel to the product, which linked up with an ordinary trailer hitch. The product had a nice benefit and was reasonably priced at $70. What gave the product a chance to succeed was that motorcyclists who travel are easy to reach. Fred needed only to purchase a booth at some of the big summer motorcycle events or purchase a list of motorcycle owners with incomes over $30,000.

How can you tell whether your product's consumers will be easy to target? Your product's users must be clearly defined and easy to locate. Motorcyclists who travel have both characteristics.

In contrast, consider a product that protects paintbrushes for reuse. How can you identify the people who will want this product? If they own paintbrushes, they may have already solved the reuse problem. Even if you could identify potential users, how could you find them? There is no reliable source of names of people who would want this product.

A product like the paintbrush protector would need to be placed in a retail store or mail-order catalog. Don't look down on this type of distribution network; many products are sold successfully this way. However, in this type of network, a product creator won't have control of how the product sells; the retail outlets will control its success. There isn't much that can be done if stores or catalogs won't carry the product.

The motorcycle device's inventor, however, had several options if retailers wouldn't carry his product. He could run an ad in a motorcyclists' magazine, buy a mailing list from a magazine or from another manufacturer, or display and sell the product at motorcycle shows.

You might wonder why I'm not recommending advertising the paintbrush protector. In most advertising campaigns, you pay on the basis of the number of people who will potentially read, hear, or see the ad. When your market is unclear, as it is for the paintbrush protector, you end up advertising to a broad audience, such as homeowners, even though only a few of those you reach might want to purchase the product. That spread of advertising doesn't pay off. The motorcycle product's ads will reach a much higher percentage of potential buyers, the key factor in having an advertising program that has a chance to be cost-effective.

Is the Distribution System Concentrated?

When I first investigated the market for my tire cutter (see Chapter 1), I was happy to learn that there were only about 45 key distributors throughout the country. That meant I had only 45 customers to call on.

A concentrated market allows you to better estimate your chances of success. With the tire cutter, when I talked to 5 distributors, I had surveyed over 10 percent of the market. If I had had a gift item, which could have been bought by thousands of shops, talking to 5 stores wouldn't have helped much at all. With only 45 tire cutter distributors, I was able to obtain accurate market research without spending any money. On a gift item, I'd never have been able to conduct any reliable, inexpensive research.

A concentrated market has two other advantages:

1. Promotional expenses will be lower.
2. Inside contacts will be extremely helpful because they will know most, if not all, of the people who control the market.

Rarely will you find a market as nicely concentrated as the market for tire equipment. The entrepreneur's job is to find ways to make a market smaller. For example, let's consider several ways in which a product creator can concentrate the gift market, which is extremely fragmented:

- Sell the product as an executive gift, through advertising specialty companies. These companies call on large and medium-size corporations to sell products suitable for sales and other incentive awards or customer gifts. Typically, any city has only a few large advertising specialty companies.
- Sign an exclusive distribution agreement with one of the large department store chains in your area. Department stores like having an exclusive offering. If your product sells well, you can expand to stores in other cities.
- Set up your distribution through one or two mail-order catalogs. If you offer an exclusive contract, you may be able to get priority position.
- Offer your line, on an exclusive basis, to a large gift distributor. You may have to offer an introductory price or a promotional program to sign up a distributor, but once you have one, its promotional muscle will help sell your product.

Many inventors are reluctant to give anyone an exclusive distribution agreement because they believe an exclusive agreement will limit sales volume. Potentially, it can eventually be limiting. However, an exclusive agreement is often the only way you can start to sell a product.

When you talk to possible sales outlets, remember their desire to be different from their competitors. Sales outlets don't want their merchandise to be like everyone else's, because then sales are governed by which outlet has the lowest price. Stores want products that are unique and different.

Concentrating your market will also help your sales efforts. You'll be able to customize your product, your sales literature, and your sales approach to the needs of a specific market.

Is the Market Open?

Martha M. was a great cook, and she made a cheesecake that all her friends loved. They persuaded her that she should market her cakes. Martha started selling her cakes first to a local family restaurant. After her product was selling there, she purchased a booth at a small trade show for restaurant owners and food buyers and received a tremendous amount of interest from several restaurants and some food stores. Martha soon received an order to supply cheesecakes to a chain of 30 family restaurants.

Martha's friends were ready to invest in her cheesecake and put it into every grocery store in America. But their enthusiasm immediately ran into a dead end: The food distributors that supply grocery stores typically place orders for 250,000-case lots from manufacturers. They didn't want to buy in smaller quantities, because of the cost involved in processing small orders.

When the friends went to talk directly to supermarkets, they got a negative response toward purchases of small quantities from an individual manufacturer. The supermarkets wanted a slotting allowance, which is a payment made in return for shelf space. Martha M. discovered that supermarkets are not an open market.

This didn't mean the cheesecakes couldn't be sold. It meant that they couldn't be sold through a distribution network that included supermarkets. When Susan Schwartz ran into the same problem with her Dakota Seasonings product line, she started to sell the product, packaged as a gift item, in gift shops in North Dakota. Susan started to attend gift shows and found a distributor to sell her product across the country. Gift stores don't sell the same volume as supermarkets do, but their sales level is more than enough for a profitable business.

Besides supermarkets, closed or restricted markets can occur when there are too many similar products being offered and when two or three manufacturers dominate the market.

Too Many Similar Products

Buyers, whether industrial buyers, store owners, or consumers, don't like too many choices; they get confused. Most people respond to a market that has too many choices by buying the best-known brand. How do you react when you're shopping for a toaster, a coffeemaker, car wax, a shaver, or any other product that has a multitude of brands? You're probably not willing to carefully evaluate each choice. You buy the brand you know best, the brand that's the cheapest, or, for some products, the brand that's most expensive. An entrepreneur faces tremendous resistance when introducing a product into a crowded market.

James S. created a cutting board with a three-inch-high vertical board on one end. People could hold tomatoes, cucumbers, apples, sausage, and other foods against the vertical board for fast, precise slicing. I thought the product had a great benefit, especially for people like me who know how to cut only thick slices. The product sold briskly at home shows and fairs, where Jim demonstrated it, but retailers didn't want to carry it. They were already selling cutting boards and saw no advantage in carrying a new board. When Jim succeeded in placing the product on the shelves of a store, consumers wouldn't buy it. There were too many cutting boards to choose from. The cutting board needed an advertising program, which was an expense Jim couldn't afford.

Major Players' Control of the Market

The power tool market is controlled by Black & Decker and Sears. In some industrial markets, one or two major suppliers control 60 to 75 percent of a market. Heinz and Hunt's dominate the ketchup market, Campbell's outdistances all competitors in the soup market, and Nike, Reebok, and L.A. Gear control the sports shoe market.

Markets dominated by one or two companies are difficult for new entrepreneurs to penetrate. The companies' promotional programs encourage retailers to buy as many products as possible from them, and they have been known to use subtle pressure to keep new products from getting shelf space. Marketing can be a power game. In markets that have many competitors, the power lies with the retailer. In markets that have only a few dominant manufacturers, the power belongs to those manufacturers.

I once introduced to metallurgical laboratories an industrial product that measured very thin layers of industrial coatings. The product was a variation of a traditional product line that was purchased primarily from two companies. Our product was superior in applications where the coatings were less than two microns thick, which is much thinner than a piece of paper. The traditional product line worked better for thicker coatings. Our product cost $8,000, a small percentage of the $200,000 to $500,000 that a new laboratory had to spend on traditional equipment. But the two traditional suppliers didn't want us in anyone's laboratory. They disputed some of our technical findings and tried to discourage potential customers from contacting us. Their resistance turned what should have been a simple introduction into a difficult one.

Even if dominant manufacturers don't offer active resistance, they still can present problems to a new entrepreneur. Retailers and other customers often enjoy the simplicity of ordering from a large product line. Sales call frequency is another advantage of dominant companies. They might call on larger retailers weekly or biweekly, but an entrepreneur has time to call only every few months. Dominant manufacturers' promotional programs, which offer retailers a discount based on purchase volume, tend to prevent product creators from establishing their products.

For example, a retailer might be able to obtain a 10 percent discount by buying $15,000 worth of products. Retailers don't want to lose that discount, and their sales might drop if they bring in another, less proven product line.

Ease of distribution is a crucial go/no-go decision, but it is not the final answer. The next section explains ways to overcome distribution problems. My key advice here is to keep expenses to an absolute minimum until you're confident that you've found a way to put a product onto the market.

TACTICS FOR RESOLVING DISTRIBUTION PROBLEMS

Dave S. discovered a new process for impregnating air freshener chemicals into a variety of materials. He created a line of products for homes, autos, and lockers. Although his product line was appreciably better than other air fresheners on the market, he wasn't able to penetrate the distribution network. The market wasn't concentrated, and there were already too many air fresheners on the market.

Dave decided to change tactics. He approached a sports shoe manufacturer, offered a special air freshener for shoes, and persuaded the manufacturer to buy his product as a sales premium for its shoe customers. The company ran a six-month promotion that included the freshener, and the product was a hit with shoe customers. When consumers started returning to buy more freshener, some shoe stores started to carry Dave's product.

Dave was resourceful; he kept looking for a distribution outlet for his product. Product creators often end up with good products that they can't launch into the market. Some of the tactics you can use for market launch are:

- Selling your product as a promotional item
- Using another manufacturer as your distributor
- Driving your business through distributors
- Combining your sales efforts with those of other inventors
- Initiating another distribution channel

At a minimum, you'll need a model and some market research to use these tactics successfully. You might have to invest in a limited production run to secure an order. If at all possible, try to have exploratory talks with potential customers before you spend too much money.

Sell a Promotional Item

Dave S.'s air freshener was sold originally as a promotional or premium item. Dave sold the product to a company that then gave it away, or sold it at a large discount, to a purchaser of one of its products. Premium items are constantly sold through soft drink, cereal, food, and sporting goods companies, as well as fast-food restaurants. Virtually every company is a candidate to buy a promotional item if it can be persuaded that the item will increase its sales.

The advantages of selling your product first as a promotional item are:

- The marketing power of a large company helps to establish your product.
- A large order may be obtained before you make a significant investment.

The disadvantages are:

- A steep discount has to be offered.
- Large companies can be very slow deciding whether to use your idea.
- Competition for promotional items is fierce: 20 to 30 items may be involved.

I like this tactic because an entrepreneur needs only a few models and can then approach a manufacturer or other company. If the idea doesn't sell, only a minimal investment has been made. If the idea does sell, a lot of the ground toward success has been covered for very little money.

Use Another Manufacturer for Distribution

The cheesecake venture I mentioned earlier had a tough time getting its product into supermarket freezers, primarily because its volume was too low. The company arranged to sell its cakes through a frozen-pie manufacturer. Distributors started to carry the product because the combined volume of pies and cheesecakes was acceptable.

Manufacturers are often willing to buy and then resell products that fit into their product lines. They receive several benefits, including expanded product lines with little or no risk, more commission opportunities for their sales forces, and extra income.

Entrepreneurs who have inexpensive products that complement costlier items should consider private-labeling their products through other manufacturers.

Susan Anderson developed an antistatic kit for computers. Her product was inexpensive and her potential customers—primarily computer users at companies—were easy to identify. The users were easily reached through a host of computer magazines and computer sales outlets. Susan's problem was that most sales methods, such as placing magazine ads or having a sales force call on stores, cost more money than Susan could generate with her inexpensive antistatic kits. Rather than trying to sell the product directly to end users, she sold the kits to computer manufacturers. They had Susan put their own names on the kits they ordered, and then sold them as part of their product lines. By selling through established companies, Susan was able to quickly penetrate the market.

An inventor benefits when he or she can utilize a larger company's distribution network. There are disadvantages. You'll have to give a large percentage of your profit margin to the manufacturer, you won't be able to control your business, and you run the risk that the manufacturer will develop its own product and drop yours.

Still, this is another tactic that I like, primarily because the marketing arrangement can be set up with a minimal investment; often, only a few models are needed.

Drive Your Business through Distributors

Richard Worth, the founder of R. W. Frookies cookies, wanted to develop a healthier cookie. He created a cookie that had no cholesterol and was sweetened with fruit juice, but he wasn't able to get food distributors to carry his line. Richard attended the 1988 Fancy Food trade show. When he received some orders, rather than deliver the product himself, he took the orders to a distributor. Not wanting to turn down a guaranteed sale, the distributor agreed to handle the product.

The dental supply company that I worked for started the same way. The founder, John Naughton, invented the first reclining dental chair, a product that is now used in virtually every dental office in the country. When John started out, dental distributors would not handle his product. They already had dental chair suppliers and they weren't interested in buying a product from an underfinanced inventor who was producing the chair in his garage. John went from office to office, selling his chair directly to dentists. When he got enough orders, he gave them to distributors that would agree to carry the product.

Most product creators fill orders themselves, rather than pay a distributor a percentage on sales they have generated. Although they make more money filling the orders themselves, these entrepreneurs are really losing out. Having a distributor might increase their sales five to ten times. You should use whatever orders you get to gain distributors.

The big drawback of this tactic is that you have to start production and incur marketing expenses before you can find and obtain customers. This means you need to invest a substantial amount of money before you know whether you're going to succeed. I'd recommend using this tactic only if you're already producing your product or if you can make an initial run for a minimal investment.

Combine Your Sales Efforts

One-product companies are under tremendous pressure. They run into resistance from stores or end users who prefer to buy from companies with broad product lines. The costs of selling their one product to a store or company are so high that they often can't sell enough units to cover the costs they incur.

One solution to these two problems is to combine efforts with several other one-line entrepreneurs, to be able to promote a broader product line. There are two ways to combine: Have each entrepreneur pay the others a sales commission for crossover items that they sell, or have the inventors join their resources to form a company.

This is a good tactic if you can find two or three other people offering similar products. Whenever you start a project, be sure to look for other inventors. You can find them by attending flea markets, fairs, trade shows, and inventors' conventions, and by watching for product ads in local magazines. Another way to locate inventors is to look through the *Patent Gazette* at a large library, which lists all the patents issued each week and has an index that lists inventions by state as well as by category. By looking through back issues, you should be able to find local inventors with similar products. Some of those inventors might still be trying to take their ideas to market.

Be sure that any inventors you consider combining with have a professional approach and are willing to work as hard as you are. You'll become frustrated if you continually work with an inventor who refuses to take a realistic approach toward marketing a product. If you're willing to spend 40 hours a week trying to promote everyone's ideas, be sure your partners aren't planning on spending only 10.

Initiate Another Distribution Channel

Interplak developed a rechargeable electric toothbrush. Its main feature was a series of small rotating brushes that not only cleaned the teeth but also massaged the gums, a benefit that can minimize periodontal disease. Interplak's problem was that the toothbrush's initial price was $149, a price so high that it scared retailers.

The company sold the product through dentists, with a multilevel marketing program. The company lined up a core group of dentists who supported the product, and then had those dentists recruit other dentists. After the product started to sell throughout the country, stores were willing to stock it.

Another entrepreneur, Terry Sachetti, created a bedspread with fluorescent strips that emitted a low-level light. The idea was targeted at children who are afraid of the dark. When Terry couldn't get any stores to stock the product, he started selling it at kiosks in malls, in the hope of eventually selling franchises of his kiosk concept.

I don't recommend this method. You have to spend too much money before you know whether your product will sell. Typically, you need both a marketing plan and a production plan before attempting an alternative distribution system, which requires a considerable investment. I'm mentioning this method because readers may at some point have substantial inventories that they need to sell. An alternative distribution channel may resolve their overstock problems.

THE IMPORTANCE OF PROPER TIMING

There are three reasons for establishing a distribution network *before* you invest in a project:

1. You must know your market potential. Remember, total market size is not relevant to you at the start. The only market that matters is the one your distribution network will reach. You may be able to expand later to reach the entire market, but that might take years. Confine your investment to a level that's justified by your immediate distribution plans.
2. You have to know how best to package and promote your product. Each distribution network may require different types of packaging and promotion.

Figure 6-2   Distribution Go/No-Go Decisions

---

1. If a distribution network exists, does it have product support costs that you can afford?
2. Is the market size of the existing network large enough to justify your initial investment?
3. Can you afford the cash investment required by the network's payment schedule?
4. Is the product easy to distribute?

---

3. You need to know what margins to incorporate into your product costs. Each distribution network requires a varying percentage for the people or companies selling a product. Be sure your product has enough built-in profit to cover your distribution costs.

Figure 6-2 summarizes the go/no-go decisions for distribution of a new product.

7

PRODUCT APPEAL: WILL CUSTOMERS BUY?

"I know my product will sell. It's a brainteaser that has two parts that will come apart when twisted just right. I leave it on my coffee table and everyone who comes over picks it up to play with."

Over 50 percent of the product creators I talk to will go ahead and invest in their ideas with little more than this amount of input. These people aren't careless; they just don't know how to conduct market research.

Jim T., the creator of the puzzle, made several research mistakes, but his biggest error was not simulating the selling situation. Customers don't buy puzzles off a coffee table. They select them in stores from among dozens of similar products. Jim needed to know whether people would buy his product instead of one of the other twist-apart puzzles.

In the movie *Big*, a toy company is doing market research with a group of children. A room is full of toys—theirs, competitors', and the new toys being tested. The marketers want to see whether kids will play with the new toys. If the kids pick up a new toy and then put it down after a minute or two, the marketers know that the product won't sell. If the kids pick up a new toy and play with it for an extended time, the marketers know that the product could be a winner. That's the type of research an inventor needs to do.

Jim should have had six or seven other brainteaser puzzles along-side his puzzle on his coffee table. If his product fared well, then he should have placed the products on the table unopened, to test reactions to their packages. The research would have improved a little more if his friends didn't know which product was his.

The market research cycle has two steps:

1. Initial research, to see whether a product concept has merit
2. Research with a model or prototype, to determine whether people will buy the actual product

These steps follow the preliminary research that precedes the start of any project: compiling all available background information regarding competitors, pricing, distribution networks, and manufacturing techniques (see Chapter 4). That preliminary research is the only research you should consider having someone else do for you. All the research that follows it concerns how people react to your product. I believe it's crucial for a product creator to hear this input firsthand.

Marketing research is important not only because it helps you make the go/no-go decisions, but also because people's reactions to your product may lead to design, marketing, and packaging changes that might make the difference between success and failure.

PRELIMINARY MARKETING GO/NO-GO DECISIONS

Product entrepreneurs need to decide early, before they invest any money, whether their products can survive in today's self-service environment. Consumers' shopping habits are dominated by quick glances. Whether they're walking down a department store aisle, scanning a mail-order catalog, or skimming a direct-mail piece, consumers give a product entrepreneur only a few seconds to convey a message. Inventors trying to reach industrial buyers often get about as much time. The buyers quickly scan trade magazines and product literature before deciding which one or two companies they'll talk to.

The self-service environment places considerable pressure on product entrepreneurs. Not only do they need to fight off competition from other entrepreneurs, but they also have to reach consumers who are over-exposed to advertising, promotion, direct mail, telemarketing, and other marketing messages.

You should carefully choose product ideas that meet three preliminary marketing criteria:

1. The product's benefit can be shown quickly.
2. The product is clearly different from others in the market.
3. The product has a significant benefit.

The Benefit Can Be Shown Quickly

You have, at most, 5 to 10 seconds to communicate a product's benefit. For some products and packages, you will have just 2 to 3 seconds to persuade a potential buyer to pick it up. If your product's benefit can't be communicated quickly, you'll need an extensive advertising campaign, which most product entrepreneurs can't afford.

Communication problems are compounded because, besides telling people a product's benefit, you have to convince them the benefit really exists. Sam R. and Jeff L. created a handle that attached to the middle of the shaft of rakes, hoes, shovels, and similar garden tools. Sam and Jeff came up with their idea because they thought people would have fewer back injuries if they didn't have to bend over as far as they did when using conventional garden tools. The product's package was adequate: It clearly indicated that the product reduced back strain while gardening. Sam and Jeff's problem was that people couldn't understand why an extra handle on a garden tool would reduce back strain. The product failed.

Chip Clips have been a big seller. Their initial package simply showed how an opened bag of snacks was sealed with a Chip Clip. Consumers quickly grasped the product's intended use and its benefit. Compact disks, on the other hand, succeeded only after a great deal of promotional publicity from major electronics companies. Consumers initially couldn't understand a compact disk's benefits.

The products that succeed grab consumers' attention immediately. You must have a way to show people a benefit. When we developed our tire cutter, we didn't show the cutter itself, because people wouldn't understand what it did. Instead, we showed a cut-up tire, a benefit customers immediately recognized.

Don't try to market a consumer product unless people can understand its benefit in less than 5 to 10 seconds. Don't try to market a nonconsumer product unless customers can understand in less than 15 seconds how you're solving a problem.

The Product Is Clearly Different

Products can be clearly different in many ways. For example, a cordless drill, a rechargeable flashlight, a fishing reel that doesn't get tangles, or a T-shirt with a new slogan can all be different because they're innovative. But a clear difference can also be introduced in a product's operation, size, or weight. For example, a faster-running drill with more torque, a lighter, smoother-functioning hedge trimmer, or an easier-to-apply car wax could all be products that are clearly different. How do you know when a product is clearly different? When a potential customer can look at it and recognize within 1 to 2 seconds that the product is unique. If consumers can't make that snap judgment, then a product doesn't pass this go/no-go decision test.

A product entrepreneur needs a distinctly different idea to have a chance of selling a product to a distribution network. As an example, consider Phil Q., who created a new walleye-fishing lure that combined the benefits of a jig and a slip sinker. Walleyes can't be caught on the surface, so bait must be placed near the lake bottom, which requires a weight of some sort. A jig is a weighted hook, usually made partly of plastic, with some feathers or other appetizing-looking material on it. Besides the advantage of being weighted, the jig can be jiggled around to attract a fish's attention. The jig's only drawback is that walleyes will often spit out the bait when they feel the jig's weight. The slip sinker, which corrects this problem, is attached a short distance from the hook. When the walleye takes the bait and starts to swim away, the line slips through the sinker so that the fish doesn't feel the weight. The problem with a slip sinker is that the person fishing can't put any action or jiggle on the bait. Phil's product was the first one on the market to combine the features of a jig and a slip sinker.

Even though Phil's product was different, he ran into heavy resistance from fishing retail stores. They weren't anxious to take on a new product from an unknown supplier: They were already buying from two or three major lure manufacturers and didn't want the paperwork of adding another. The stores were also afraid of losing their promotional allowances. Typically, manufacturers of seasonal items (such as fishing lures) offer promotional discounts that are prorated for the volume purchased by a store. For example, a retailer might receive a 10 percent discount for a $10,000 purchase. A store will be reluctant to take on an item from a new-product entrepreneur if its promotional discount will be jeopardized.

Finally, the stores wanted to see an advertising program to support the lure. Retailers don't like to give up shelf space to an unknown product. A retailer can minimize the chances of a rejection by being sure that a new product is advertised. Phil was undercapitalized and couldn't afford advertising.

Although Phil has been able to overcome all of this resistance and place his lure in several stores, it's too soon to know whether the product will succeed. A product creator's idea must be clearly different if it is to overcome the built-in inertia that prevails in most distribution networks.

The Product Has a Significantly Better Benefit

Mosquitoes are a constant hot-weather problem. Just outside my front door in summer, I often have anywhere from 20 to 100 mosquitoes hovering, waiting for their next meal. When a company introduced a small electronic device that repelled mosquitoes, I bought one for $5.95. The product's benefit was very appealing to me.

Another inventor had devised an innovative spice rack that was designed to be pulled in and out of a kitchen cabinet. The product was an improvement, but because its benefit wasn't important to most people, the product failed.

When consumers look at a product's benefit, what matters is how much better that benefit is than the benefits of competing products. The mosquito repeller's competitors were bug sprays. By comparison, the repeller didn't smell, lasted forever, and was environmentally safe. The spice rack's 10 to 20 percent improvement wasn't enough to attract consumers.

Product creators often become confused over this issue because companies repeatedly introduce products that offer only minimal improvements. The position of those companies is completely different from that of product entrepreneurs. The companies often replace their own products on store shelves. The retailer isn't faced with making supplier changes. If a company has a strong brand name, stores will want to stock its products—most hardware stores, for example, will carry any new product introduced by Black & Decker. Finally, companies have established distribution networks and promotional programs. They have contacts in place to help introduce products. Product entrepreneurs don't have these advantages. They must rely on having products with superior benefits.

How do you know when a product has a significantly better benefit? When consumers say they'd really like to have it or exclaim: "That's fantastic! Why didn't anyone think of that before?"

CONDUCTING INITIAL MARKET RESEARCH

You should do the initial marketing research in two steps. Decide whether your idea meets the three criteria I've been discussing. If you believe it does, then confirm your decision with input from potential customers, using the market research tactics listed in this chapter's next section.

During your initial research, you won't necessarily have a model or prototype. You might have only a drawing or a crude model, which won't yield perfect input from potential customers. You can still get valuable input by using two simple tactics.

The first tactic is to verify your premises. Suppose you have a product that kills flies. Your premise—that consumers need a better way to kill flies—is the reason you developed the product. You want to be sure that people agree with your premise. The best way to verify consumers' needs is to show people products that are currently being sold and ask them:

1. Have they used the products?
2. Do they think the products work effectively?
3. In what way should the products be improved?

People will give you a wide variety of answers, but you should be able to tell, for example, whether or not people believe there is a need for a better way of killing flies.

If your product doesn't have competitors, then you should ask people how they currently meet the need you've identified and whether they would like an alternate solution to the need. Charlie R. designed, for condominium owners, a bed that could double as a locked storage space. The inventor needed to ask whether owners who sublet their units still kept items such as golf clubs, tennis rackets, and other valuables in their units, and whether the owner-landlords were interested in having a secure way to store their valuables.

A premise doesn't have to be as dull as a better way to kill flies. Do-it-yourselfers might want an inexpensive power tool; bike riders, tired of ten-speed bikes, might want a more comfortable bike—like a mountain bike; people of all ages might find a novelty item a lot of fun.

The second tactic is to verify that potential customers can see how your product will meet the preliminary go/no-go marketing decisions. Show people the idea, have them compare it to competitive products, and then ask how long it took them to understand your product's benefit, how it differs from other products, and how important the new product's benefit would be to them. If competitive products don't exist, show your product and ask people how long it takes to see the benefit and how important the benefit is.

You're asking the same question twice when you ask someone to verify a premise and then to tell you how important a product's benefit is. I like to do that because people won't always realize how important a product's benefit is if they see only a drawing. They need to see the product. Asking them to verify a premise is a double-check to see whether a product will have an important benefit. Another reason to check twice is that people sometimes get confused by a drawing and, rather than tell you they're confused, they'll give you an answer without thinking. People usually don't have any problem explaining why they think a premise is valid or invalid. Ask both questions just to improve the accuracy of your research.

FREE OR LOW-COST MARKET RESEARCH

Product creators tend to think that market research is something that only big companies can afford to do. In fact, most individuals can gather almost as much quality information relative to their potential markets as large companies do, without spending a fortune.

Most of the tactics listed here can be used for both the initial and final market research steps. I recommend using as many tactics as possible in the initial research; your first research efforts occur *before* you spend much money. Do the best job you can when you gather initial research, to avoid spending money on a product that can't be marketed.

Gather Input from Friends

I don't recommend investing any money based on friends' input, but there is nothing wrong with doing some preliminary research with them when you're deciding whether you should even start a project. Don't tell your friends that you have a great idea and then ask them whether they agree. Instead, use your friends as a research panel. They can provide you with an initial response to the validity of your product premise and further proof that a product meets the preliminary go/no-go decision criteria.

Set Up an Impartial Research Panel

If you're developing a consumer item, you can distribute to your neighbors a flyer offering $10 to anyone willing to participate in a market research study. Explain on the flyer that you've created an exciting new product and you need people to evaluate it. You can even list on the flyer the type of people you're looking for: fishing enthusiasts, women who have jobs, people who like to do home woodworking, and so on. You'll pique people's curiosity with the flyer, and some calls will start to come in.

Among other tactics you can use to find people for a research panel are joining any relevant clubs in the area, such as woodworking or garden clubs; posting a flyer in a store that sells products in your category of research; and asking friends to give you names to contact. To research nonconsumer products, you can attend trade association meetings and set up appointments with appropriate engineers and marketers from companies in the market you hope to penetrate.

Use Industry Insiders as Paid Consultants

An industry insider is someone who is already involved, as a manufacturer, distributor, or retailer, in the market you're trying to enter. Insiders don't have much free time during the course of a day. If you get to talk to one of them, the conversation will be held to about 15 minutes. One way to get around this is to offer to hire the insider for a couple of evening hours. Some people are flattered to be asked to consult, and they'll give you a tremendous amount of input. Usually, you can find someone to help you for a fee of about $100. Chapter 9 covers how to find and use insiders.

Run Ads

Sometimes research will show that a product has potential, but it will leave you unsure whether people will quickly grasp the idea's benefit and then buy. A good tactic to use in this situation is to run an ad and measure the response.

Gary O. developed a smelter system that attached to a woodstove. His product could be used to melt down aluminum and metal cans. Once the metal was liquid, it could be poured into a mold to produce a metal ingot, which is a large bar that can be sold to a foundry. The product was targeted primarily at people living in rural areas, who had no convenient way of recycling food and beverage cans. Gary's product was difficult to research because only a small percentage of people were potential customers.

Gary ran a classified ad in the magazine Mother Earth News. *The ad offered, for $12, plans for the smelter. He received enough orders from the ad to convince him that his product might succeed.*

I worked on a fly trap, which competed with electronic bug killers and fly strips. Everyone told me the product was great, but I was worried that people wouldn't be willing to go to the trouble of setting up and then emptying the trap. I ran ads in small local papers in Georgia, offering two traps in a kit for $4.95. The ad response was pitiful and I dropped the product.

Newspaper ads are generally too expensive to be used for research. Magazine ads tend to be much cheaper and you can usually find a magazine that is specifically targeted at your potential customers. For example, NordicTrack manufactures a cross-country skiing version of a treadmill. Its primary customers are affluent people who can afford to spend $500 and more for home exercise equipment. Its initial advertising appeared in airline magazines; most airline travelers/readers have incomes of over $40,000. You don't have to restrict your advertising to small local magazines. Many larger magazines will inexpensively run an ad in a small geographic area. *TV Guide*'s rate for an ad in a limited urban area is under $500. Your ad should invite people to either buy the product or request more information.

Incidentally, be careful if you decide to run an ad that asks for advance payment. After receiving an order, you have only 30 days to either ship the product or offer a refund. Otherwise, you might be violating postal regulations. Plan on sending out refunds, or offer only a free information package in the ad.

Interview Store Owners

Once you have a model or prototype, along with a product's packaging, you're in a position to talk to store owners, distributors, and other prospective sellers in a distribution network. If you have an industrial or other nonconsumer product, call on distributors or manufacturers' representatives who sell the product. You can also contact people in companies that might use your type of product.

It's imperative that you obtain some input from people who sell to your market. Their input is more reliable than that of consumers. You can't be sure that consumers will buy a product, even when they tell you they will; people don't like to give other people negative feedback. Consumers won't always know what other products are available to buy instead of yours. People in a distribution network, besides being informed, are always evaluating objectively the ideas proposed by salespeople and employees. They won't feel guilty about telling you that they don't like an idea, and they're usually honest about the reasons they won't buy. Consumers often try to soften the impact of negative comments.

Another reason to talk to store owners or industrial buyers is that you can give them a sales presentation. When you deal with consumers, it's dangerous to try to sell them a product, because your presentation may influence them too much. People in a distribution network are not so easily swayed. Give them a presentation and you can find out not only whether they'll buy your product, but also whether your sales strategy is on target.

Attend Flea Markets or Trade Shows

The advantage of selling a product at these outlets is that you can contact a large number of potential buyers in a short time. Flea markets are handy because you don't need a polished product. (Flea markets or craft shows often rent table space for under $20.)

Lou B. created an improved wheelbarrow. Lou had several working but rugged-looking prototypes; he had made them by modifying existing wheelbarrows. Lou knew he could test the product at flea markets if he could also sell old wheelbarrows. He visited flea markets and garage sales for a couple of months, rounding up as many used wheelbarrows as he could find. Then he took them, along with two of his improved version, to a flea market. After a weekend of concentrated sales effort, Lou concluded that people didn't understand his product's benefit.

Trade shows are usually not open to the public; they are held for retailers, wholesalers, and distributors who are in a specific market such as gifts, toys, or sporting goods. You can rent a small booth at a trade show, and you will receive valuable input by showing the product to both buyers and sellers. Trade shows cost more than flea markets, but you can hold down your expenses if you attend small regional shows.

You can find out what trade shows are coming to your area by checking with your city, county, or state convention/tourist bureau; talking to retailers; reading your area's business magazines; or checking the industry's trade magazines.

Don't go to an industry's largest trade show. It will cost too much, and your product concept may need some refinements before it can be shown to a large audience.

FINAL MARKETING GO/NO-GO DECISIONS

Start a marketing evaluation with the three preliminary go/no-go decision criteria (see page 114). You can do this most often with a drawing or a rough model. Once you're confident that your idea meets those criteria, make a model that's representative of what the final product will be like. As a last step, check your idea against the final go/no-go decisions given below.

The final go/no-go decisions help a product creator to determine whether, with limited resources, he or she can introduce a product. The criteria will *not* determine whether a product could be introduced by a large, well-funded company. A product like compact disks wouldn't have passed these go/no-go decisions because the benefits of the disks weren't obvious. Compact disks were a great product for a company that could afford an extensive promotional program.

Is the Product's Benefit Obvious?

The first three final go/no-go decisions are the same as the preliminary decisions. You should check these three points again, after you have a model. The model allows you to show the product to people, who will then be able to give you a more reliable response than could be gained from only looking at a drawing.

Is the Product Clearly Different?

Ask people to look at a group of similar products that includes your representative model and to state which ones they've seen before. Then ask the research respondents to rate the products, from highest to lowest, by how unique they are. If people respond that they've seen your product before or give the product a poor ranking for uniqueness, you'll know the product is not clearly different.

Asking people to determine which products they've seen before also gives you some feedback on how aware of the target market your respondents are. If a person has never seen a product that has been on the market for years, you should note that fact when you review the respondents' comments.

Is the Benefit Significantly Better?

This is an important point to recheck. In your initial research, you told people what your benefit would be and then asked how important that benefit was to them. Most people respond with the belief that a product would completely meet the need. In reality, few products are that perfect. You need to know:

- Does the prototype meet the need people thought it would?
- Does the way the product works provide an important benefit?

For example, the benefit of the tire cutter I introduced (see Chapter 1) was that discarded tires would take up less space at a garage or dump. Preliminary research indicated that this was a big benefit. When we had a model, people could see how much space the cut-up tires required. The tires used less space than some people had imagined and more space than others had thought was needed. When people see a product and the job it performs, they can decide again how much better the benefit is.

Does the Product Have Emotional Appeal?

I have two sons, eight and five years old. They saw the Teenage Mutant Ninja Turtles in a toy store long before the Turtles were popular or even advertised. The minute my sons saw the characters, they wanted them. The Ninja Turtles were the only items in the store they wanted to buy. That's the type of appeal that helps a product sell.

A consumer product can have emotional appeal because it's "neat," like the Ninja Turtles; or it solves a problem, like a rechargeable flashlight; or it's cute, like a Pet Rock or Halloween garbage bags; or it helps a consumer to project an image.

Wayne C. and John M. created a product that appeals to people because it creates an image. They developed a storage container for fishing gear that could be permanently locked into a boat. Their idea was that the gear could be stored overnight, and the container's location allowed a person fishing from a chair to easily grab anything that was needed.

I'm not a fisherman; the product looked dull to me. But others who fish thought it was fabulous—a perfect product for fishing enthusiasts who had everything. Why did the product have appeal? Because it was new, different, and convenient to use? I don't know why people like it; I just know they did.

Wayne and John failed to put their product on the market. The initial market research was done with the product priced at $29.95, but Wayne and John couldn't keep costs down low enough to charge that price. Instead, the product ended up costing $59.95. The product's appeal vanished at that price. Emotional appeal is a combination of looks, features, benefits, and price. Changing the price changed the product's combination and destroyed its appeal.

Inventors have trouble measuring emotional appeal. They're excited about their products, and they're anxious to have people praise them. The best method I've found to gauge a product's appeal is to have people rank a group of five or six similar products, one of which is yours. Pick three types of products for the group: some with strong appeal, some with less appeal, and some with no appeal. You'll get a better idea of what category your product is in.

Can the Product Be Packaged Effectively?

Some products, especially midsize ones, are difficult to package. Tom S. created a new camping grill that hung down from a tripod so that it could be used over a wood fire. The product was targeted at boaters, hikers, hunters, and backpackers, who aren't always able to stay at a structured campground. The grill came in a cardboard box that measured 18 by 24 by 2 inches.

Tom's package posed several problems. The box was an awkward size that took up too much space on a retailer's floor. Sales volume was too low for retailers to set up a display model. The grill failed because, without a model, consumers weren't able to see and touch the product.

Packaging possibilities can add real spark to a product. Dale McGinnis came up with an idea to prevent crayons from breaking. He called the product Boo-Boo Toobs: fluorescent-color tubes, the same size as a crayon, which slipped over crayons to protect them. Dale packaged the product in sharp-looking little containers that resembled the top of a crayon, and put the product in a point-of-purchase display that had some cute pictures of a kid using the Boo-Boo Toobs. I believe Dale's package is the most important reason that his product is in over 500 stores.

Does the Product Have an Acceptable Price/Value Relationship?

When people look at a product, they decide either consciously or subconsciously what the product is worth. For example, you might look at a toy figure and decide that it's worth $5. If the product is priced above $5, you probably won't buy it, no matter how much you or your kids like it.

To check a product's perceived value, place it again in a group of similar products, and ask people to rank the products in order of their value. Because you know what the other products sell for, you can estimate your product's perceived value. For you to make money, your price normally has to be at least four times the manufacturing cost (as determined in Chapter 8).

You should experiment with a product's perceived value. Sometimes, minor product modifications can add a great deal to a product's value. Glen A. developed a plastic puzzle in which five solid rings could be linked together or taken apart. The puzzle's perceived value was only $5, primarily because it was made of plastic. If Glen had made his puzzle out of stainless steel, the puzzle would have had a perceived value of about $8.

Figure 7-1   Price/Value Chart

Features	Typical Price
1. Plastic	$ 5
2. Steel	7
3. Stainless steel	8
4. Steel with rubber handles	10
5. Upscale packaging	2 additional

As you work on your project, start a price/value chart of similar products. The chart can show you how to change a product to bring its price/value ratio in line. A chart for Glen's puzzle is shown in Figure 7-1.

Is the Product in an Established Category?

Rhonda L. developed a new, inexpensive alarm to let people know when someone was breaking into an apartment or home. The alarm slipped over a door. A 3-inch pole extended from the top of the alarm. When the alarm was on the door, the doorjamb pushed the rod back against a switch and the alarm was quiet. If the door was opened, the pole moved forward, activating the alarm.

At first glance, the alarm seemed like a great product to sell through discount stores. The problem was that discount stores didn't have a place for this type of product. If it were stocked with locks, only people looking to buy locks would see it. Rhonda couldn't afford to advertise enough to make people ask for the product, and the product wasn't suited for a point-of-purchase display. The product had potential, but there was no place to put it. Product entrepreneurs have a very tough time marketing products that fall out of established product categories.

Does the Product Have a Great Name or Other Promotional Possibilities?

The "Pet Rock" was a great name. Large, fold-up windshield shades and soda or beer can huggies (coolers that fit over aluminum cans) sold because they are great ways for companies like Coca-Cola or stores like 7-Eleven to promote their names.

Slim-Fast and Ultra Slim-Fast have easy-to-promote names. Closet organizers show up well in pictures. Products that are in hot neon pink or blue are promotable because they look good in a photograph.

Other products don't adapt well to promotion. Clyde S. came out with a dartboard that included a game called Chicago. In this dart game, the players try to hit numbers 1 and 6. Each player throws 5 darts. A 1 is worth 100 points, a 6 is worth 60 points, and all other numbers are counted at their face value; for example, a 5 is worth 5 points. The game's benefit was hard to show both on the product's package and in an advertising program.

I once saw a novelty product that featured clock components that rocked back and forth. The only way the product's feature could be shown was in a demonstration, which made it hard to package the product effectively.

GOING FORWARD

I don't think you should try to market a product unless it meets at least six of the eight marketing go/no-go decision criteria—and I don't mean *barely* meets. You should display your product with six others, to allow you to see not only whether your product has a selling point, but also how strong that point is.

Some readers may think that my criteria are too tight. Other manufacturers are certainly introducing products that don't meet every point. One of the book's main points is that product creators have to introduce products when they have a fraction of the marketing power of a large company. They must compensate for their deficit by choosing ideal products.

Brian P. came into my office with fashion sports shoes that everyone else thought would be an enormous hit with teenagers. I didn't. I have trouble getting excited about a product before comparing it to the competition. I gathered a few brochures showing shoes that were coming out in the next season (a manufacturers' representative who had attended the last major shoe trade show loaned them to me), along with a few comparable products that were already in stores. People lost much of their enthusiasm after they saw what other shoes were available.

The moral of the story is to take one step at a time. One of your most important steps is to carefully check whether people will buy your product.

8

MANUFACTURING COSTS: CAN YOUR PRODUCT MAKE A PROFIT?

I met Jim E. at a boat show. Jim had created a small wheel device that fit underneath the front of a boat's hull and made it easier to pull the boat up onto a beach. Jim sold his product only at boat shows. When I asked him why he didn't sell through distributors, he told me he couldn't afford to sell the product at wholesale because his manufacturing cost was higher than the product's wholesale price.

Where did Jim go wrong? He had to know the perceived value of his product because he was a boat owner. What he didn't know was that, to make money, his manufacturing cost couldn't exceed 25 percent of the product's retail price. Jim used high-quality materials, and one of his friends was his contract manufacturer. His production costs were 75 percent of his retail price.

Manufacturing is an area where you must be a hard-nosed negotiator. If a cost should be no more than $3, then it *must not be* any higher. If you look again at the cash flow-through chart in Chapter 4, you can see that there's no margin for errors in costing. Errors will make an already slim profit margin disappear.

In addition to final manufacturing costs, a substantial investment will be needed to put your product on the market. Models, prototypes, tooling, setup charges, and packaging are all areas that can consume a tremendous amount of money. I've talked to many product entrepreneurs who've spent over $50,000 just to get ready to produce a product.

You should concentrate on three manufacturing concerns:

1. Can you hold a product's manufacturing cost down to less than 25 percent of its perceived value?
2. Can you hold the model, prototype, and first production costs at a level you can afford?
3. Can you afford, or get a contract manufacturer to absorb, the tooling and start-up costs of putting your product into production?

THE PRELIMINARY EVALUATION

The two major product cost components are manufacturing and packaging. The two minor cost components are product liability insurance, which typically runs about 1.5 to 2.0 percent of sales, and scrap/product returns/shrinkage and so on, which usually total about 5 percent of sales. All four cost components added together equal a product's total cost.

Before you start spending money on a project, be sure that you can make your product at a cost that's less than 25 percent of the proposed retail price. You won't have a product or a prototype to cost out, but you can utilize comparison products and estimating techniques to decide whether an idea can make a profit.

Estimating Manufacturing Costs

Your first step is to find a product that is about the same size, is made out of the same materials, and has about the same complexity as your projected product. You'll receive more accurate cost quotes from manufacturers if you can give them a clear idea of what the product will be like.

If at all possible, try to find a product that is handled in the distribution network you hope to use and that has a sales volume similar to the volume you expect your idea to achieve. You can find a similar product in a mail-order catalog, magazine, or retail store, or at a trade show. Be sure to purchase the product. You won't be able to get by with just showing the manufacturer a picture.

The next step is to make a mock-up (a crude model of an idea). You can use cardboard, papier-mâché, wood, or other inexpensive materials. The first thing you need to do when you're making your mock-up is to list every feature the product will have. If possible, include all those features in the mock-up. If that's not possible, then make a model or another mock-up that shows only what that feature will look like and how it will work. For example, when I was working for the dental supply company mentioned earlier, we developed a new dental chair with a feature we called "compensating traverse." This feature kept a patient's head in the same vertical plane, as the rest of the chair was being reclined. Our mock-up of the chair represented what the chair would look like, but it couldn't simulate compensating traverse. We constructed a small wooden model, about 6 inches high, that demonstrated how that feature would work. If your product includes a feature of another product, such as a nozzle from a spray paint can, be sure to obtain a sample of that part. The manufacturer must understand every detail of your product before offering a quote.

A model or prototype will generate more accurate quotes than a mock-up, but I don't believe the quotes will improve enough in your favor to justify investing in a prototype just to obtain price quotes. On the other hand, I've always been disappointed with price quotes based on drawings. The problem sometimes lies with the manufacturer, who may leave off or may not understand features that are shown in a drawing. More often, though, the problem lies with product entrepreneurs who forget or don't explain important features. A mock-up forces you to explain all the details of the idea.

The last step is to obtain price quotes from several manufacturers for both your product and a similar product. Tell the manufacturers that you may be introducing a new product and that you need two price quotes, one from a mock-up of your idea and one from the similar product. When you receive the quotes, be sure to ask why the quote for your product is different from the quote for the established product. You might find that one or two features cost too much or that the low-cost material you've chosen has left you free to consider a higher-grade option and still stay within budget. At the very least, you'll learn quite a bit about how to convert an idea into a manufacturing process. When I first received quotes on my tire cutter, the estimates were too high. But I found out from the manufacturer that one feature of the product, a handle that attached at a 90-degree angle, was difficult to manufacture. I was able to cut the quote by $4 per unit by switching to a differently angled handle.

There are many ways to find manufacturers that can give you a cost quote:

- Ask some of your contacts in the industry.
- Look in the Yellow Pages or in a business-to-business telephone book.
- Look in your state's industrial directory, available at your library. The directory will list manufacturers by the type of products they produce.
- Keep copies of want ads published in your city. Often, the ads tell what type of products a company makes. Ads for salespeople are especially informative.

- Use the *Thomas Register of American Manufacturers* at your library, to find local companies that manufacture products similar to your idea.

Should you get quotes even if you're planning on making the product in your basement? Yes. When you do your initial production runs, you may not make any money on your sales. That's okay; your initial production run should be used only to prove that your product can be sold. Sooner or later, you'll have to go into full production in order to succeed. You must be sure that you'll be able to make money when you reach a normal production level.

Estimating Packaging Costs

This is the second of a product's two major cost components. For some products, especially those in lower-priced ranges, packaging will be 25 to 30 percent of total costs.

Packaging costs are dependent on a product's sales volume. A small consumer product in a blister pack (a clear plastic molded piece glued onto a cardboard backing) might have a packaging cost of 8¢ at high volume or a cost of 25¢ if volume is low. In Chapter 6, I discussed how to estimate a product's sales volume. Be sure to check your volume estimates carefully before you talk to packaging suppliers. You can find suppliers through your contacts, the phone book, state industrial directories, or the *Thomas Register.*

Packaging costs have two components: up-front costs for tooling and artwork, and a per-piece packaging cost. Your estimate might list a cost of 25¢ to package each product, plus setup charges of $1,000 for color artwork and $1,500 for a blister-pack mold. Keep these charges separate. The 25¢ will be a part of the product's ongoing cost. The artwork and mold charges will be one-time start-up expenses.

Calculating a Preliminary Manufacturing Cost

After obtaining the first two estimates, you'll have a packaging cost, which should be reasonably accurate, and a manufacturing quote, which will normally be higher than you had expected to pay. You still don't have enough information to make a wise decision. You need to utilize the comparison product to evaluate your product's cost. The comparison procedure has four steps (see Figure 8-1). In the first two, you'll calculate the manufacturing cost of the comparison product; in the last two, you'll estimate your product's total cost, using the following ratio:

$$\frac{\text{Your product's manufacturing cost}}{\text{Similar product's manufacturing cost}}$$

Figure 8-1   Product Comparison Procedure

1. Multiply the retail price of the similar product by 25 percent. This figure should be close to the product's total cost.
2. Subtract the average packaging estimate you received for the similar product. The number you obtain is the estimated manufacturing cost of the similar product.

   Example: To determine the manufacturing cost for an existing hardware product that has a retail price of $8.95 and a wholesale cost of $4.47 (wholesale cost is typically approximately half the retail price):

   a. Multiply the product's retail price by 25 percent
      to obtain total product costs ($8.95 × .25) $2.24
   b. Subtract packaging costs   −.42
      Similar product's manufacturing costs $1.82

   Now you're ready to calculate your product's costs.
3. Calculate your projected manufacturing cost. Take the cost from step 2 and multiply it by the cost ratio that results from the two manufacturing quotes. To get the ratio, if your product's average quote was $2.75, for example, and the similar product's average quote was $1.96, the cost ratio is $2.75/$1.96, or 1.4.
4. Add on the projected packaging costs to determine your product's total cost.

   Example: To determine your product's total cost based on the similar product analyzed in steps 1 and 2:
   c. Calculate your manufacturing costs by
      multiplying the similar product's manufac-
      turing cost of $1.82 by the cost ratio of 1.4 $2.55
   d. Add packaging costs   +.52
      Total product cost $3.07

This is the cost you should use in your preliminary evaluation of whether your product can make money. Your initial production costs will probably be quite a bit higher, but you can't expect to make money with low-volume production. Your goal here is to be sure that you can make money once you reach *normal* production levels. The total cost gives you a target amount to shoot for. Keep searching until you find a contract manufacturer that can hit the required price for your projected production levels.

Comparing Costs to Perceived Value

In Chapter 7, I explained how to estimate a product's perceived value. Take that value and compare it to your manufacturing costs multiplied by 4. For example, for the hardware product in the example, multiply $3.07 by 4 to arrive at a minimum final retail price of $12.28. The product can make money as long as its perceived value is more than $12.28.

After your preliminary evaluation, you must make your go/no-go decision: Can your product be made for less than 25 percent of its perceived value? If the product's perceived value is too low, review the price/value chart shown on page 126. Is there any way to add value to the product?

At least 50 percent of the time, product entrepreneurs need to adjust the values of their products. It's important to keep track of what features add value and what features add costs. Always ask manufacturers for detailed explanations of their price quotes.

BUILDING A MODEL OR PROTOTYPE

If a preliminary evaluation indicates that a product can make money, the next step is to decide whether you can afford the necessary models or prototypes. If you can't, you'll need to either get an investor or arrange in some way for a below-cost prototype. You can get a below-cost prototype in three ways:

1. Find an industrial designer who will build your prototype at cost in return for a small share of the invention. This is especially important if your idea is more complicated and needs a designer.
2. Find a prototype builder who will build your prototype at cost for a share of the invention.

   Note: For these two tactics you need to find designers or prototype builders who have some spare time. Since their rates are typically $40 to $75 per hour, you can save a great deal of money if you can get the prototype for your actual material cost. In most cases, you'll need to offer 10 to 20 percent of your idea in exchange for low-cost help.
3. Offer to eventually have your product produced by a manufacturer if it will help you develop the prototype for a below-market cost. This tactic is most effective if one of the manufacturers that gives you a manufacturing quote also likes your idea. This is typically the best tactic to try first, as you don't need to give away a part of your invention or idea.

A prototype looks and functions exactly like a finished production unit. A model may be slightly different in size and function from a production unit. You'd have a model if you bolted two plastic pieces together to represent a one-piece production unit. Use a model for a complex part or for a product that has very high tooling costs. Some models show only one or two functions of a product—the improvements the idea has introduced for existing technology. A model may be made of a material different from that of the finished product.

As I mentioned earlier, you should always make a model or prototype before investing in production tooling. You can't do your final market research accurately without prototypes, and you'll often learn from them that your product has a few flaws that need correcting. It's not unusual for a product to have three or four different prototypes before the final version is ready to be introduced.

Unfortunately, many first-time product creators skip the prototype stage. They are positive their ideas will sell and/or they don't know how to make prototypes inexpensively. They decide the investment for a prototype is unnecessary and proceed to buy expensive tooling and go straight into a production run. This mistake often leaves an inventor, after an investment of $10,000 to $50,000, with a garage full of unsalable inventory.

Underfinanced inventors can't afford to skip the prototype stage. Not only do they lose an opportunity to perfect their products, but they lose the advantage of market research data that might convince a contract manufacturer to pick up their tooling costs.

I believe that prototypes for at least 95 percent of all products can be made in a person's garage or basement. I rarely even consider the expense of a prototype to be a go/no-go decision. I've included models in this chapter because so many product creators look at prototypes as an expense that only big companies can afford.

Did I really mean that you can make virtually any prototype in your basement, perhaps with just a little help from a machine shop? You have a plastic product that needs to be injection-molded, or a metal product that needs an investment casting, or an intricate piece of machinery that has 15 to 20 parts. *You can make all of these in your basement.* You may need to spend two weeks working out all the details, but that alternative is a lot better than spending $10,000 to $25,000 to have a manufacturer make a prototype.

How should you go about making models and prototypes? I can't offer you complete details for every type of product, but, when you get to the prototype stage, you should be able find information for your type of product. The "Helpful Sources" section at the end of this book lists several books and magazines you can consult. My favorite book on prototypes, by far, is *The Modelmaker's Handbook* by Albert Jackson and David Day (Knopf, 1981). The book is written for hobbyists, but it contains most of the information you'll need. Its best feature is that it demonstrates how you can make virtually anything.

A magazine I highly recommend is *Fine Scale Modeler.* In addition to informative articles, the magazine has ads from companies that sell the supplies and equipment you need to make prototypes. Visit hobby shops, bookstores, and your library to find other books and magazines that might be helpful.

The materials you need for making prototypes are not always readily available. I list several sources in this chapter; more are listed at the end of the book. I've found the best source for information to be the specialty trade magazines—*Fine Scale Modeler,* for example, or similar magazines listed in *Gale's Source of Publications.* Both sources can be found in large libraries.

Builders of model airplanes are great contacts. At any model display, look for modelers who've used your technology or ask around until you get the names of people who know how to make a good model. These people can be of great help. If you're a klutz who isn't handy with tools, these hobbyists might also make your prototype for a very low price.

Wood Models

These models are useful for a variety of applications: to simulate plastic or metal parts, as reference parts that can be used by a machine shop to manufacture a prototype, as models for molds for injection-molded parts, and as actual molds of vacuum-formed prototypes.

Balsa wood, which is readily available in hobby stores, is the best wood to use if you have to bend or curve parts. Otherwise, you can use almost any wood that is available. You'll find an ample supply of woodworking books at any library, and most cities have several woodworking shops. Any model airplane hobbyist will have a sizable amount of woodworking equipment. If you don't want to make the model yourself, ask at a woodworking shop for the names of people who have large home shops. They might enjoy working on your project for a nominal fee and perhaps even at no charge.

Clay Models

If you're going to make a mold for a plastic or metal model, you will usually start with a clay model. Use the modeling clay sold in art supply stores. Its soft pliability allows you to add all the intricate features you'd like. The model should be as smooth as possible because every feature will come out in the final mold. Be sure to sand out any imperfections after the clay dries. Clay models make useful guides if parts have to be machined.

Plastic Models

You can make plastic parts out of a plastic mold (usually used for small parts), from temporary tooling (the best method for intricate parts), with a

vacuum-forming process (the easiest way for doing larger parts), by simply bending the parts (the cheapest and simplest way to make uncompli-
cated parts), and with fiberglass layup (typically used for very large parts).

Using a Plastic Mold

Hysol Electronic Chemicals (see the "Helpful Sources" section at the
end of this book) has a line of plastic tooling materials, all of which cure at
room temperatures. You can use the chemicals to make either a one-part or
a two-part mold. A one-part mold is used when product features are on
only one side of the product and the other side is flat. A two-part mold is
used when features are on both sides of the product; each part of the mold
has half of the product's features. To use the mold, you clamp the two
parts of the mold together and leave a plug, which is a small hole through
which you pour the molten plastic. After the part is molded, you can cut
off any excess plastic from the plug.

To make a plastic mold, start out with a clay, wood, or machined
(made from metal) model. Next, make a wooden box that is about 40 percent bigger than the model. For a one-part mold, fill about 25 percent of
the box with mold-making plastic, such as Hysol's TE6345NA. Apply a
mold release compound to your model, and then place the model in the
box so that it is about a half inch from the bottom of the box. Add molding
plastic until it comes even with the back of the part. After the plastic cures,
you will have a mold. You can use the mold while it is still in the box.

A two-part mold is made almost the same way. The only difference
is that you'll use two boxes, and each mold will handle half of the part.
After you do the first half, turn the product upside down, place it in a box
25 percent full of molding resin, and bring the plastic mold material up to
the same spot where the first mold stopped. Once the molding compound
cures, clamp the two parts together, drill a small plug through the bottom,
and you are ready to start making parts. After the mold is ready, coat it
with a layer of nonsilicone wax, and then pour in plastic that you've
heated over a Bunsen burner or stove. You can use this procedure with a
silicone rubber compound from a company such as Castolite. Hysol's
plastic products are handy because you can machine the plastic mold to
correct imperfections or to add features.

Your plastic mold can be used for a prototype and for your initial
production run. Hysol's catalog, *Plastic Tooling Materials*, is very informative. The best plastic to use is polystyrene, which you can get from a hobby
shop or virtually any chemical distributor.

Temporary Tooling

Some parts need a lot of pressure to force the plastic into all the
crevices; an injection-molding machine is required, but an expensive mold
is not. Instead, use temporary tooling. When you make a mold, you start
out with a metal molding form, which functions as the wooden box does

when you're making a plastic mold. Instead of buying brand-new forms, look for used molding forms that are slightly bigger than your product. You usually can buy these from distributors of molding machines. Next, you need a metal or plastic model. For temporary tooling, aluminum is used instead of molding plastic as an insert in the used mold. A temporary mold may cost only 10 to 20 percent as much as a permanent mold. You'll need to find a small plastics manufacturer or a company specializing in prototypes to make the aluminum insert. The best sources for finding these companies are local distributors of plastic molding equipment. You should be able to find their names in a phone book or an industrial directory.

Some plastic products are too large for temporary tooling but need more strength than a vacuum-formed part can provide. An example of this type of part is a 6-inch-long scoop, with a 4-inch handle, that can be used to throw and catch a ball. Prototypes for this type of product are best made with temporary rubber molds. To do this, make a model of wood or sheet metal, and then cover the model with a silicone rubber mold material from a company such as Castolite (see "Helpful Sources").

Vacuum-Formed Products

Parts that are vacuum formed are usually larger and simpler than plastic molded parts. A mold for a vacuum-formed part is different from a plastic or temporary mold. For those methods, your model would be exactly like your product. In vacuum forming, the plastic wraps around the top and sides of the mold, and the part looks like a thin shell that would cover the mold. For example, a plastic canopy or a tray or a box could all be vacuum formed. The mold would look like the inside of the part.

The easiest way to make a vacuum-formed part is to complete a wooden mold in your basement and then take the mold to a vacuum-forming shop to have it made into your prototype. As long as you have a mold, the cost will be reasonable. Buy a sheet of ABS plastic for making the parts. ABS is readily available at any plastics distributor, or you can buy it from the vacuum-forming shop.

Another option is to buy a small vacuum-forming machine. Some cost less than $1,000. You can use the machine for models and prototypes, as well as for an initial production run.

Bending Plastic

Plastic is fairly easy to bend and reshape. You need only to wrap the plastic in aluminum foil and hold it over an electric stove until it softens. (An electric stove's heating area is more even than a gas stove's.) Be sure to wear insulating gloves. Bend the soft plastic around a block, a can, or other surface, to form the plastic into the shape you want. Once the plastic cools down it will hold its new shape.

Bending plastic and then machining it or reworking it is one of the fastest ways to make a model or prototype. You can successfully bend plastics into models without any experience. Buy acrylic and acetate sheets or rods from a plastics distributor, or bend an already existing part.

Fiberglass Layup

This process, which is used in making boats and other very large shapes, is really a layering process. Start with a wooden (or even cardboard) mold or base that looks like the outside of the part. Put down a coat of polyester resin, a layer of fiberglass, a layer of resin, and so on, until you build up enough strength for the product. Let the resin dry thoroughly between applications.

Fiberglass has very high strength and can be used in models in place of metal. On a dental chair, a large back portion required tooling that cost $45,000. The part could have been made from fiberglass, and then painted. It wouldn't have been as strong as metal, but it would still have been acceptable for a model. Small chemical distributors often carry fiberglass resin. It can also be found at some hobby shops.

Machined Parts

Machining refers to modifying or working a model by machine. Drilling, punching, turning, shaping, planing, and other operations are all machining processes. Most models require at least some machining. You can do it yourself if you have the proper equipment, or you can take your model to a machine shop or hobbyist for completion.

One of the easiest ways to make a model is to find similar parts or products, and then contact the manufacturer to see whether any old or discontinued molds are available. If they are, you may be able to have a mold machined so that it will make your part. This requires less work than starting from scratch, and you'll often get a better-looking model. Occasionally, you might pick up a free mold.

Charlie R. invented a new applicator for floor wax. He found a medical supply company that made a part similar to the one for which he needed a mold. He talked to the company and was given a mold from a discontinued product. Charlie had the mold machined into the shape he needed for $250.

Most machine shops work from engineering drawings, which are expensive. But I've found that many smaller shops will duplicate a part from a model. This approach has several advantages: It saves on expensive engineering time, it minimizes the effect of drawing mistakes, and it provides the machine shop with a better idea of what the product will be like.

You might want to consider buying the machines you need to make your model. If you need only one or two machines, the expense won't be terrible. You'll actually save money by owning them, if you have to make three or four models before you create one that sells. You might then be able to make the initial production run yourself. Look for sources of small machining equipment, listed in modeling magazines. (Another good source is Micromark Corporation, listed in "Helpful Sources.")

Sheet Metal Models

Sheet metal is economical to work with and can be substituted for plastic in some large parts. A drain tray designed to go under washing machines will probably eventually be made of plastic, but the product's features can be demonstrated from a sheet metal model.

As mentioned earlier, the best way to obtain a model is to make a crude mock-up out of cardboard or papier-mâché. Take the mock-up to a sheet metal fabricator who can make the final prototype. For most parts, you can obtain the model for under $300.

Fabric Models

Most fabric or vinyl models can be made either with a home sewing machine or through a contract manufacturer. If the fabric is heavy or if the item is fairly complex, I'd try to have the model made by a manufacturer. It won't cost any extra money because there won't be any tooling and setup charges, and the manufacturer will have the equipment to make a professional-looking prototype.

Metal Models

Some metal parts can't be machined or bent; they must be cast. This process is similar to making a plastic mold, except that you use a cold-curing silicon rubber as a mold and a metal casting alloy as the molten material. Castolite Corporation has a large line of casting compounds and molds, as well as a very informative catalog. The company sells an introductory kit that can help you become familiar with the metal-casting process. Another product for making a temporary metal mold is General Electric's Construction 1200 glazing compound.

Cannibalized Products

You can take apart already existing products and use their parts to make a new product.

Donna K. created a new stationery product that helps people budget their incomes. She bought two products at Kmart and two at a stationery store, and she ordered another from a catalog company. She then combined parts of each product to make her product.

Cannibalizing products won't always work, but it can be an excellent tactic. Combinations of cannibalized parts can create new working models. For example, if your new product requires an electronic switching mechanism, you might be able to remove one from a product you already have at home or can buy at a flea market or discount store.

Packaging

For some market research, you'll need to show the product in its package, to help you decide whether consumers can quickly grasp the purpose and benefit of a product. I recommend that you make several packaging models and then evaluate which one—or which combination of packaging—will work best for you.

Choice of packaging can affect cost. I once made a packaging evaluation for presenting an improved clothespin design, which was easier to use and caused fewer wrinkles than a standard clothespin. The product (a set of 12 clothespins) was suitable for a blister pack. Another possibility was placing the product on a piece of cardboard and then shrink-wrapping both the card and the product. (Many packaging houses will shrink-wrap a product for a minimal fee.) A third alternative was to attach the product to a thin cardboard with metal clips. The comparative costs per sales unit were: blister pack, 55¢; shrink-wrap, 20¢; metal clip, 12¢. That's quite a price spread for 12 clothespins with a manufacturing cost of only 4¢ per clothespin. The 12¢ package worked best, saving the product creator a tremendous amount of money.

Package models can usually be made from standard packages, close to the size you might eventually use, which are available from packaging suppliers.

When testing the packaging models, be sure to include graphics, which means both pictures and copy (the words on the package). Graphics is an area where costs can get out of hand. Color artwork can cost $2,000 to $3,000, an expense you shouldn't incur during your research phase. Be prepared to improvise. Choose a black-and-white or color photograph, clip art, or a picture from a magazine as your artwork. Add copy to the package, displaying prominently the product's name and benefits. If you don't have an artistic touch, take your artwork and copy to a freelance artist or art student. You should be able to get final package graphics done for less than $100.

Take the completed package graphics to a copy center that has a color copier and have one or two copies made. Glue the color copies to the cardboard backing of the package or to a point-of-purchase display. If you intend to use the display, make it last longer by having it laminated. Keep the original artist's version of the graphics for possible future use.

Budgeting

Once you've sorted through all of your options and all the steps of building your model, determine what your model costs will be. The second manufacturing go/no-go decision is: Can you afford to produce the models and prototypes required for your project? Plan on having to pay for them from your own financial resources, and try to hold model costs below 25 percent of your available money. Holding model costs down will leave you with the money needed for an initial production run. If the model cost is too high, you need to find either a contract manufacturer who will absorb the cost, a lower-cost method of building the model, or a prototype builder who will work at cost in return for a share of your idea.

CONTRACT MANUFACTURERS

A manufacturer that agrees to make a product for another company or for a product entrepreneur is acting as a contract manufacturer. Any manufacturer can be a contract manufacturer, even if it makes and sells several products of its own. Most underfinanced entrepreneurs have to rely on a contract manufacturer to put a product on the market. Setting up a manufacturing operation is too expensive and complicated for most inventors. I recommend that you try to find a contract manufacturer after you finish conducting your market research with a model or prototype.

Finding the right contract manufacturer provides tremendous benefits to a product entrepreneur. The manufacturer might have a prototype lab or machine shop capable of making revised models or prototypes as well as the initial production run. Besides helping to find ways to economically produce the product, a contract manufacturer might agree to amortize tooling and final engineering costs over the product's manufacturing run. The entrepreneur would then pay back the tooling costs through a per-unit surcharge. For example, the manufacturer might charge $15,000 to cover start-up expenses. The product entrepreneur would pay an extra 56¢ per unit until the manufacturer recoups the $15,000.

If a manufacturer is not fully utilizing a plant, a contract arrangement can be lucrative. The arrangement provides profit on new production, helps cover overhead expenses, improves plant productivity, and increases production without incurring the financial risks of developing a new product.

Contract manufacturers prefer to invest in an idea after the end of the first sales period. However, sometimes the models or prototypes are too difficult or complicated or expensive for you to make. Then another manufacturing go/no-go decision becomes: Can you find a contract manufacturer that will help defray some of the cost for any required prototypes?

Does it sound like the manufacturer is giving everything away? If the product succeeds, the manufacturer will recover all its costs from a per-unit amortization charge. If the product fails, the failure will cost a lot less than if the manufacturer had tried to develop and market a new product on its own. New product failures are a part of business that companies learn to accept.

Not all manufacturers are good candidates for a contract manufacturing agreement. Some may already have high production; others may be introducing their own new products. Some manufacturers feel that contract arrangements are big headaches. To a manufacturer looking for more production, however, your product might represent the difference between making and losing money.

To be successful with a contract manufacturing agreement, you have to find a manufacturer with the right attitude and circumstances, and you must be able to show that your product has a reasonable chance of success.

To find the right manufacturer, first go through your files and find friends of friends or anybody who might have manufacturing contacts. If they aren't in a position to help, they may know someone who is. Another approach is to look through trade magazines and find ads for companies that supply raw materials for products. Call the companies' headquarters and ask what salesperson, distributor, or manufacturers' representative covers your area. Call those contacts and tell them that you're an entrepreneur with a new product and that you're looking for a contract manufacturer that might be willing to amortize tooling costs. You may have to call several contacts, but you'll get a list of manufacturers that might work with you.

You can also pick up contacts at trade shows. Some manufacturers attend shows to promote their contract services. The phone book is another source. If nothing else works, go to the library and find potential manufacturers in your state's industrial directory.

Check out small-town manufacturers up to 200 miles away. They'll have lower labor costs and, on occasion, they can get financial aid from their communities to pay for new molds, as long as a product will increase employment.

You must show that your product has a good chance to succeed. Manufacturers are constantly approached by entrepreneurs, and they also have products of their own to introduce. Show that your product has the best chance to make money.

In Chapter 4, I told you to record every contact you made and to follow up each contact with a letter. Some readers may have thought I was crazy to suggest such a time-consuming task. But when you try to convince a manufacturer that your product will sell, you'll have proof of whom you have contacted and what each person said. In Chapter 4, I also covered how to package an idea. That advice will help you to convince a manufacturer to support your product.

When you find an interested manufacturer, be honest about any problems you're facing. Most manufacturers have experience in introducing new products, and their people may be able to resolve puzzling situations. An important point: Make the manufacturer responsible for the quality of your production units. Frank Q. had a room full of defective manufactured units of a hardware product. The manufacturer said the defect was the fault of the supplier; the supplier blamed the manufacturer. Frank didn't have enough experience or know-how to solve the dispute, and he ended up paying for products he couldn't sell.

There are three areas where you might have conflicts with a contract manufacturer:

1. *Simplifying your product to cut both tooling and production costs.* Sometimes simple changes can reduce costs without impacting a product's perceived value. Other changes might have a negative impact on how customers respond to your idea. Resist any negative changes.

2. *Finding the best technology for your product.* One inventor I talked to had lined up a manufacturer with vacuum-forming equipment for a product that should have been injection-molded instead. Keep informed on technology through trade magazines and various manufacturing contacts.

3. *Getting a lower per-unit price from another manufacturer.* When this happens, conflicts can arise because entrepreneurs resent paying more than necessary to a manufacturer. Keep in mind that your contract manufacturer may have absorbed tooling and other costs that have been added to your per-unit price. Be loyal to any manufacturer that helps you get started, and be sure that a price from another manufacturer includes all charges, including initial setup.

FIRM PRICE QUOTES

After you finish conducting your market research with a model, get a firm quote for the actual manufacturing cost. Can the product be sold for four times its cost? Whether you would make money on the project was a go/no-go decision in the preliminary manufacturing evaluation. You must review your decision again, after your model has been built and tested.

You can develop a firm price quote yourself, or you can use a contract manufacturer's quote. I strongly recommend that you base your product's cost on a quote from a manufacturer, even if you are planning on making the product yourself. People who have no manufacturing experience have a very tough time generating a manufacturing cost. I spent ten years working on new products in companies that had established manufacturing cost systems, and I thought I understood the systems quite well. I never once was able to estimate a final manufacturing cost with an error of less than 30 percent.

Why is it so tough to estimate a cost? Doesn't a product creator know what raw materials are required and how long each product will take to make? Unfortunately, an estimate is not that simple. A key question is: How many units a day will a person be able to make? Suppose you know that you can make 25 units per hour. But a worker won't produce constantly at peak efficiency. Time must be given to breaks, lunch hours, holidays, stocking materials on the line, cleaning up, packaging, delivering, reworking, and rejecting parts, all of which affect a worker's output. There are many hidden expenses: supplies, freight on incoming orders, unemployment taxes, social security taxes, and phone bills. The list of areas where a product entrepreneur might make costing mistakes is virtually endless. Your best bet is to get a quote from a manufacturer that estimates cost on a regular basis.

THE INITIAL PRODUCTION RUN

The initial sales period is designed to prove only that a product can be sold. A small production run of somewhere between 25 and 200 units will do this. This is *not* the time to invest heavily in tooling and other expenses, because many products never make it past the initial sales period. Instead, build or manufacture the number of units that represents the smallest possible investment. Holding down tooling costs will raise your unit cost to a high—and sometimes extremely high—level. That's okay, as long as your initial production run is small. Your go/no-go decision at this stage is: Can you afford whatever investment is required to produce a small number of units?

Bob D. created a ski bag that had a number of special pouches for virtually every item a skier would need. Bob had a sewing machine in his basement and his "production" runs came out of his "factory" every Saturday morning. Bob's costs were high because he was buying all his supplies at retail prices. His manufacturing cost was $24, and his wholesale price was only $22, a price that guaranteed Bob would lose money. Bob could have had lower costs working with a sewing manufacturer, but he would have had to produce patterns, drawings, production specifications, samples, and instructions for the inspection department. Bob found it much more practical and inexpensive to produce his product at home.

If you're forced to use a manufacturer, the burden of finding a low-cost production method will still fall on you. Some of the best ways to hold down manufacturing costs in the initial sales period include modifying other products, making the product out of another material, or using temporary tooling. All of these tactics require finishing work such as sanding, drilling, and polishing. Manufacturers don't like to work on a product twice; they prefer straight-line production of a unit.

To benefit from the up-front cost savings of temporary tooling and other low-investment production techniques, be prepared to "volunteer" to do all the finishing work yourself. Your willingness to help will be appreciated by the contract manufacturer and might prod the manufacturer into picking up the costs of temporary tooling.

Watch for alternate manufacturing methods during the entire time you work on a project. Read every trade magazine you can—both the articles and the ads. Get on the mailing lists of appropriate catalogs that you see advertised in magazines. Often, your ability to hold down costs will be directly related to how much you know about alternate manufacturing techniques.

Modifying an Existing Part

Nick T. and Andy S. were going nowhere with a plastic tool that attached to a roller and prevented paint from splattering. A quote of $25,000 for tooling stopped them cold on their idea. No manufacturer would absorb the tooling cost without a firm order from either a retailer or a wholesaler. Nick and Andy shouldn't have been moping about their lost opportunity; they could have easily solved their problem.

Their product had a one-piece design, but it had two parts: a top and a side. Those parts could have been made separately out of readily available parts. Only a small amount of machining would have been needed to allow the parts to be snapped together with a small plastic clip. The initial-run product would have cost $2.00 to make, compared to a retail price of $1.50. This cost difference is all right during the initial sales period, when Nick and Andy's only goal was to show that their product could be sold.

Making the Product from Another Material

Nick and Andy could have made their painting product out of aluminum and dipped it in a plastic coating compound such as Plasti Dip, or they could have painted it. Another option was to make the product out of fiberglass. A successful inventor of a plastic spice rack made his initial production model out of wood. I don't normally like to use different materials; I prefer to sell a product that's representative of the final version. However, using alternate materials is a viable option if you're having trouble getting a contract manufacturer to invest in tooling or if you need some sales momentum to generate financial support from your family, friends, or investors.

Using Temporary Tooling

Most plastic products and all metal products can be made using temporary tooling. For plastic parts, the temporary tooling could be an aluminum insert in a used mold, or a plastic or rubber mold; for metal parts, it could be a silicone rubber mold or a sand casting. Temporary tooling usually costs only 10 to 20 percent of the cost of permanent tooling. The biggest drawback to temporary tooling is that no one knows how long "temporary" will be. The tooling might last a week, or it might last several years. No matter how long it lasts, you should be able to get enough initial production to know whether your product will sell.

Temporary tooling is a good option when you have a contract manufacturer. Alternatively, have your initial production run made by a prototype shop. These shops put together prototypes and small production runs for established companies. They have a lot of experience with temporary tooling and short runs. You can locate prototype shops in the Yellow Pages, by contacting manufacturers' representatives of production equipment, or by calling the purchasing departments of larger companies and asking them for names of any prototype companies in your area.

Again, your go/no-go decision here is: Can you afford the cost of your initial production run? You don't want to spend all your money on your initial run. You'll still need money to help finance the transitional sales period.

START-UP MANUFACTURING COSTS

After you've completed your initial sales period, you enter the transitional sales period, during which you start producing larger quantities of units. You may be forced at this time to make the tooling investments you've avoided. You face the last manufacturing go/no-go decision: Can you raise the money to cover the start-up costs?

Manufacturing costs involve more than tooling costs; they also include engineering documentation, inventory, labor, packaging, instruction manuals, and consignment units. Remember, as you add up these projected costs, that you may be able to persuade a contract manufacturer to absorb some of them. The advice in Chapter 9 will help you find insider investors. You might also be able to find investors among friends and family.

This last go/no-go decision is difficult to make until you've completed your first sales period. Only then will you know how well your product is accepted and how much help you can expect from contract manufacturers and investors. Knowing the start-up manufacturing costs before starting the first sales period can help you decide whether your research is positive enough to justify entering the first sales period. If start-up costs are high, you'll want to be sure your product does very well in its initial research. You'll also want to be sure of help from several insiders. If your costs are lower, you might proceed with a little less positive input.

Most start-up manufacturing costs are fairly high. Along with your start-up marketing expenses, they may be more than you can afford. Don't worry about that just yet. Before you incur these costs, you'll have some limited sales history, you'll have a product that has survived several rounds of market testing, and you'll have a fairly well-defined manufacturing process. These factors might be all you'll need to line up investments from family, friends, or insiders.

Let's examine start-up costs category by category.

Tooling Costs

Gather estimates from several manufacturers to determine these costs. Try to get a contract manufacturer to pick up some of them, or look for discarded tools that you can modify. You'll be responsible for raising the money to cover this expense.

Temporary tooling has a negative connotation to many product entrepreneurs, but I've been involved with products that have been marketed for over five years with "temporary" tooling. Try to wait until the product is selling well before purchasing permanent tooling.

Engineering Documentation

Before a product goes into standard production, a package of information is needed so that other people can produce the product. This package is referred to as *engineering* (or *manufacturing*) *documentation*. It includes drawings, a bill of materials, assembly instructions, specifications, inspection requirements, and assembly times. The package is not easy to put together. You might be able to prepare the initial sketches, but you'll need a professional draftsperson to do the drawings and an engineer to rework your initial wording into the proper format and language. If your product is not complicated, your contract manufacturer may do the documentation package at no charge.

If your product is complicated, you'll probably need to cover at least some of the cost of preparing the package. Professional drafting charges range from $25 to $50 an hour, and 20 to 100 hours may be needed to complete the drawings. The total costs can be quite high.

On complicated products, find an engineer who will be one of your inside advisers. Ask him or her how long it will take to prepare the engineering drawings for your product. Add about 30 percent to that estimate (to cover unexpected cost overruns) and then call up engineering drafting firms, as well as temporary help agencies that offer drafting, and ask for their hourly rates. Ask friends if they know of any draftsperson who might work on the project in the evenings for about $20 per hour. You can also check technical schools for student draftspersons. On some products, documentation costs might be as high as $10,000 to $20,000. A manufacturer might share the expense with you if your product has strong sales potential. However, because most complicated products are geared toward small markets, many inventors of complicated parts end up making the products themselves. Labor costs stay low, and the need for a documentation package is reduced.

Inventory

You probably will have inventory costs for both supplies and finished goods. You need to buy supplies in order to start production, and you will have to pay the contract manufacturer for the units produced.

Try to work with your suppliers to keep your inventory costs low. Most suppliers want payment within 30 days. If you are an unproven product entrepreneur, a supplier may want full payment in advance or require a 25 to 50 percent deposit with your order. Rather than paying in advance, your goal is to have 60 to 90 days to pay for inventory. You should try to work on payment terms early, because only a few suppliers will offer 60- to 90-day terms. Even with long payment terms, you will have trouble generating sales *and* collecting money before 90 days have passed. You should include in your start-up costs the inventory costs of both the raw materials and the finished products for one production run.

Labor Costs

If you're not going to use a contract manufacturer, you may need to hire a few people. You should have the equivalent of six months of their salaries on hand before you hire them. Incidentally, labor costs are another reason I recommend that you use a contract manufacturer. During your first year, when sales are low, you'll probably need only occasional help. If you hire workers, you'll have to pay them regularly. With a contract manufacturer, you'll pay for labor only when you need it.

Packaging Costs

These costs can be considerable, yet they are often overlooked by entrepreneurs. The product creator almost always has to pay all packaging costs. Artwork, the biggest cost, includes the initial drawings or photographs, the color separations, and the printing. The drawings, photographs, and color separations could easily cost $5,000. For black-and-white or two-color artwork (black and one other color, on a white background), costs will still run $1,000 to $2,000. Most printers won't do a run of less than 1,000 pieces, so your minimum printing cost will be $400 to $500 for two-color artwork, and $1,000 to $2,000 for full-color artwork.

You'll also have to pay for the package itself. A mold for a blister pack can run a minimum of $500 to $2,000, depending on the size; special cardboard packaging costs at least $500 to $1,000.

A contract manufacturer won't pick up the packaging cost because it won't be doing the work. Your artist, color separator, printer, and packaging supplier will be completing the work. Contract manufacturers might pick up their own costs, such as for inventory or labor, but they typically won't pick up costs paid to someone else.

Instruction Manuals

Any costs for instructions, whether assembly or operational, are paid by the product creator. Most creators do a poor job of writing instructions. The result is product returns, the major reason that retailers or distributors drop products. Tom L. created a board game that I put into seven stores. I got all the games back after three people returned them because they couldn't understand the instructions.

Instructions require printing and preparation. The printing cost can be estimated by finding similar instructions and getting a price quote. A local print shop can do most instruction manuals.

Preparation refers to the pictures or drawings and the written descriptions in a manual. If you are using pictures, have them done by a professional photographer. Lighting has to be just right if a picture is to print well. Professionals have that know-how, and a good-quality photo is important. Expect to pay $75 to $125 per picture.

Part of the reason for poor instructions is that entrepreneurs aren't experienced writers. A second reason is that they don't spend enough time on instructions. I've taken as long as two weeks to write instructions that were only two pages long. The secret to writing good instructions is to give them to people who don't understand the product and test whether they can follow them. If they can't, the instructions need work.

Figure 8-2   Manufacturing Go/No-Go Decisions

---

1. Do the preliminary cost estimates indicate that the product's perceived value is four times the product's projected manufacturing cost?

2. Will the model and prototype cost be less than 25 percent of the money you have to invest?

3. Can you find a contract manufacturer that will work with you on favorable terms?

4. Can you afford the investment required to produce a small initial production run?

5. Will you be able to raise the money to cover the start-up manufacturing costs?

Consignment and Demonstration Units

If you sell through manufacturers' representatives or distributors, you may need consignment units—units you lend to distributors so that they can promote a product. You may also want to lend or give products to potentially large customers. You won't be getting paid for these units. Include their costs in your start-up expenses.

Figure 8-2 summarizes the go/no-go decisions for manufacturing a new product.

9

INSIDE HELP: EVERYONE NEEDS KEY CONTACTS

When I worked for an industrial equipment supplier, we developed what we thought was a great new product for assembling large, low-volume, surface-mounted, printed circuit boards. The product was unique and cost-effective, and appeared to answer a large, unmet need. Our main stumbling block was that a working model would cost $50,000 to $60,000, which was more money than we wanted to risk.

We moved ahead with the project, for less than $30,000, with help from key inside people. I located two people who were responsible for specifying this type of equipment for their companies. We hired each one (for about $200 apiece) as a consultant for an evening. They provided us with the following:

- An evaluation of our product's features and benefits
- A list of features they thought we could drop
- The names of contacts at several manufacturers that might field-test the product
- Local distributors (again, with the names of contacts) that would probably be willing to sell the product
- Estimates of our potential sales volume

When my partner and I were introducing the tire cutter, we weren't sure whether we should try to license the product or try to start a business.

We didn't know whether we could sell the product for $70, or whether we could set up a distribution system without an advertising program. We talked to key people at a distributor that sold tire-mounting equipment and to a store manager for a tire dealership. We found out that our idea had merit, the cutter had to work when tires were on or off a wheel rim, and the companies would help us with our initial market research.

This inside advice steered us in the right direction, not only for product design, but also in our subsequent efforts to set up a sales network. On other occasions, inside advice convinced me to drop products, but at least I dropped them early, before spending too much time and money.

Another important reason to use inside contacts is that they can become investors, partners, or future employees. Most people dream about being involved someday in their own businesses, and the ideal businesses for them are those they know a great deal about. Most product entrepreneurs hate to give up part of their company, but I think it makes sense for an entrepreneur to take on an insider as an investor. The company gets involvement from a knowledgeable source, an impressive management team for future loan applications, and additional capital to fund the business.

I once took a new inspection microscope to Digital Computer. The product had a 3-inch by 4-inch viewing lens, rather than the traditional two eyepieces. The product greatly reduced operators' back and neck strain, which resulted from bending over the traditional eyepieces. When I first showed the product, two of the people who specified microscope equipment immediately asked to invest. That type of insider can help a product by contributing both market data and money. Unfortunately, the inventor of the microscope couldn't consistently put enough light on the screen. Operator eyestrain resulted and the product failed.

This chapter has only one go/no-go decision: Can you find the inside help you need to introduce your product?

INSIDE CONTACTS: WHY YOU NEED THEM

Inside contacts have the experience, connections, and knowledge that can help put a product on the market. They can offer many pieces of valuable information.

Sometimes you won't be able to find an insider in your specific market. You still have to have an insider, even if the person works in another market.

Dennis Courtier created a new cider drink. It's not easy to find a helpful insider in the beverage market, which is ruthless and dominated by large companies; insiders are too busy to help a new entrepreneur.

Instead, Dennis found help from a radio station contact. The station used the cider drink as a promotional item. The exposure helped Dennis to set up a small distribution system.

History

What similar products have been successfully introduced? How long does it take for a product to become established? What percentage of users will buy a new product in its first years? What mistakes have caused other products to fail? What is a typical first-year sales volume for a new product? What companies have been able to continually introduce successful new products? Every answer to these questions can give you key insights into the steps you'll have to take to introduce a product.

Product Review

Most product categories have several nuances that aren't apparent to everyone. For example, a hedge clipper might need a grease fitting to lubricate the gear case. Product entrepreneurs often overlook little points, much to the detriment of their products. Insiders will usually spot design defects, primarily because they've seen them cause other new products to fail.

Besides noticing product nuances, insiders can offer a fairly accurate review of your product's main features and benefits, including how well they work, how important they are, and what their perceived value is. Getting insiders to evaluate a product while it's still in the mock-up stage can minimize the number of product changes you might have to make later on.

Manufacturing Help

Insiders can give you names of companies that might make a product on a contract basis, tell you what manufacturing process the market likes for a certain type of product, and generate negotiating leverage. You'll probably obtain more help from a contract manufacturer if you can show that you've received input from both the general manager of a major distributor and the merchandise buyer of a large retailer.

Distribution Hints

Insiders often know which distribution networks are easiest to enter; what networks are most likely to take on a product from a small, one-line company; the best price point for a product; how much marketing a product needs; and what type of payment terms you should expect.

Connections

Insiders know the people and companies in the market. The names of new contacts will help expand your potential sales base, and you'll have much better luck approaching those contacts when you can say that the insider suggested the call.

Promotional Help

There may be certain trade magazines that generate high numbers of ad responses. Particular trade shows may be crucial for you to attend. The market may respond to only certain types of promotions. Your product literature and price lists may lack essential information. There may be certain mailing lists that are very effective or an ad format that has always worked well. All of this information may be available from insiders.

Help during Initial and Transitional Sales Periods

Finding your first few sales outlets, before you have any sales momentum, is difficult. Often, insiders become your first customers, or they help you find your first customers. Once insiders help you to start sales, you'll be able to build on your initial momentum and line up additional distribution outlets. Without insiders' help, you might not even be able to place a product in front of customers.

FINDING THE RIGHT INSIDERS

I've talked throughout this book about how to find manufacturers' representatives or salespeople. Their help is valuable, but they don't qualify as key insiders. They probably know how only a portion of the market works, they don't always carry enough clout in the market to help during the initial sales period, and their backgrounds usually aren't strong enough to provide the management experience needed on future loan documents.

Your goal is not necessarily to work with the best-known person in the market. He or she is probably too busy to help you, will cost more than you can afford, and will be too difficult to contact. But you should try to find someone who is significant in your local market. For example, if you have a hardware product, your insider might be a buyer for a local chain of hardware stores, the president of a large distributor, a key executive in the local hardware association, or the marketing manager of a local hardware products manufacturer. Any of these people will have enough contacts in the local market to help get a product established.

John Naughton is an example of an entrepreneur who knew how to take advantage of inside help. When he created the first reclining dental chair, John had the initial support of a core group of several well-known dentists. With their help, John started selling chairs one at a time throughout the Midwest. Through the dentists, John contacted the most successful district sales manager in the industry. John made an attractive offer to him. Within two or three years after the offer was accepted, the company was selling well over $1 million worth of chairs per year.

Scott Turner developed a new product to measure diffusion depths in silicone wafers, a crucial test in the early production of semiconductors. One of the reasons Scott succeeded was that he had, at one time, worked for a key semiconductor production manager in the Philadelphia area. That contact initially helped Scott to sell some machines and gave him the names of people to call at other prospective customers. I worked with Scott for two years, and he taught me the value of the question: Do you know anyone else I should talk to? This question will help broaden your base of insiders.

Graham Lovelady, a California dental equipment servicer, put together a vacuum pump specifically designed to provide all the needed suction during dental procedures. Graham enlisted the aid of the western regional manager of the industry's largest distributor to generate his pump's initial sales. His company's sales quickly rose to over $5 million per year.

These key people are harder to find than manufacturers' representatives or salespeople, but you should be able to meet them if you learn to use your initial contacts and if you make a dedicated effort to become involved in the activities of your chosen industry.

Using Initial Contacts

I was trying to help Craig N. conduct some California market research on a new bracelet for kids. The research was important because California is by far the biggest market for fad products. Dave Butts, with whom I worked at the time, had a sister who sold products to California convenience stores. She got a few stores interested in the bracelet, and she had the store managers mention the product to a rack jobber distributor that sold them cheap costume jewelry. The store managers also mentioned my name to the jobber's merchandise buyer. Finally, I talked to the buyer, who liked the product, wanted just one change in its packaging, and agreed to sell it at a suggested retail of $1.99—provided he could buy it for 70¢. Craig is still trying to find a way to make the product in volume for 35¢ to 40¢, but the important point is that Craig got all this information for a minimal price. He has a potentially valuable contact if he can find a low-cost production method.

If initial contacts give you insiders' names, you can either have the contacts arrange a meeting, as in the previous example, or call the insider yourself. I usually prefer to call the insider, unless an initial contact can provide leverage because he or she is a customer or an important supplier to the insider. When you meet or talk to the insider, explain that you're working on a new product. Describe what benefit the product offers: why you feel the product is marketable, what response you received in your initial research, and how you've heard from several people in the industry that the insider is an important person to talk to. I recommend that you offer to pay the insider to be a consultant.

This approach tells several things about you:

1. You're serious; you're taking a professional approach.
2. You have a chance to succeed because you're seeking expert help early in the project.
3. You probably have only a rough mock-up.

Trade Associations

Drugstore owners, toy manufacturers, industrial distributors, and countless other groups have associations that meet regularly to discuss common problems or opportunities. Many of these associations have local chapters; one may meet in your state. If a local chapter doesn't exist, attend any local trade show and find out whether any associations will run meetings in conjunction with the show.

Trade associations are great places to meet insiders. Not only are members of the association knowledgeable, but they have more than the typical number of connections.

Chambers of Commerce

Chambers exist to promote business growth. They do this primarily by lobbying for business interests, but they also are supportive of new business ventures. By attending their meetings, you might meet some key people. Tell the chamber what you're doing and ask whether it can recommend anyone who would be able to help you. Chambers often have important business leaders as members, and such help can be valuable. A woman I know went to a Minneapolis Chamber of Commerce meeting and met Harvey McKay, the owner of his own envelope company, a key Minnesota businessman and the author of *Swim with the Sharks without Getting Eaten Alive.* Harvey suggested several contacts that helped the woman expand her business.

Magazine Articles

When I needed technical insiders to evaluate equipment for a surface-mounted assembly, I found them by looking through a year's back issues of trade magazines. Two people had written lengthy articles regarding equipment similar to the new product I was researching. I called the people and set up appointments. I started both conversations by mentioning that I had read the magazine articles. About half of all the people I've found through magazine articles have been cooperative.

Many product creators are not experienced in business. They're apprehensive about calling up and talking to a businessperson. Their fears are groundless. Some people will be rude and others won't have the time to talk, but many more people will not only talk but will offer their help and advice.

Speakers

Another tactic is to check trade magazines for speakers at local association meetings or trade shows. You can also obtain speakers' names from the trade association itself or from chambers of commerce. Other sources of speakers' names are newspapers and magazines, where experts in a market are frequently quoted.

WHEN TO USE INSIDERS

You should use insiders on every project, but you must be careful to use them sparingly. Don't make them feel you're taking advantage of them, even if you reimburse them for their time. There are critical times during a project when you *must* consult insiders, either because you're about to invest a considerable sum of money or because you need their help in selling the product. Save your consulting requests for those times.

When You're Starting Out

After you have a mock-up or a drawing of an idea, you should consult with one or two insiders. You won't have spent much, if any, money, and you don't want to make an investment if there's a reason the product will probably fail. This is also an ideal time to gather as much market information as possible.

Some product entrepreneurs are reluctant to show ideas when they're still in their initial, rough stages. They're afraid people won't understand the ideas or won't like them because of their crude appearance. These points are valid. I've found, though, that insiders will still offer valuable advice if they're informed in advance that they'll see rough products. See an insider after you've received positive input from your initial market testing.

After You Have a Model

With a model, for the first time you'll have something concrete to evaluate. Until you have a model, people's evaluations are based on what you say— or what they imagine—your product will be like. People won't need to speculate after you have a model; they'll be able to see, touch, and use it.

Insiders will be able to tell whether your product provides its expected benefit, to identify any drawbacks the product might have, to estimate the product's perceived value, and to know whether its benefit is obvious.

Before the Initial Sales Period

Insiders can steer you to stores, distributors, and companies that may buy a product. If at all possible, you'll want to use these contacts to set up an initial distribution network. This momentum will help future sales, because the product will look like a winner to potential sales outlets and distributors.

When You Enter the Transitional Sales Period

In this phase of an introduction, a product moves from having just a few isolated sales to having a solid sales base in a small part of a market. For example, a hardware product might have its initial sales in eight regional hardware stores. The transitional period would be marked by expansion of sales throughout half of the company's home state.

This is a difficult period. You can do almost everything yourself in the first sales period; in the transitional period, you'll need to rely on other people to sell a product. Insiders can help you make contacts with key distributors or manufacturers' representatives. They might even know of a recently retired salesperson who could help your sales efforts on a part-time basis.

The transitional sales period is almost impossible to survive without insiders' help. Some product entrepreneurs succeed because insiders happen to notice their products and decide to help them.

Lynn Gordon of French Meadow Bakeries, who made bread from a fermented mix of grains and water, happened to call on a grocery store buyer who was on a special diet that didn't allow oil, honey, or dairy products. Lynn's bread was just what the buyer needed. You shouldn't make your future dependent on luck. Find your insiders early in a project, and use them during the introduction process.

ASKING INSIDERS TO INVEST

The two times to ask insiders to invest are before starting the transitional sales period and when expanding sales into a larger market area.

To quickly review, the stages of a project are initial conception, first sales period, transitional sales period, and sales expansion period. Almost every product entrepreneur needs financial help in the latter two stages. At those times, insiders' investments can provide not only needed capital but also the cash leverage required to obtain additional loans from banks or finance companies.

Why Wait Till the Transitional Period?

Most product creators ask: "Why shouldn't I get insiders to invest right away?" If you are going to keep control of a product, you must provide more than just a good idea. If insiders think you have a great idea, they might move to take over the idea and just give you a 5 or 6 percent royalty.

Instead, you should postpone asking for money until you can prove you have management capabilities and an established sales pattern.

Most new product entrepreneurs don't have extensive management experience. The one way they can show they're capable of handling a project is to complete the initial stage of the introduction cycle. Survival through the first sales period shows insiders that a product entrepreneur has devoted the time and effort required to put a product on the market and is resourceful enough to find ways around the numerous introduction problems everyone encounters.

You should be able to show that a product is actually selling before asking insiders to invest. Even if the product is in only four stores, at least you will have evidence that people are buying it. A product becomes more and more attractive to investors as its sales level rises.

Lloyd G. created a lure retriever, a fishing product that retrieves lures when they get caught in weeds or among rocks. Lloyd had sold about 500 units for $9.95 at trade shows and flea markets. Then Lloyd got tired of attending the shows and allowed a friend to try to sell the product to stores and distributors. The friend then went two years without selling any product.

Lloyd decided to try to sell his product to a manufacturer after the two-year delay. He had invested $30,000 in the idea and thought it had "million-dollar" potential, so he decided to ask for $100,000. The manufacturer's president told Lloyd that, without ongoing sales, he would consider offering only $5,000 and a small royalty.

The key to establishing a company's or a product's worth is potential sales volume—what it will sell in the next year. Where does that leave you, if you're trying to raise money in a project's initial phase? In trouble. Insiders like to see some proven sales history before they invest.

What's a Product Worth?

There's no firm formula for determining a product's or company's value. For two similar products, the value can vary tremendously. Still, I think product entrepreneurs can say that an established product is worth its annual sales volume. If a product is new and its sales are steadily increasing, the product is worth about twice its expected sales for the following year. As an example, if you've completed your initial sales period with sales of $5,000, and you project, based on distributor commitments, to sell $30,000 in the transitional period, then the company would be worth about $60,000. A product's worth can change if it has a high margin, a large capital requirement, or an explosive growth potential.

Every time you put a price tag on a product, you must start with a sales projection. This isn't a problem if a product has been sold for several years. However, a sales estimate is very difficult when you dramatically increase sales in the first year of the transitional sales period and again in the early part of the sales expansion period.

There are three methods to estimate sales during sales growth:

1. Average the sales estimates you received from industry insiders and sales representatives.
2. Analyze the sales of one or two similar products in the targeted market.
3. Use the actual sales per outlet or per salesperson that were achieved during the initial sales period.

As an example of the third method, suppose you approached 50 convenience stores in your initial sales period, and you were able to persuade 10 of them to carry your product. After four months, each store averages 10 units sold per month. If the transitional period's target market has 800 stores, and you can call on them with the same success rate (20 percent) as with the 50 stores, you could expect to sell to 800 stores times 20 percent, or 160 stores. Each store could sell about 120 units per year (10 units per month times 12 months per year), for an estimated annual sales volume of 19,200 units.

Product entrepreneurs often like to estimate sales using the first two methods, primarily because they're a lot easier than the third method. Estimates under those methods, however, are almost always too high. A new entrepreneur doesn't have the promotional muscle of an established company, and he or she won't be able to achieve the same market penetration. The third method, using actual sales results, is the most reliable. When you obtain an estimate based on past experience, divide the number by 2 to estimate the next year's sales potential. Dividing the sales level in half takes into account the time you'll need to sell to the larger market.

Compare your estimate based on actual sales to the estimate based on input from insiders and salespeople and to estimates based on sales of similar products. If the sales level is lower, that's OK; you can expect it to be lower. If the estimate is higher, go back and lower your estimate. Sometimes higher estimates from actual sales are the result of initial sales at some friendly outlets that provided premium shelf space. You probably won't get favored treatment in the rest of the market.

How to Ask for Investments

If you've been working with insiders all along, you'll find that they're easy to approach for an investment. The secrets to success are approaching them at the right time, having a presentation package, and asking for a modest investment.

When approaching potential investors, tell them that you're looking for people who'd like to invest $5,000 (or another appropriate amount) in the company. Explain that you've prepared an information package and ask if they'd like to look it over. You should receive a fairly positive response if your contacts like the product and if they have some money available to invest.

What's in a Presentation Package?

Your presentation document doesn't have to be an extensive business plan. Your insiders have been working with you all along and should know the product fairly well. The following topics are essential.

1. *A brief history.*   Provide a short summary of why you came up with the idea, what made you think of your particular product design, and why you think it will sell. Include a list of any insiders you've been working with.

2. *A competitive products chart.*   Analyze the products that are already on the market, what they cost, and what their strong and weak points are. Include your product in the chart.

3. *Current sales efforts.*   Provide a listing of where the product has been sold and a summary of the sales results at each location.

4. *A transitional sales plan.*   Explain how you're planning to expand to a larger market. For example, you might have decided to take on three more distributors or three more salespeople, or to attend two trade shows to line up manufacturers' representatives. Chapter 14 contains additional information about the transitional sales plan.

5. *The product's profitability.*   Include the product's expected margin, which is the net profit (after all expenses) divided by the sales volume. If you expect to make $10,000 after expenses, on sales of $100,000, the product's margin is $10,000/$100,000, or 10 percent. Include a profile of what happens to the dollars generated by a retail sale. The profile should look like the hardware product's breakout chart in Chapter 4.

6. *The product's value.*   Use the methods discussed earlier (see pages 117–126) to determine a product's value.

7. *An orderly financial plan.*   Show how you're going to finance the business's growth. You don't need an operating pro forma that lists your projected cash flow; you won't have enough information to create one. First, detail how much money will be raised in

the transitional period, what percentage of the business will be sold, and how the money will be used. For example, if you project sales of $100,000 per year, you might have a goal of raising $40,000: $20,000 from investors, to whom you're offering a 20 percent share of the business, and $20,000 from a commercial finance company, to fund an initial marketing program of ads, product literature, and promotional support materials.

Next, explain what expenses you'll pay for personally in this period—for example, certain manufacturing and packaging start-up expenses. Show that you're covering certain costs, either out of your own pocket or, preferably, by having them absorbed by a contract manufacturer.

Finally, show how you'll finance future growth. For example, after the product is established in the transitional market, you might plan to raise an additional $200,000, half by selling another 20 percent of the company and half from a bank loan.

Two points are important when considering a financial plan: (a) Try not to sell more than 20 percent of the company in the transitional period. You may need to be able to offer additional shares of the company at a later time. Another advantage of limiting sales to 20 percent is that your early investors will realize they're buying shares at a much lower price than will be offered to investors who will buy later. (b) Always show that you realize additional money will be required to fund the sales expansion period. Businesspeople expect that you'll need additional financing, and they expect you to realize it too.

8. *The size investment you're looking for.*   I know that entrepreneurs do a tremendous amount of work to get through the first phase of a product introduction. But most insiders will still view a project as an iffy proposition. Try not to ask for an investment that's greater than $5,000 to $10,000 in return for a small share of the business. As an example, you could offer 5 percent ownership in return for a $5,000 investment. People can always ask to buy a bigger share later, but try to make their initial investment an easy step. Remember, you're interested in the insiders' help as much as in their money.

Figure 9-1 lists the 12 key go/no-go decisions for continuing with a new-product introduction.

If your product doesn't meet all 12 criteria—and very few, if any, ideas do initially meet the criteria—it becomes your job to go back and change your idea so it passes. Not every idea can be modified to pass, but many can. The next chapter will explain how to rework a product so it can be introduced.

Figure 9-1   The 12 Key Go/No-Go Decisions

In the Introduction, I listed the basic criteria that determine whether an individual product creator can successfully take a product to market:

1. Is the product easy to distribute?
2. Is the technology simple?
3. Is the product perceived to be unique?
4. Is the benefit obvious?
5. Can the product be sold for three to five times its manufacturing cost?

The go/no-go decisions are designed to help you know when your product meets these criteria. In some cases, the relationship between the criteria and the decisions may not be obvious; for example, one reason you need insiders is so that your product will be easy to distribute. Other decisions, such as whether the product is perceived to be unique, are directly related to the criteria.

I've covered quite a few decisions in Part 2, but I believe you must answer yes to all of the following 12 questions, in order to continue moving forward on a project:

1. Can potential customers quickly understand your product's benefit?
2. Is your product clearly different from others in the market?
3. Does your product have a benefit people want?
4. Can the product be packaged effectively?
5. Is the market open?
6. Does a distribution network exist with product support costs you can afford?
7. Are your customers easy to target?
8. Can you afford to make your models, prototypes, and initial production runs?
9. Can you find a contract manufacturer that's willing to absorb some of the start-up manufacturing costs?
10. Can you find market insiders to help you?
11. Does your product have a perceived value that's at least four times its manufacturing cost?
12. Is the market size of the distribution network large enough to justify your time and expense?   (*Continued*)

Figure 9-1   *Continued*

Entrepreneurs often overlook the last question. If you're going to sell through two or three catalogs and the average sales for products sold that way is $200,000 per year, you're likely to make about 10 percent of your sales dollars, or $20,000. Is that amount enough to justify your effort? It all depends on you. One product might not require that much effort on your part, and $20,000 might be a nice annual return. Another product might require a full-time effort on your part, along with a large investment, and not be worth the effort. That's a decision only you can make. The important point is that you make it. Too many hopeful entrepreneurs keep spending money and time on their ideas when their projects have only a small profit potential.

10

REWORKING YOUR PRODUCT: HOW TO ADJUST AND PASS THE GO/NO-GO DECISIONS

I recently read this comment from Stephen Jobs, cofounder of Apple Computer: "Behind every overnight success are four years of hard work." While I certainly hope you succeed in less than four years, the fact is that most product entrepreneurs have to rework their ideas several times before they have winning product introductions.

A product entrepreneur has a tendency to look at one flaw in the product, correct it, and then move to reintroduce the product. Sometimes this approach works, but other times it forces an entrepreneur to define the problem too narrowly, missing the product's real problems. This is analogous to the person who fixes the upholstery in a car when the engine is on fire.

Joe and Mona T. invented a bumper pad that could be wrapped around a baby's walker, a device babies sit in and can move by shuffling their legs. Babies use walkers from when they are about seven or eight months old until they can walk. The bumper pad's purpose is to protect furniture. Joe and Mona sold their product with only limited success. The complaint they heard most often was that their product attached to the walker with strings, which the babies could suck on or pull apart. So Joe and Mona switched to a Velcro attachment, but the baby bumper still didn't sell, and Joe and Mona dropped their idea. However, their problem wasn't that their idea couldn't sell, it was that

*they defined the problem too narrowly (that strings were a poor fea-
ture) rather than looking at the problem broadly (is the product right
for the market and is it being promoted correctly?).*

Joe and Mona essentially were marketing their product as a furniture
protector. If they had gone back and researched their target market, which
was parents of children four to nine months old, they would have found
two segments of parents: those who use walkers and those who don't.
They would have also found that parents who purchase walkers weren't
that worried about their furniture, and those who did worry about furniture didn't use walkers. This is a much bigger problem than the fact that
the bumper needs Velcro instead of string.

To sell successfully, Joe and Mona needed a benefit that was important to either one of the two market segments. If they had checked on what
was important to parents, they would have discovered that parents want
their children to develop thinking and creativity skills, which calls for
children to be exposed to more experiences and situations. This is a benefit that baby walkers offer, because it enables the babies to see another part
of their world. Joe and Mona were selling a furniture protection device.
They should have been selling a child development aid.

The goal of this chapter is to help you go review your product's marketing basics, so that you can introduce a product that will sell. The three
marketing basics you need to cover are:

1. Understanding your target customer
2. Building a product that hits prospects' hot buttons
3. Finding the distribution system that works for your customers'
   needs

The final topic in the chapter is product design and development, which
covers how to address design and manufacturing issues.

UNDERSTANDING YOUR TARGET CUSTOMERS

Figure 10-1 is a tool that will help you decide if you have a winning product. The bottom axis is a scale of the importance of a feature or benefit to
the target customer. The more important the feature, the farther to the
right it is placed. The vertical axis indicates how unique the feature is to
your product or company. Products in the upper right-hand corner are
unique to a company and important to the customer. That's the situation
in which your product will make money. The fact that the baby bumper
pad protects furniture is a feature that ranks low in importance and high
in uniqueness, an area outside of our target box.

Figure 10-1   Target Customers' Desired Features or Benefits

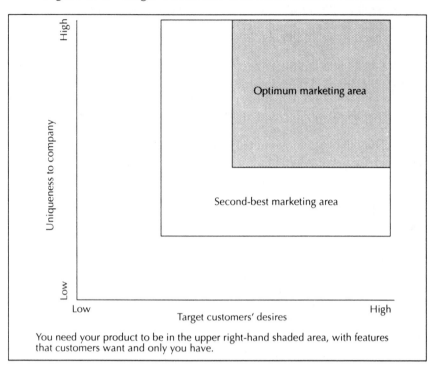

You need your product to be in the upper right-hand shaded area, with features that customers want and only you have.

There are three ways to reposition your product into the target area:

1. Change your target market.
2. Reconfigure your features and benefits.
3. Add additional features.

Changing Your Target Market

Changing your target market can also be looked at as reducing it to dimensions in which your features become important. This is more commonly called *segmenting a market*. I'll use Joe and Mona's baby bumper pad as an example. Joe and Mona face a confusing situation in which their target customers are parents with children six to nine months old. Some parents care about protecting their furniture, while others don't. The same applies for fostering children's creativity: Only some parents will consciously try to increase their children's exposure to more and different experiences. The result is that Joe and Mona's product is not perceived to have a meaningful benefit.

But what happens when Joe and Mona limit their market to parents who make a dedicated effort to develop their babies' thinking skills? Suddenly, the baby bumper pad can be placed in the upper right-hand corner of the desired features chart. Those target customers could be reached through educational toy stores, parenting magazines, and specialty education catalogs.

Targeting a smaller market is something that even big companies frequently do. Figure 10-2 shows a desired feature chart for Suddenly Salad, which is a mix you add to boiling water for a quick, nutritious pasta salad. This product is available in most major supermarkets and is produced by a major consumer products company. If Suddenly Salad's market consisted of all families in general, the feature chart would be different: Low cost would be more important, and ease of preparation would be less important. By targeting working families, Suddenly Salad moves into the upper right-hand corner of desirable, unique features.

The drawback to targeting a smaller market is that it's not as glamorous or as profitable as a big market. Targeting the baby bumper for parents who are willing to spend money on their child's development places the product into educational toy stores instead of Target, Kmart, and Wal-Mart stores. The advantage in choosing the smaller market is that your product features will be important and meaningful, and you'll have a

Figure 10-2   Target Customers' Desired Features
or Benefits for Suddenly Salad

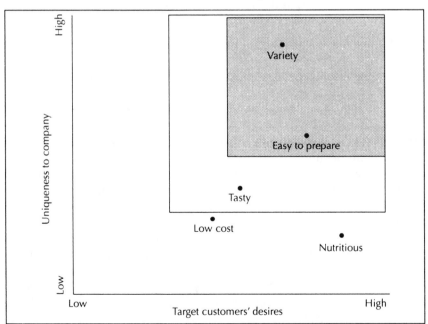

much better chance of securing sales. Once you have a successful track record, you can attack other markets.

Reconfiguring Features and Benefits

Inventors, as well as many companies, have a tendency to focus on their product features instead of customer-desired benefits when they sell products. The result is that a product that might be just right for the market won't sell. Products sell well when they meet customers' wishes or needs, and it's a product entrepreneur's job to make sure customers realize that the product meets their needs.

As an example, one inventor developed a mobile truck-washing unit for cleaning truck trailers. Primary customers were bus companies and trucking companies, and the unit sold for $40,000. This was a great product for its market because it could clean a truck in eight minutes and recycle all wastewater for proper disposal, in addition to being easy to operate. The company's competition consisted of bay washing systems, which cost $200,000, and mobile truck-washing businesses, which visit trucking company sites once a week to wash trailers.

This company promoted the following product features:

- Self-contained unit
- Lower cost
- Ease of maintenance
- Air brushing
- EPA compliance
- Mobility
- Ease of use
- Four-wheel steering
- Hot water
- Indoor or outdoor washing

These product-oriented features were all nice but they didn't address directly what customers wanted, which was a clean, high-class image. The inventor sold his product as a maintenance item, when the customer was looking to attract more business.

All the inventor needed to do was present the features of his product as what the customer wanted. He could promote his product with the tag line, "Never send a truck out dirty again." The product's benefit is that a truck can be cleaned in just eight minutes. By anyone in the yard. Without any setup time. Inside a bay or out in the parking lot. Up to 15 trucks in a row can be cleaned. There just wasn't any reason a trucking company couldn't have a top-of-the-line image.

This inventor didn't have to change one thing about his product to sell it effectively; he just had to present its features in such a way that customers would want it.

Adding Product Features

John K. developed a camping pillow that could be folded over itself once to be a seat cushion and then folded over again into a very small package that would fit easily into a backpack or could be clipped to a belt for travel. John thought his product was ideal for campers. They would have an easy-to-transport pillow and a seat pad for whenever they sat down on the trail.

These all seem like great features, but how do they fit into what campers want? Not very well as it turns out. A camper who drives to a campsite doesn't worry about a pillow's size—a regular pillow can be stuffed somewhere into the car, and having a seat cushion just isn't that important. Backpacking campers also didn't think sitting cushions were important, and most used sweatshirts or coats as pillows. Family campers didn't have any strong desires for pillows and weren't good candidates for a new product.

However, some backpackers, did mention two desired features: a pillow that would keep the head warm on a cold night and easy access to aspirin and other items on the trail. So John added to the pillow a fleece cover that pulled up so a camper could put his or her head between the fleece and the pillow on cold nights. This enabled him to use the slogan "stay warm on a cold night." He also added a small pouch to the pillow that was accessible when the pillow was rolled tightly for carrying on a belt, a feature that backpacking campers found appealing.

A PRODUCT THAT HITS PROSPECTS' HOT BUTTONS

Once you know what customers want and your product has the necessary features, you have to be sure it communicates the right benefits and features to your target customer. You can do this most easily by making sure you can answer a short series of questions about your product.

What Is Your Buyer's Motivation?

People usually have one of four motivations when they buy products:

1. *Goal-oriented motivation.*   For example, people might buy products that enable them to cook gourmet meals in half the time.
2. *Image- or status-oriented motivation.*   Cars and clothes are often bought for status, but so are camping products. Some campers want the best-looking products on the market and others buy only well-known, name-brand products.

3. *Usage-oriented motivation.*   A more comfortable bicycle seat has a usage-oriented motivation. So do a blender with improved mixing capabilities, a mulching lawn-mower blade, a database software program, and a composting chemical.

4. *Entertainment-oriented motivation.*   These are products that people buy at least in part to have fun, such as toys, a swing for the front porch, wind sails, unusual golf equipment, and any other product that will make people smile.

What you need to do is make sure your product, the ad layout you've designed, and your package fit the motivation of the people in your target market. The image your product gives people in one to two seconds needs to convey your product's positioning. The following list indicates the look your product and packaging should have to correspond to each motivation category:

1. *Goal-oriented:*   Products and packaging should match the look of other products used to meet the same goal. For example, bread-making machines match the look of food processors and look like they fit right into the kitchen.

2. *Image-oriented:*   Products should contain features that are associated with a high-priced image—for example, a small understated logo, leather pieces, silver or gold trim, or a fleece liner. Product features should reflect their respective market's own image. Be sure to include in your product one or more features that are indicative of the desired image.

3. *Usage-oriented:*   The feature or benefit that makes your product better should be obvious. For example, a more comfortable bike seat needs to *look* more comfortable. You also should have a trademarked name for your feature. For example, in the advertising slogan, "exclusive toroidal tension inner-spring design balances weight distribution for maximum comfort," the trademarked name would be "toroidal tension."

4. *Entertainment-oriented:*   The product has to look like it's fun, with bright colors and a funky design—perhaps a bit overdramatic. The Super Soaker's most innovative feature was its ability to shoot water more than 50 feet. But what sold the product was its oversized water canister. That made the shooting-distance feature of the product jump out at the consumer.

Does Your Product Look Different but Still Belong?

Your target customers have certain predispositions that are very hard to change. For example, a product for a machine shop needs to be rugged looking and dark colored, and typically it should have a backlit LCD display. A new product will be difficult to sell if it looks totally different from this expectation. The key to success is to make your product look unique and different, but still make it look like it belongs. The new breed of bread-making machines did an excellent job of meeting this requirement, as did automatic drip coffeemakers, which used traditional-looking coffeepots. It wasn't necessary to do that, but it made the product fit customers' predispositions.

Is Your Product's Purpose Clear?

The purpose of some products is very clear—for example, a new style of hairbrush will almost always look like a traditional hairbrush. But people won't recognize a plastic tray with various-size slots as a junk drawer organizer without seeing the product's name. I can't determine the purpose of 25 to 50 percent of inventors' products. Sometimes I can't even determine it after the inventor explains to me what the product does.

Underfinanced entrepreneurs can't afford to offer products with unclear purposes. Prospects must be able to tell in one or two seconds if a product addresses one of their needs or wants. If a product alone can't stand on its own, the package and name have to do the job. Fix-A-Flat is a product whose name tells its story. But a product still gets only one or two seconds in which to do this.

Can Prospects Quickly Understand Your Product's Benefits?

If people can understand what your product does, can they also understand what its benefit is? People might understand that your product is a hairbrush, but do they also understand that the brush rotates so it can pull out tangles?

To be successful, products have to convey four critical messages within seconds:

1. What the product is
2. Why it's better or why you should buy it
3. Why it will do what you say
4. Why your message is credible

An example of how a product can do this is the Junk Drawer Organizer. The product's package includes the word *kitchen* at the top, making it clear where the product fits. The inventor, Devee Philpot, fulfilled steps two through four first by having each compartment specifically sized for different items in the kitchen, which showed how the product was better. Devee then demonstrated that her product would work by placing decals in each compartment, which showed how kitchen items would fit. Finally, she packaged the product in shrink-wrap so people could see it, which built credibility.

Every one of these steps was necessary so that Devee's product would sell. You probably have noticed that none of the items I've listed has anything to do with the product. The decals are quickly discarded and the shrink-wrap is really the most cost-effective package. But almost every product needs just a few little twists to make it sell. Kodak uses bright yellow cardboard on its single-use cameras. This wasn't just a randomly chosen package. Bright yellow is a color associated with outdoor use, implying rugged, almost indestructible products. And the cardboard emphasizes the product's disposability. The cover targets the camera as the perfect fit for occasions that might be too rugged for a standard camera.

One of Devee's best marketing moves for the Junk Drawer Organizer was shrink-wrapping her product. Although the major drawback of shrink-wrapping is product returns due to damaged packages, the advantage is that people can see the product. Customers today are very skeptical, especially about products from one-product companies. It is important to let people see your product so they know exactly what it is like. If your product needs a box, you might consider adding a plastic window similar to the packaging of many toy products.

If you can't show your product because of your distribution channel, your product's configuration, or another reason, you still need to develop credibility. One way to do that is to offer convincing proof of the product's functionality. For example, the packaging for the Junk Drawer Organizer might use a photo of the product holding 48 items. Another tactic to build credibility is to give very clear, concise claims. A claim such as "this product will organize every item in your junk drawer" is vague. A claim should be much more specific, such as "this product holds 65 common kitchen junk drawer items."

A final tactic for building credibility is to add a personal touch to your product. Devee might put her picture on the box with the caption, "Devee Philpot, inventor of the Junk Drawer Organizer." This tactic has been used by companies such as Orville Redenbacher and Kentucky Fried Chicken. People will believe in a product that displays someone's name.

Where Is Your Mystique?

Hope is an important, though rarely discussed, factor in every customer purchase. Customers hope you solve their problems, offer them new excitement, or make their lives a little easier. You should try to add a little intangible mystery to a product to help it sell. You can do this in many ways. For example, bread machines have a much different look from toaster ovens. They look space-age and convey the image of high-tech mystery. Food processors have the same look.

You also can create a mystique with a trademarked name (such as "Chrysalis Arts for All"), a trademarked feature (such as a "patented synthesized silicon lubricant"), or an unusual process (such as "recycled from used tires").

FINDING THE RIGHT DISTRIBUTION CHANNEL

Most new-product entrepreneurs tend to lock into one product distribution channel early and never consider other distribution options. This can be disastrous, especially with a new product.

"Dr. Juice" is a Minnesota inventor who created a series of small packets of liquids that fishing enthusiasts could place on their lures to attract fish. Dr. Juice's products are fairly well known in fishing circles, and they sell in fishing stores. But when Dr. Juice started out, nobody had heard of his product and people thought his idea was a little crazy.

Dr. Juice's products probably would fail the initial go/no-go decisions if the distribution channel was fishing stores. When a distribution channel's response is unfavorable, the trick is to go to the most favorable channel possible, no matter how small it is. In the case of Dr. Juice, the most ideal market was to sell through fishing guides and outfitters. The product's lack of credibility could be overcome if guides were to use and endorse the product. Dr. Juice needed to give samples to guides and show them how to use his product. Dr. Juice could succeed if at least some of the guides would try the product and agree to promote it if it worked.

Once Dr. Juice was able to sell through guides, he would know he had a base from which to build. This example points out several considerations that product entrepreneurs overlook:

1. The amount of support your product needs
2. Your size versus the distribution channel's size
3. The percentage of customers that could buy the product
4. The degree of competition in the channel
5. The sales effort needed to get a positive response

Amount of Product Support

A convenience food store offers a product little if any product support. Office supply or electronics superstores, such as Office Max or Circuit City, offer a limited amount of support, but much less than a computer reseller with trained salespeople that focuses on business applications. Your job is be sure your product is positioned in a distribution channel that offers enough support to sell your product. Product support can be from a specialized store or catalog, such as a camping store that sells only backpacking supplies; a well-trained, expert sales force, such as dentists or podiatrists through whom you sell products; a distribution channel that can demonstrate a product, such as an auto dealer or independent individual distributors that attend trade shows; or a distribution channel that focuses only on a small, specific market, such as a distributor that handles only Victorian products.

You'll need a distribution channel with support if your product:

- Needs to be demonstrated (e.g., a new musical instrument)
- Has technical features that people aren't familiar with (e.g., a device that attaches to a car's carburetor and will turn the gas stream into a gas spray for better fuel efficiency)
- Is one that people normally aren't looking for (e.g., Dr. Juice's fish-attracting products)
- Doesn't have a benefit people immediately recognize (e.g., the camping pillow)
- Doesn't meet customers' predispositions (e.g., a Velcro-applied strap that you wear on your forearm instead of your elbow to prevent tennis elbow injuries)

Big companies also try to avoid products that need support, but they can afford advertising support when a product needs it. Most new-product entrepreneurs can't afford advertising and, instead, need to rely on distribution channels to provide the sales support their products need.

If you are unable to find a distribution network that will take your product, you have to ask yourself whether the network is capable of selling your product. People in distribution channels know what products they can't support, and they will turn those products down. Your product can still be marketed if you find the right channel.

One product entrepreneur, for example, had a product for an outdoor deck that consisted of rows of clear, very strong plastic that let sun shine down to windows below. The product was designed to attach to standard deck framing and it allowed the windows below the deck to get sunlight, which was a great feature for split-level homes. But it was a new product that people weren't predisposed to buy. Building supply stores, such as Knox or Builders Square, provide little sales support and are unlikely to take new products from small vendors unless they are certain that people will buy them.

Another product channel open to this inventor, which does provide enough sales and product support, is contractors who build decks. The product entrepreneur could sell decking material to the contractors, who would then use it on the decks they build. The custom deck builders could use the product as a selling feature of their service, offering a product that couldn't be purchased at a store. Once the product was sold through deck installers, the large building supply chains would be more likely to stock the product.

To decide if the product will pass the go/no-go decisions, the inventor can contact 15 to 20 deck installers and ask them if they would become distributors. Once some say yes, this product entrepreneur knows he has a path to market his product. If you have a product that needs support, don't be afraid to consider using small, part-time distributors that will take your product and demonstrate it at trade shows, county fairs, and other appropriate gatherings. Many fishing and household products are sold that way. For example, one product entrepreneur developed a home soda machine. Users would buy syrup to place into the machine, which would then produce soda just like a fast-food restaurant does. The company then set up a network of 25 distributors throughout the country. These distributors obtained leads at home shows and county fairs and then sold the product through in-home demonstrations. You can find part-time distributors through ads in the business opportunity sections of local papers or through ads in business opportunity–type magazines.

The Size of Your Targeted Channel

Big market channels like large suppliers, and big suppliers like to sell to large market channels. This leaves the smaller distribution networks to smaller suppliers. There are many reasons that small, one-product suppliers find big channels hard to penetrate. They include the cost to a company of adding a supplier, the unreliability of small companies when it comes to returns or warranties, and companies' lack of familiarity with each small supplier.

Inventors frequently try to approach the biggest market available. They may fail, even though they have excellent products. When you don't receive support from a big market, try a smaller one.

Stan and Gladys Friesen, for example, turned their product around simply by going after another market with their snack-food product,

*Glad Corn. Stan originally came up with the idea when he was try-
ing to make ethanol in his kitchen from field corn. When the corn
exploded, he discovered a new snack. The corn isn't like popcorn,
but instead produces a kernel that is five or six times larger than
normal and quite tasty. At first the Friesens sold their product as a
fund-raiser to 4-H clubs, which is a small and appropriate market
channel. Then the Friesens thought they'd approach convenience
store chains, a big, hotly contested market. After they failed in this
market, they regrouped and went after gift shops and natural food
stores. Glad Corn is expected to have $250,000 in sales in 1996—
not a big company, but a good start to what could be a very profitable venture.*

_____

The Percentage of Customers That Could Buy the Product

Only a small percentage of target customers buys any product. Stores and
distribution channels know that, and they are reluctant to stock a product
unless virtually anyone who walks in the store might buy it. Retailers just
don't think a product will sell fast enough unless it appeals to the vast
majority of their customers.

An example is the Space-Saving First Aid Medical Drawer. This
product mounts under a kitchen cabinet and folds up tightly against the
cabinet when it's not in use. The product is barely visible, but is very
easy to pull down if an emergency should arise. This is a nice product,
but a little hard to sell because it is hard to find a distribution channel
where virtually everyone will be a potential buyer. The product was
targeted at parents with small children. The original target distribution
channel was kitchen stores and housewares departments of discount
retailers such as Kmart. The kitchen store channel wasn't opened to
the product because its target market was homemakers who like to
cook, and a major percentage of those customers doesn't have small children. Discount retailers were unwilling to stock the product because
it didn't appeal to most of the people who walked into the kitchen
department.

The product belonged in clothing, furniture, and toy stores that were
targeted at parents of young children. The product didn't sell initially to
that channel when it was first on the market because it was sold without
supplies and people didn't connect immediately to its benefit of better
first aid. The product did sell once it was filled with emergency first aid
supplies, as it then offered a complete solution for the customer, as well as
an obvious benefit.

Degree of Competition in the Channel

Inventors will have a difficult time breaking into new distribution channels anytime they run into stiff competition. Returning to the example of first aid drawer, another reason that attempts to sell into the kitchen store market failed was that those stores are approached by hundreds of suppliers of similar plastic parts. The product entrepreneur looked just like one of the crowd in those markets. The product became unique only when it was offered to people in the children's clothing, furniture, and small toy store markets.

This step is almost the opposite of what most inventors and product entrepreneurs do. You have a kitchen product. What better place to sell it than at a kitchen store? Rather than look for distribution channels based on what they sell, look at them for who their target market is. Do this first by listing your target customer and then listing all the distribution channels that service that target customer.

As an example, consider a biodegradable paper diaper that sells for 20 percent more than standard diapers. The product's benefit is that it completely degrades in three months after use as opposed to the non-biodegradable status of diapers currently in use. The ideal market for diapers is grocery stores and drugstores. But those channels would be very competitive and hard to penetrate. The product entrepreneur introducing this product should list the target audience and then list distribution channels where this audience might shop.

Target customer:	Environmentally conscious parents of babies
Distribution channels:	Co-op food stores featuring natural foods, catalogs from organizations such as Greenpeace, health food stores, catalogs of organically grown food

This product could also be sold into any of these channels much more easily than into supermarkets. These channels don't carry many, if any, diaper products and competition will be light. After sales are developed into these channels, the inventor might be able to penetrate supermarkets.

Sales Effort

Devee Philpot introduced the Junk Drawer Organizer mentioned earlier. She has well over a hundred accounts now, but she had to call most of them four or five times before she got their business. There are five main reasons people don't buy products: (1) no need, (2) no trust, (3) no interest, (4) no hurry, and (5) no ability to pay or decide. The second biggest reason people don't buy is that they haven't developed trust in the person selling the products.

When I first started working, I attended a course that addressed salespeople one week and purchasing groups the next. The instructor asked our sales group how many times we would call on a buyer before giving up. The average answer was five times. The week before, the instructor had asked purchasing people how many times a salesperson needed to call before getting a big order. Their answer was seven times. You need to see a person four or five times before you can really know if he or she will buy your product. Most buyers will wait—especially when dealing with a new supplier—until they see you or hear from you for three to six months before they buy from you. When you don't really have a product to sell, it is a little difficult to decide if someone will buy, so you need to pick out four or five people to contact and then preplan a sequence of calls to build trust. A four-call sequence that I recommend is as follows:

1st call: Show the idea to the buyer and ask if there are any improvements he or she would suggest.

2d call: Approach the buyer and mention ideas other people have suggested to see if the buyer has a positive response to them.

3d call: Show a picture of the final version of the product you've decided to develop and ask for comments.

4th call: Call on the buyer and mention that you are doing a survey to see if people will actually buy the product. Then ask whether the buyer would take the product, and if so, how large would the order be.

PRODUCT DESIGN

Inventors often pay too much attention to how their products work and far too little attention to what their products look like. I believe in the motto "look like success" for new products, which means your product needs to be well designed, up to date, and pleasing to look at.

Ten to fifteen years ago many products were built with sheet metal designs, sand castings, or basic bent-plastic shapes. The inventor's world has changed quite a bit over the last ten years, primarily due to advances in molding technology. You just can't get away with a crude product appearance anymore. People expect products to have a modern—and often futuristic—look. Inventors and product entrepreneurs have always had ideas rejected because the look of their products was outdated, but this problem is greater now than ever.

The main reason inventors run into trouble with an outdated look is that they compare their products to those already on the market rather than to products that have been recently introduced. For example, if you have a small, new kitchen appliance you can't compare its look to that of a toaster oven or blender. Those products have been available for years and have an established market position. Instead, you need to look at new products, such as bread machines or food processors. You can tell immediately that new products have vastly upgraded designs.

Better-Looking Drawings

After you have completed an initial design for your product, find, either at retail stores or through trade magazines, five to seven recently introduced products. If your product design isn't comparable, you'll need to upgrade it. Since you are simply trying to make your go/no-go decisions, you should be able to get by with just a picture.

The best place to get someone to do a low-cost product design is through an art school or university. Look in your phone book for local art schools. Ask the placement or employment office to place an ad for a one-time project to design the look of a product. The graphic arts instructor may be able to recommend a student to you. These students like design projects, because they can be added to their portfolios. Students are good resources for product entrepreneurs because they don't charge much and typically will spend a lot of time on your product. You can also call universities in your area to see if they have industrial design departments (which should be your first choice) or graphic arts departments. Contact the departments directly for the names of students looking for a project like yours.

One last choice is to contact industrial designers. They'll be more expensive, but they will do an excellent job. You can sometimes get a better price if you explain that you are working on a new product and have very little money. You can offer to give the designer the entire project if your initial testing goes well and you are able to attract investors.

Appearance Models

Sometimes a drawing doesn't show enough for people to get an accurate picture of what your product will be like. In this case you may need to make an upscale appearance model. Again, you can rely on art schools, prototype shops, and universities. If those avenues don't work out, you can consult back issues of *Design News, Machine Design,* and *Industrial Product Design* (see "Helpful Sources" at the end of this book). These magazines will run ads for prototype shops and CAD (computer-aided design) shops that will make appearance models for you. You might also contact your state's small business development center, which you can find by calling the nearest Small Business Administration office.

When considering whether you need a drawing, appearance model, or prototype, remember that people usually will not look beyond what you show them directly. For example, if you show a person a rough prototype and state, "On the real model we will have a structural foam cover with a sweeping arch over this area of the product," what the person will see is the rough prototype and not your more elaborate image.

This is a crucial mistake that product entrepreneurs make over and over again. They live with their products, sometimes for years, and have visions of what the final products will look like. They don't see rough prototypes, they see final products. But that's not what anyone else sees—they just see the products in their present forms. The result is that entrepreneurs think they are showing space-age products, while the manufacturers, retailers, or investors just see the rough prototypes. Don't fool yourself into thinking you can explain how great your product will be with a few modifications. Instead, get a drawing or an appearance model that shows what the product will really be like.

Rechecking the Go/No-Go Decisions

Everyone is in a rush to make money with an idea, but rushing to put an idea on the market often results in a failed introduction. You might need to go back through the go/no-go decisions three or four times before you are ready to proceed. Some people even have to go through the decisions as many as ten times. Don't worry about your timing. Introducing a product is far too hard to do unless every feature and benefit is just right. In the end, spending time in the beginning of a project to create the best product idea is your quickest path to success.

PART THREE

SELLING YOUR PRODUCT

If your product idea earns a yes on all the go/no-go decisions, you may be so excited that you can't sleep at night. You can't wait to take your product out to where customers can buy it. You probably feel like your project is a freight train running at top speed, ready to burst through any barrier. Right?

Wrong. You've climbed the first 30 feet of a 50-foot cliff. You've made a lot of progress and your future looks bright, but you still have a long way to go before you can call yourself successful.

Gary F., along with three partners, tried without success to introduce a hairbrush that untangled hair. The partners had rushed their product into production, assuming that it would sell. Gary told me that he had recently watched a TV show that covered all the preliminary work the marketers had performed for the Teenage Mutant Ninja Turtle toys. Gary's reaction was: "Who did we think we were, expecting the brush's introduction to be such a snap?"

Don't run headlong into the market and then find out you can't sell a product. Continue with the step-by-step approach I've been advocating all along. Part 3 explains the actual process of selling a product, which is really the heart of a winning introduction. Your idea won't succeed unless you can sell it.

Be prepared for a great deal of rejection when you start to sell a product. You might have only one sale after making ten calls—or maybe even twenty. That's normal. Every company runs into sales resistance from customers. Don't let it discourage you as long as some people are buying your product.

11

THE FIRST SALES PERIOD: PROVING A PRODUCT WILL SELL

After a product has passed the go/no-go decisions, the next step is to prove that it can be sold. This is not the time to gear up production and try to saturate a market. At this stage, you produce as few as 100 to 200 units and then see whether customers will buy them.

Manufacturers almost always take products to small test markets before they launch them nationally. Product entrepreneurs often think testing cycles are unnecessary. Unfortunately, bypassing this key step is usually disastrous.

When I worked at the dental supply company, we introduced a product for cleaning out root canals. The product's benefit was that it minimized the problem of files breaking in canals—an important benefit because a dentist might need an hour or longer to extract a broken file. We invested $25,000 in market research studies; the results were so positive that we were afraid we couldn't make enough units. We introduced the product with a double-page ad that drew a response from 8,000 out of 120,000 dentists, by far the highest response rate we had ever heard of. We couldn't even supply literature to every interested dentist.

In four months, with 25 salespeople and 400 dealers, we were able to sell only $150,000 worth of product, which was less than 20 *percent of what we thought was a very conservative budget. Dentists weren't buying the product, despite its tremendous benefit, because the product sold for $995. Another product of ours, similar in appearance, sold for $495. The new product's technology was different, but the dentists didn't care; the products looked the same. Our mistake was that we hadn't had a first sales period to see what problems we would encounter.*

During the first sales period, product entrepreneurs are better off if they're undercapitalized rather than well funded. Someone who is short on funds doesn't have money to waste. Keep your expenses low. You don't know whether your product will sell, what price consumers will pay for it, and how many units need to be produced. (See Figure 11-1.)

GOALS OF THE FIRST SALES PERIOD

Financial

I'm discussing the financial area first because many product creators mistakenly try to make money in the first sales period.

Cliff L. had an ice-fishing product that both skimmed ice out of a fishing hole and grabbed a fish on the line after boring below an ice hole. Cliff didn't want to invest in expensive tooling—a smart move on his part—but he made another mistake. He spent all the money he had ($3,000) to buy material for 1,000 units. By buying that much inventory, he got a 40 percent discount. At the discounted price, he could make and sell his product for a profit.

Figure 11-1   Goals of the First Sales Period

Business Area	Stated Goal
Financial	To break even
Manufacturing	To make a product for the lowest possible total cost
Sales	To sell a minimum of 50 to 250 units, through the targeted distribution network
Market research	To establish the ideal price point, the packaging required, the best name, the most important features, an effective distribution network
Scheduling	To complete the preceding goals in 3 to 15 months

Cliff placed the product in six stores on a consignment basis. The product didn't sell. Customers apparently weren't able to understand the product's benefits, primarily because of its poor packaging. Unfortunately, Cliff didn't have any money left to modify his package.

Cliff should have made up only twenty to thirty units. When it became obvious that he needed new packaging, he could have taken one or two photographs that demonstrated the product's benefit, made thirty copies, attached them to the packages, and tried to sell the product again. Twenty or thirty new packages could have been made for $50 or $60.

A friend of mine, who is a small entrepreneur, likes to say, "Now is the time to show intestinal fortitude and put your money on the line." A lot of product entrepreneurs would agree. I don't. Ninety percent of all products fail within three years. No one knows for sure whether a product will sell until someone buys it.

Manufacturing

You should make your product for the lowest possible *total* cost. You must include tooling, setup charges, packaging, manufacturing, reworking scrap, and everything else. Most entrepreneurs tend to look at the final product costs, not the total cost. For example, an entrepreneur might be able to make 1,000 units for $4 each or 30 units for $9.50 each. Many people would choose to make 1,000 units. But 1,000 units will cost $4,000, and packaging and setup charges can run another $750. The total cost for 30 units will be $285 plus packaging and setup charges of $175. Per-unit costs are high for limited production runs, especially when temporary tooling is used, but your goal is to spend as little money as possible.

Sales

Your sales goal at this stage is to prove that your product will sell. You don't have to sell a carload of units to get that proof. As a rule, 50 to 250 units are enough. Be sure that they're sold in a situation that simulates actual selling circumstances as closely as possible.

Greg H., the creator of a new type of bracelet, asked my help in placing the item at convenience store and drugstore checkout counters. Greg produced 200 units. I made four point-of-purchase displays out of bakery boxes. Photographs of teenagers wearing the jewelry communicated the product's benefit, and I used press type for a few lines

> *of copy. I put the displays into two convenience stores and two drug-stores, and then watched to see whether the product sold.*

Rarely is advertising worthwhile during the first sales period, primarily because advertising results are very limited on a short-run ad campaign, and because any demand created by advertising might be lost if buyers can't find the product. Instead, the focus should be on creating demand with clever point-of-purchase displays and on placing the product in stores where it can be bought.

If you think your product won't get a fair trial without advertising support, run a specific store promotion. One inventor placed an antifungal product in a local drugstore and then ran ads that featured the drugstore's name in the local paper.

Market Research

A product doesn't rest—or sell—on its merits alone. Its total package of features, which includes its price, packaging, name, unique benefits, and marketing campaign, contributes to its success. Try to gather as much research as you can on your product's total package during your initial sales period.

Price

Try out two or three prices, even if you lose money on the lowest one. When we were introducing the tire cutter, we found that a similar product had been introduced earlier for $149. No one bought the product because it looked like it had a manufacturing cost of about $15. At $60, our product could sell; after a product redesign, it could sell for $100.

> *Tom R. developed a writing board that slipped over a steering wheel. It could be used by delivery drivers, law enforcement officials, and service people. Tom's manufacturing cost was about $5, which meant the product should retail for about $20. When the product didn't sell at all at $20, Tom tested it at $14.95. It sold quite nicely at the lower price. Tom knew that he would have a viable product if he could lower his manufacturing cost to 25 percent of $14.95, or about $3.50.*

Not every product sells more at a lower price. Some products sell at about the same volume at any price. Adult toys often fit into this category.

For a while, I sold digital diaries at Macy's. Casio sold a model for $109; Selectronics sold a similar product for $79. Casio's diaries, at the higher price, always sold considerably more units than Selectronics' diaries. People bought what they thought was the best product, and they interpreted Casio's higher price to mean the Casio diary was better.

On some products, price doesn't significantly impact sales; a 10 percent price increase might cause only a 5 percent drop in sales. On these products, entrepreneurs are better off with a higher price. Car and truck accessories are good examples of products for which price will have only a small impact on sales volume. When I started to sell the lottery pen, I tested it at three prices: $1.99, $2.49, and $2.99. The sales volume per store changed only slightly as the price changed. People either liked the pen and bought it at any of the tested prices, or they didn't like it and wouldn't buy it at any price.

Packaging

Your choice of package can be a major cost consideration. A blister pack with four-color artwork might cost 50 to 85¢ per unit; a two-color card with shrink-wrapping might cost 25¢—a big difference when the product costs less than $2. Still, a package must convey the message of a product; for that to happen, you may need the blister pack. The only way you can know which combination will produce the best results is to test several options.

Name

A well-chosen name can add 30 to 50 percent, or even more, to a product's sales volume. For some markets, the name will dictate whether a product will succeed. "Chip Clip" is a great name; I doubt that the product would have sold without it. "Hula Hoop" is another name that clearly added to the product's sales appeal.

Unique Features

Some products have one or two features that add a disproportionate amount to their cost. Try to sell the product without the feature(s), to test their importance.

Ray A. created a basketball game targeted at the adult market. One feature of the game was that its shooting positions could be rotated to allow bank shots. This feature represented 40 percent of the product's final cost.

Most product creators are tempted to skip any testing of product features. If you look back over your product's development, you might find that a feature is the result of input from only one or two people. Perhaps one friend told Ray that his game got boring after an hour or so, which inspired Ray to add the bank shot. Most products have one or two features that are responses to limited input, and a great deal of money could be saved if the features could be dropped.

Stores/Distribution

If possible, try to sell your product through a variety of stores or other sales outlets.

A fishing product that keeps leaders straight illustrates the benefits of trying new distribution outlets. A leader, a heavier piece of line that attaches to a hook, has two benefits: It minimizes the chances that a fish will bite the line in two, and it makes it easier to change hooks. Unfortunately, leaders can be easily tangled. The straight-leader product was initially sold through bait-and-tackle stores. A distributor took the product to a fishing trade show and found that charter fishing-boat captains would buy the leader holder. The new market that opened up turned out to be much better than bait-and-tackle shops.

Not everyone can do all the testing I've outlined here, but each entrepreneur should do all the testing that's possible. It will pay off. I held marketing positions at the dental supply company for seven years and introduced one or two new products every year. I thought I knew the market about as well as anyone could, but there were always a few surprises in every introduction. To succeed, you need to be able to adjust to those surprises.

Scheduling

Product entrepreneurs like to look at the first sales period as a single effort that might take a month or two. Sometimes that happens, but more often the first sales period is a series of activities. Ted Z., who created a knife-sharpening device, started selling his product at flea markets, then moved up to rod-and-gun shows, and finally placed the product into four retail stores.

Manufacturing delays can stretch out a projected timetable. Delays can result from making a few units at a time or from a need to make product or package modifications.

Art T. had a new face shield that was designed to keep construction workers warm in the winter. During his initial sales period, a new hard hat was introduced. A construction worker couldn't use Art's shield while wearing the new hard hat. Art solved that problem but then discovered that his shield didn't provide enough airflow. Each modification took time and money.

Most readers probably reacted by saying "No way!" when they saw a scheduling goal of 3 to 15 months. New entrepreneurs are anxious to bring their products to market and start making money. They must worry first about taking the right product, in the right package, at the right price, to the right distribution outlets. For product introductions, slow and steady usually wins the race and preserves enough cash to cross the finish line.

PREPARING TO START

Incorporate

You open yourself up to tremendous legal liabilities when you sell a product. If it should injure someone or if another type of calamity should occur, you could be personally liable. One way to protect yourself is to incorporate, which insulates your personal assets from business claims.

Numerous books on incorporating a business are available in libraries and bookstores. The office of the secretary of state in your home state will send necessary forms and filing instructions, when requested. *Entrepreneur* magazine sells booklets showing how, in each state, to incorporate a business without a lawyer. Most incorporations can be effected for under $200. If you're reluctant to incorporate on your own, contact a lawyer but be prepared to pay for his or her professional time and services.

Buy Liability Insurance

Product liability insurance protects you if someone claims your product caused an injury. Some stores and distributors will not carry a product unless it has insurance. Even if you can sell a product without insurance, you should obtain it if a product might cause an injury.

Liability insurance can be expensive: A typical insurance company will want a payment ranging from $2,500 to $10,000 to set up a policy. One way to avoid this steep expense is to attach an insurance rider to a contract manufacturer's policy. This tactic is effective because your contract manufacturer will also be liable for damages if your product causes an injury. If a product that you're producing isn't dangerous, you can usually avoid any insurance problems by selling to smaller stores that don't require insurance.

Maintain an Active Contact File

Go back through your notebook and your previous contacts, and find people who could assist your sales efforts. These contacts will usually make it fairly easy for you to place a product in a few sales outlets. To place a new clothespin that could be opened at either end, Craig D. called up a variety store owner whom he knew. His call resulted in the product's placement in two stores. Another contact, a manufacturers' representative, placed the product in three drugstores.

Some of your earlier contacts should be willing to help. They know you and what you're trying to do, they may have already offered you input and advice, and they may enjoy contributing further to a product's success.

Seek Community Help

I've mentioned throughout the book that community groups can be helpful, especially chambers of commerce and trade groups. I highly recommend that you go back to these groups whenever you have a problem, such as finding a store in which to place your first product. Ask the chamber for names of retailers that might be willing to help a new manufacturer.

Find Out Why People Don't Buy

Many people will not buy your product. Plan in advance to take advantage of information you can receive from surveying people, stores, or distributors that don't buy. Why don't certain customers buy? Why does the product sell better in a particular type of store? Why isn't the product selling through catalogs when it's selling at flea markets? The answers to questions like these will often tell you a great deal about a product. For example, if you fail to sell a product to a store owner, you can ask for an honest reaction to your sales pitch. The answers might be: "The product just doesn't look sturdy," or "I can't make any money at that price," or "I already have six products like yours on the shelves." These answers can steer you to a new course of action that might help the product sell later.

Compare the rejection answers to the reasons store owners give for buying a product: "I'm not sure why I bought it. I guess I just like it and I think it will sell," or "I think the product provides a unique benefit," or "I would like to use the product myself." These are helpful, but they don't define your market as well as the reasons that customers won't buy.

Product creators don't like to ask why people don't buy, primarily because they feel that someone who doesn't buy the product doesn't like it. Any one person doesn't buy most of the products on the market. Many of the answers you'll get to "Why didn't you . . . ?" questions won't reflect badly on your product. Statements such as "I'm trying to focus my sales on a different type of product," or "I prefer to carry products that have a higher price," or "I just don't have any money," or "I've committed my shelf space to another supplier" are all possible and legitimate reasons for someone's not taking your product.

Keep asking questions when people don't buy. You'll be able to find out:

- Is your sales approach working?
- Is the product's benefit obvious?
- Is the package appealing?
- Does the product have any major flaws?

Questioning why a product will sell at one outlet and not at another can tell you how quickly people perceive a product's benefit.

At a fair, I watched Jason R. give a three-minute demonstration to sell a unique tool pouch with a better organizational system than that of a traditional pouch. When I asked Jason whether his product had been selling in stores, he gave me a litany of his rejections. I wasn't surprised that the product could be sold only at fairs. Its benefit wasn't obvious; the pouch needed a demonstration.

WHERE AND HOW TO SELL A PRODUCT

Entrepreneurs have a wide variety of possible places where they can sell products. One of the goals in the first sales period is to sell the product to your target customers through the distribution chain you plan on eventually using. Some outlets, such as flea markets, can give you valuable market information, but you still have to simulate your eventual distribution network before you can declare the first sales period a success.

Fairs, Flea Markets, and Trade Shows

George T. attended a home show with a tool apron that, when laid over a five-gallon paint bucket, became a painter's bench. George sold 300 aprons at $15.95 each. Two days later, he received an order for 100 aprons from a chain of paint stores.

Trade shows offer major benefits:

- You're able to sell a product; you can then parlay your trade show sales to penetrate other sales outlets.

- You can meet valuable contacts.
- You receive immediate input about a product.
- You can adjust the product's price.
- You can sell a product with and without certain features and measure each group of sales.
- You can sell the product when you have only a few demonstration models.

The last benefit, taking orders without immediate delivery, is extremely helpful. George took 400 aprons to the show. I wouldn't have done that. I would have made, at most, 50 units. When I was selling out, I would have taken orders for later shipment. Taking orders allows you to invest in minimum inventory, in case the product doesn't sell.

Bob S. created an adjustable outdoor bench swing that could recline. He took five units to a state fair and took orders for 30 more units to be delivered in four weeks. Those orders helped his small business keep growing.

If you're going to take orders, try to arrange to accept Visa or MasterCard as payment. Because you're a small manufacturer, some people will be reluctant to give you checks (they might not get refunds). They can always get refunds by disputing credit card charges. This added security will increase your sales. Apply to your bank for an imprinter (it will cost about $75).

Two approaches can help you get a booth at a show at a discounted price. Don't contact the show until about a month before it opens. Delay your actual buying decision until the last moment. If the show is not sold out, the promoter might offer you a booth at a 50, 60, or 70 percent savings. The risks of waiting until the last entry day are that you might get a poor location and you might get no booth at all. A second approach is to tell the show promoter that a full booth is too expensive and ask whether any potential exhibitors might be willing to share a booth.

When visiting a show, as an exhibitor or an attendee, arrive a little early so that you can meet other exhibitors. Try to find out how often they've come to the show and how many units they usually sell. Talk to other exhibitors about their distributors, suppliers, and sales outlets.

Retail Stores

Owners of small retail stores are often operating on their own shoestrings; they're not always willing to take a product from a new entrepreneur.

However, large stores can be even harder to get into because they often place restrictions on new companies, such as mandating a large inventory level or requiring 60- to 90-day payment terms. I believe new entrepreneurs are better off starting with small stores.

Whenever you're dealing with stores or distributors, you'll find resistance to ordering a new, unproven product. You'll need to be creative in setting up an order pattern that is as risk-free as possible.

One tactic is to put the product in the store on consignment. The store owner won't pay you until the product is sold. There are advantages to this method: Stores will take your product, and sometimes you can request a favorable shelf position. The disadvantage is that you're putting yourself in a weak position because you don't obtain an actual order. An order puts you into a business relationship with the store or distributor, and an order history will help you obtain loans.

Another way to structure an order is to offer 60-day billing with a guaranteed sales clause. Under this arrangement, you ship in inventory, and you come back to the stores after 55 days and count how many units have been sold. The store pays you for the goods sold, and you take back any unsold products. This tactic ends up netting you payment in about 60 days, which is as fast as you'll usually be paid from any source.

When you're starting out, offer an extra discount. Give a 50 to 60 percent discount, instead of 40 to 50 percent, to retail stores. When you call on any potential customer, you'll be bucking an established set of distributors or manufacturers. An extra discount will make people more willing to interrupt their normal buying routines.

When you approach a retail store, take with you the product in its package or display, a layout of a sales brochure, and a selling sheet (a list of a few of the benefits of the product, along with the retailers' and suggested retail prices). Figure 11-2 shows a sample of a selling sheet. Create a sheet listing any positive results or endorsements you've obtained from market research or sales outlets. It would be helpful to be able to show a retailer that a product is averaging 10 units per month at a competing store.

Start by approaching any retail contacts you've made during the go/no-go decision process. Sales to these contacts should be relatively easy, and you can then use those sales to persuade other retailers to take the product. To know whether your product was a success in a store, be sure to ask the retailer how many units per month the product needs to sell to stay on the shelf. You should also, if at all possible, try to learn the approximate monthly volume of the products near yours in the store.

Stop into the store every two weeks to see how the product is selling. Ask if there is anything you can do to encourage sales. Find out whether there has been any customer reaction. One simple tactic that can help establish a smooth relationship is to send in a friend to buy your product. An early sale will convey an impression that the product has appeal, which might encourage salesclerks to promote it.

Figure 11-2   Sample Selling Sheet

THE LUCKY LOTTO PEN™

Increase your profits from the lottery with a fast-selling impulse item

Use for both the Daily Pick 3 and Lotto America

Directions	A Sure Winner to more Lottery Profits
1. Tip the pen over so balls go to the top of the pen.	
2. Turn the pen back over so the pen points down.	Suggested Retail — $2.49 Retailer's Cost — $1.25
3. Roll the balls in your fingers so the balls roll into the lottery slots.	P.O.P. Box of 24 Pens
4. Pick the numbers next to the blue balls.	Suggested Retail — $59.76 Retailer's Cost — $30.00

PLACE YOUR ORDER TODAY   Mail to: **SLICK PIC CORP.**
5200 West 73rd Street
Edina, Minnesota 55439

Quantity	Description	Price	Extended Price
_____	**Lucky Lotto Pens**	**$30.00**	_____

Store Name _____

Contact _____

Address _____

City, State, Zip _____

Make checks or money orders payable to *Slick Pic Corp.*

All prepaid orders shipped freight prepaid
All C.O.D. orders shipped freight paid by store

All orders shipped within seven (7) days

Entrepreneur Salespeople

Industrial and other nonconsumer products aren't sold through retail stores; they're sold through salespeople who call on companies. This type of sale is a real asset to product entrepreneurs because the only inventory they'll need is a demonstration unit. As a result, entrepreneurs can handle fairly complicated products, because they'll have orders in hand before they have to produce the products.

I mentioned earlier that I worked for Scott Turner, who invented a piece of semiconductor inspection equipment. When he started his business, he took his product to Texas Instruments and landed an order for three units. He borrowed enough money off the order to produce the units in his basement before heading back on the sales trail. Often, early sales are all made by the entrepreneur.

Preparing a winning sales script is a challenge. I've sometimes developed three or four sales presentations before finding one that worked. Don't be discouraged if your first attempts fail. Instead, keep asking customers what they're looking for in your type of product. Vary your approach until customers perceive that the product meets their needs.

Mail Orders

The mail-order market has expanded rapidly during the past ten years, but it has not become an easy market for product creators. Some of the problems in dealing with mail-order companies are:

- They want a product with an established demand.
- They don't like to handle product introductions.
- They sometimes want discounts that could run as high as 70 percent.
- They worry that a small manufacturer won't be able to ship the orders they receive.

You can run your own mail-order ads in magazines and card packs. This tactic can be dangerous because the cost of an ad can easily be two to three times higher than the profit on sales you might generate. Before advertising in a magazine, find copies of the previous 12 back issues. Count how many advertisers repeat their ads. Call one or two advertisers to see how many sales their ads generated.

I once sold a book through general-product card packs. Each issue of the packs contained about 20 book ads. When I called an advertiser, I learned that one company was promoting 80 percent of the books in the deck, and that it was receiving a 60 percent discount. My contact told me I'd need a similar discount before I would have a chance of making money.

If you want to try a magazine ad, *don't* start by advertising in the magazine with the largest circulation. Ask at your library for *Gale's Source of Publications*. Find your product category and pick out five or six magazines with small circulations. Compare the ad rates and select those that look least expensive. Don't be afraid of the high prices; ad rates are listed for full-page ads, but the magazines do sell smaller spaces. Call the magazines and inquire whether they have a first time or introductory discount. Be sure to include a cutout order coupon in your ad. Before running your ad, find ads for similar products. Imitate the format of the ad that has been running the longest.

You might try sending out a flyer on your product as an enclosure with another company's invoices or order acknowledgments. Most companies have trouble selling mail-order products unless they have large lines of products. The big profits in the mail-order business come when customers buy two, three, or more products. Companies that are short on products might be willing to work with you for a percentage of your sales. Save every piece of direct mail you receive that offers products that are anything like yours. Contact those companies before you are ready to start production. Be prepared to offer at least a 25 percent commission to entice the company to send out a flyer.

The main disadvantage to mail-order sales is that you won't receive any feedback. You know a customer didn't buy, but you don't know why. That missing information hurts your ability to adjust your marketing efforts.

Mail orders can be useful to generate sales momentum at retail stores. Showing a product advertised in a magazine, along with some proof that orders have come in, will sometimes help get an order from a retailer.

Dennis Sperling is trying to use mail-order sales to generate orders from retailers for Solar Stat, an easy-to-apply vinyl window tinting. The expensive ads might not produce a profit, but they could help Dennis start to sell the product.

I usually discourage people from running their own mail-order campaigns because it's expensive and it may not work. Instead, try to sell a product to a catalog company to hold your costs down.

Distributors

I consider distributors or manufacturers' representatives to be the key to successful products. You can sell only so many products yourself. To expand further, you need other people's sales help.

When approaching distributors, keep in mind that time and customers are their big concerns. A distributor's personnel have to utilize their time in a manner that will produce the highest possible sales volume. New customers are important to them. To a distributor, a new customer doesn't represent just a one-time sale; each new customer could be an ongoing consumer who might conceivably add significantly to sales volume.

As with retailers, start with any inside contacts you might have and then expand to unknown distributors. Use the same sales tools as before: the product, the package, and, if appropriate, the point-of-purchase display. Include a selling sheet (see Figure 11-2) and fill in the distributor's price below the retailer's cost. For the lottery pens, the distributor's price could be 75¢ per pen, or $18 per box. This schedule shows a distributor how much profit can be made per unit or per display.

The basic business points to make to a distributor are:

- The product has been selling well.
- The product is a natural fit into the distributor's line and will require only minimal time and effort.
- The product will generate inquiries from new customers.

Those points will start you off well, but to succeed you should make some or all of these offers:

- You'll travel with each salesperson, if necessary, to show how to promote the product.
- You'll turn over existing accounts to the distributor.
- You'll give the distributor a six-month exclusive in his or her geographic area.
- You'll run promotions over the next six months to support the product.
- You'll handle all product complaints and returns.

Work out all the kinks in your sales strategy before seeing distributors or manufacturers' representatives. If they don't generate immediate sales results, they'll drop your product or stop pushing it. During the entire initial sales period, you must continue to build on successes. Momentum is especially important when you're trying to persuade a distribution network to handle a product.

Product entrepreneurs are typically shocked when they realize how much their sales messages are diluted before they reach customers. An entrepreneur starts out with a passionate message. A distributor's selling pitch might be: "This product is selling; you ought to buy some." A store clerk's response usually is: "How do I know what the product does? I just work here." Take a proactive approach with the distributor. Provide a simple one-page selling card that highlights your product's key selling points.

"I'm on my way now, I've got a distributor!" crowed a proud entrepreneur. I asked: "How many units do you think the distributor will sell?" This question totally stumps most people. Distributors talk about their contacts and the sales they can get you, but some of them have only small operations that they run out of their houses. A small distributor can be valuable and should not be overlooked, but you need an estimate of how many units the distributor will sell. Otherwise, you won't know whether your initial sales period will be a success or a failure.

When you first meet distributors or manufacturers' representatives, ask for their line cards (a listing of the companies' products that they carry). Call a few of these companies and try to obtain ballpark figures on what the distributors can be expected to sell. Don't be disappointed if the number is small. You need to know only whether your distributor or manufacturers' representative is selling your product at a typical rate.

In Chapter 9, I described the importance of obtaining inside help from industry veterans. This help is crucial when dealing with distributors. Mention the names of your inside contacts to the distributors to broadcast your chances of success. Enlist your insiders' help in convincing distributors to choose your product for special sales efforts. Most distributors strongly promote only 15 to 20 percent of their product lines. You want your product to be among those that are promoted.

A tactic that is especially applicable to nonconsumer items is to offer extensive sales support. For our tire cutter, my partner offered to accompany the local salesperson on sales calls to all of the local tire dealers. Our goal was to build up a history of success in our own town as leverage for sales outside our metro area. The distributor appreciated the support because it enabled the salespeople to spend time actively selling a product instead of merely servicing accounts.

MAKING ADJUSTMENTS

If a product is not selling, don't drop it too quickly. The price might be out of line, the product or packaging might need some minor changes, or a new distribution network might be the solution.

Price

An instant coupon is a tactic for determining whether people think a price is too high. Offer, for one week only, a 40 percent discount. Place the coupon alongside the product, and make it clear when the discount will expire. If a big discount doesn't perk up sales, then customers either don't see or don't want the product's benefit. I tried selling wrap sunglasses at $2.99. Because of poor response, I dropped the price to $1.99 and finally to 99¢. The product didn't sell at any price, and I discontinued it.

If you are having trouble signing up retailers or distributors, offer a special one-month sales incentive. For example, if you attend a trade show for giftware, you'll notice many manufacturers promoting a "show special," an offer of a 25 to 50 percent discount for any order placed at the show. This incentive generates a great deal of business. I've often offered distributors a first-order discount of 25 percent so that they could test how well a product would sell. A product has severe problems if you can't get distributors to handle it with a large discount, 60-day terms, and guaranteed sales.

Don't offer discounts too quickly or you'll defeat your goal of seeing whether your product will sell at a profitable price. But if you're running into sales resistance and your product won't get a fair trial, try a discount to get sales started.

Product and Packaging

This topic was discussed in detail in Chapter 7. I mention it here because most product entrepreneurs don't like to change their products, primarily because changes are usually expensive and cause manufacturing delays. A small change can make the difference between a product's succeeding or failing. If you visit a retailer or jobber that sells discontinued products, you'll see items that look pretty close to successfully marketed products. Take the time and effort to give your product the best possible chance of succeeding.

Distribution Networks

Sometimes, you'll be able to tell right away that your product isn't selling in a distribution network. Don't be afraid to try another distribution network.

Jake S. created a variation of a grater that both grated and sliced food. Jake was a great showman, and he sold lots of his product at fairs. The product had several drawbacks. Its price of $29.95 was expensive for small hardware or variety stores. Big stores wouldn't take Jake's product until he had an established sales pattern. Because Jake had no early sales momentum, distributors and manufacturers' representatives weren't interested in carrying the product.

Jake decided to explore other distribution channels. He offered a limited quantity of his product free to a marketer of cleaning chamois *who sold products through magazine ads and who had a network of salespeople selling products at state fairs. In return, he asked the marketer to test his product at three fairs. Jake then persuaded a small, independent TV station to run his commercials in exchange for a $15 commission on every sale. Jake lost money on both of these efforts, but he learned that his product would sell in certain sales outlets.*

Selling is hard work. Don't switch distribution networks at the first sign of sales resistance. If a distributor places an established product into 20 percent of the stores it serves, then your product is doing well if it is placed in 10 percent of the stores. But if prolonged efforts are not turning up any sales, consider switching channels.

KEEPING THE LIGHT GREEN

Everyone loves a winning product. One of your early strategies should be to always appear to have a product that has tremendous momentum. If you approach a store and the manager won't take your product, don't go back until you have some initial successes. Otherwise, the store will look at your product as a failure. One entrepreneur got this response: "Are you still trying to get that product off the ground? Isn't it time you just give up?" Don't get caught in that position. Plan your efforts so you always appear to have ongoing momentum.

In the first sales period, you should let your sales drive your production. Don't overproduce the product with an expectation of selling it. Instead, be prepared to work weekends to replenish your inventory. You'll find that, 99 percent of the time, sales don't materialize as fast as you'd like. Be cautious and conserve your capital.

A dental product my former employer introduced sold sensationally in the first three months. Unfortunately, the product had an unanticipated characteristic that caused it to malfunction during repeated use. It took us six months to correct the mechanical problem, and we were never again able to regain our momentum. How we wished we had taken the time for a first sales period!

You have to be the driving force behind your product. This book should make you realize that a product creator doesn't operate like an established business owner. The creator of a new product has to be constantly searching for an angle, an advantage, or some imaginative way to make things happen.

12

EVALUATING INITIAL SALES RESULTS—BEFORE YOU SPEND BIG MONEY

Dee K. created a new storytelling board game. She placed the game in five retail stores and received a large order from an insurance company that wanted to use the product as a promotional item. After that, nothing encouraging happened. Dee had hoped that someone else would stock the game, but nobody has yet.

To increase her sales, Dee needed to go into the transitional sales period, which would have required a sizable investment in promotional, manufacturing setup, and sales costs. Dee was facing an investment five to ten times larger than the amount she had spent to make it into the first sales period.

Going into the transitional period is expensive and challenging. Before taking that step, product entrepreneurs need to reevaluate their ideas. Dee's major problem was that she didn't realize she needed another introductory step. You'll know when you need the transitional period. You'll have to decide whether it's worthwhile to enter it.

Most entrepreneurs never stop to evaluate their ideas after they start to sell products. That's not surprising; many of them have invested $50,000 to $100,000 before even starting their sales efforts. By following the action steps in this book, you will probably invest less than $5,000 to get into the first sales period. I certainly think that $5,000 is a worthwhile investment if you believe you might have a million-dollar idea. However, don't be afraid to drop an unsuccessful idea. You're better off cutting your losses rather than investing more money in a product that can't be marketed.

An X-ray screening device I worked with in the dental industry illustrates the importance of reevaluation. The product was originally designed as a small shield that attached to an X-ray head. The shield was to pick up scatter radiation that could potentially harm dental assistants.

Several leading dentists supported the concept, and we had a positive response from dentists during our initial market testing. In our research, we received some constructive advice regarding product improvements, and we incorporated those into our prototypes. We made a few additional changes to adjust for variations we discovered in different brands of X-ray equipment. After a year, we had a product that cost three times the original estimate and looked like a mechanical monster. We decided to drop the product and minimize our losses.

THE INITIAL ANALYSIS

Before reevaluating your go/no-go decisions, you should do an initial analysis of your sales results. Most people, including product entrepreneurs, tend to hear only the information that supports their views. You can't afford to be swayed by what you *want* to hear. You have to force yourself to be objective by making a sales comparison, obtaining evaluations from people in the distribution network, and surveying customers. The topics covered in the following sections should get your careful, objective attention.

Sales Comparison

I've recommended several times that you find out the sales volume of products that are placed near yours in a store. To estimate the volume, you might have to count the products that are on the shelf every week. I know that's a nuisance but, as you'll read in this section, that information is essential.

To make a sales comparison, use a chart with the headings as shown in Figure 12-1. The key to this chart is the comments column. There will be many reasons that your product does not sell the same volume as other

Figure 12-1   Sales Comparison Chart

Sales of Your Product	Competitive Product's Name	Competitive Product's Sales	Percentage Difference	Comments

products. The lower volume is to be expected, but you need to understand why there is a difference in order to determine what changes a product might need, whether the first sales period was a success, and what your product's potential sales volume is.

Packaging

A package has a tremendous number of jobs to do. It must catch consumers' attention, establish that a product is worth the price, explain the product's benefit, show how the product provides the benefit—and accomplish all of these tasks in about 10 seconds. A better package can account for a tremendous difference in sales volume. Critique your packaging first when you're trying to understand why products sell at different rates.

How well two packages catch consumers' attention is fairly easy to judge. Compare two packages and decide which one looks better. Or isolate two products and ask five to ten people to point out the package that first catches their attention.

It's a little harder to evaluate whether a product is showing that it's worth its value. People like to see, touch, hold, and examine products before they buy them. That's why you see floor displays of products at Kmart, department stores, and discount outlets. Other products require copy on the package to explain their worth. Packaging of camping equipment or sleeping bags will often list a series of features, such as down filling or special waterproofing. Camping products from major manufacturers sometimes state how they were field-tested.

How well do two packages explain the products' comparative benefits? Don't trust your own judgment on this point; you know your product's benefit too well to be able to judge how it is communicated. Three or four people who've never seen your product should be asked to compare the two packages.

A product entrepreneur once showed me a hair product that detangled hair—a great benefit, but the product didn't sell. The package didn't explain why the product worked, and nobody I knew could figure out how to use it. The product failed simply because it had a bad package.

The final packaging consideration is how much time is needed for a customer to look your package over and understand what your product is, what it does, and why he or she should buy it. This time period should be as short as possible. Your sales will be appreciably lower if a competitor's product requires 5 seconds to be comprehended and your product requires 15 seconds.

Product Benefits

Is the benefit easy to understand? Some products have easy-to-understand benefits; others do not. Compare, for example, a hair sculpturing/trim kit to a cordless mustache trimmer. The hair kit's benefit—putting stripes, or arrows, or Zs in a hairdo, usually along the scalp—isn't as apparent as the mustache trimmer's benefit, which is stated in the product's name.

Having a benefit that's harder to understand is not bad, but it offers clues about sales potential. If the hair kit outsells the mustache trimmer, you can conclude that the product's benefit is more important to more people than the benefit of the mustache trimmer. If the hair kit sells slightly less than the mustache trimmer, the market for the two products is probably about the same because the product with the easier-to-understand benefit (the mustache trimmer) should sell more units. If the hair kit sells considerably fewer units, then customers might not understand the product's benefit, or the product might have a small market.

Is the benefit different? To answer this question, you must compare your product to its competitors. For the hair kit, the product should be compared to sales of hair clippers to parents. Your product is favorably perceived by customers if your sales are equal to or greater than a competitive product. If your sales are much lower, then your product has only a small market or customers don't perceive that your product is unique.

Some of you may be thinking: "If the hair kit isn't perceived to be unique, it should sell as much as the hair clippers." That's not the case: When in doubt, customers buy the products they are most familiar with, another obstacle that makes it difficult for a product entrepreneur to introduce a new product.

Price

What if the hair kit sells for $12.95, and the mustache trimmer for $19.95? Will the hair kit sell more units? Not necessarily. The products are for different markets. The hair kit is targeted at teenagers, and the mustache trimmer is a product for adults.

The price difference would be important if you were comparing two different types of hair kits. If one product were more expensive, I'd say it was outstanding if it sold as well as the cheaper product. I'd consider the expensive product to have a market if it sold half as well as the lower-priced product.

Initial analysis doesn't offer firm yes or no answers. Instead, you'll be compiling lists of trends, feelings, or observations that will help you decide whether your product meets the go/no-go decision criteria.

Advertising

Some product entrepreneurs believe that their products are outsold simply because other products are heavily advertised. Entrepreneurs tend not to be discouraged by this situation, and they proceed with their introductions. I become wary when a product loses sales to one that's advertised.

Most product creators need products that can sell with only minimal advertising, primarily because most are underfinanced. If another product outsells yours because of advertising, your product needs advertising.

Aaron W. developed a home exercise machine. Impressed by the effectiveness of NordicTrack's ads for similar equipment, Aaron tried to duplicate NordicTrack's success with his own advertising campaign. Unfortunately, sales didn't come rolling in, and Aaron went broke.

This example points out two facts that entrepreneurs typically overlook. The first is that advertising programs fail—often. At least 25 percent of the programs I've run have produced minimal results, and most large companies have similar results. Product creators, especially those without marketing or advertising backgrounds, are likely to have much higher failure rates.

The second fact is that advertising has to be run repeatedly to generate favorable results; NordicTrack has run its ads for years. Repeated exposure increases the sales response to an ad. Unless you have a tremendous amount of money to invest, be leery of a product that requires advertising.

Competition

Entrepreneurs will inevitably lose sales to other products because those products' names are well known. If their reaction is "That's to be expected," they have a dangerous attitude.

As I mentioned earlier, people faced with a confusing choice will usually buy the best-known product. If a well-known, similar product outsells yours, you might have one of the following problems:

- People don't perceive that your product is different.
- People don't care about your product's benefits.
- The product requires an advertising campaign.

Information Evaluation

Marketing analysis usually involves sifting through a tremendous amount of subjective information. The information you receive from your sales comparison should be positive before you continue any introduction efforts.

Some readers may have noticed that I haven't mentioned using the sales comparison as a tool for estimating potential sales volume. Isn't it a reliable way to come up with a sales number? For example, if the mustache trimmer sells 200,000 units, then the hair kit's market should be 600,000, if it outsold the mustache trimmer by a three-to-one margin.

A sales comparison *is* an easy way to estimate potential sales, but I think it is the wrong approach for an entrepreneur to take. Sales levels are determined primarily by a product's distribution network. The sales comparison method of determining sales volume would be valid only if the hair kit were in as many stores as the mustache trimmer.

Distribution Network Evaluation

After you finish your sales comparison, you should go back and interview everyone who had anything to do with selling your product. Don't make the interview too long or too cumbersome, but be sure to ask the following questions.

- *Did the product's sales level meet expectations?* Most people in a distribution network will have an estimate, based on past experience, of a product's potential volume. It's a positive sign if your product's sales consistently meet their expectations.
- *Was the sales level high enough?* Every part of a distribution network has a sales threshold for a product to meet. For example, a store

might want to turn its inventory every two months. If your product doesn't sell out in two months, the store won't carry it. Be sure that your product has generated enough sales to stay on the stores' shelves. Turnover is also important for packaging and order-size decisions. Sell your product so that a store or distributor can order the right number of units. For example, if a store will sell 5 units of a product every month, be sure the store can order 10 units. You'll quickly be out of business if you insist on 25-unit orders.

- *Was the product easy to sell?* Product creators are most successful when their products sell themselves. If a product needs a demonstration or potential customers ask a lot of questions, try to find out why the product was hard to sell. Make an effort to correct the problems. If you don't, you'll be in sales trouble. Stores, distributors, and manufacturers' representatives will usually drop a product that is too much work.

- *What did potential customers think of the product?* Everyone in a distribution network likes to keep customers happy. If a product does that, the network might keep the product even if it presents some problems. If customers are unhappy, the product will fail.

- *What, if anything, can be done to increase sales?* Don't be afraid to take advantage of the business experience of personnel in a distribution network. Some helpful suggestions will result, and the same suggestion may come from several people, such as: "Offer three products for $1.50 instead of one for 79¢." Some of this input won't be given unless you specifically ask for suggestions.

- *How clear is it that your product is different?* An exclusive sales agreement is a powerful incentive, but it is only a sales point if distributors perceive a product to be unique. Before you push for an exclusive sales agreement, you must know whether retailers, distributors, and manufacturers' representatives consider your product novel.

- *Will the network continue to support the product?* Frequently, a distribution network will take on a product, sell it for a few months, and then drop it. The product may be seasonal, sales may not be high enough, or a new product may come along. This sequence can happen with virtually any type of product.

For a novelty item like the slap bracelets, you should expect only a three- or four-month run. For a long-term product, such as a new fishing reel, you will hope that retailers keep selling it. Some entrepreneurs, who have what they believe are successful first sales periods, may find that their distribution networks will no longer support their products. Find this out *before* you invest in the transitional period.

If distributors won't give you continued support, try to find out why. Distributors often drop products for reasons that have nothing to do with the products themselves. Ordering or competitive factors can be influential. For instance, the network may think that your product needs a bigger discount or that your price schedule doesn't offer high enough discounts on small enough quantities. You may have the wrong-size package, or your package may not fit into a space where retailers would like to put it. All of these problems may be correctable if you learn about them soon enough.

Your product could also be dropped because of competitive pressures. A major manufacturer might be introducing a new line of products that will take all the available shelf space; another manufacturer might be having a new promotion or introducing five or six new seasonal products right before the start of a season. A distribution network will support products that are advertised and promoted. Your unadvertised product may be a casualty.

Customer Ratings

You should seek as much customer input as possible about a product. That's one of the reasons I recommend that you attend trade shows or fairs. Another way to get input is to include a warranty card with each unit. When you receive a warranty card back, call the customer and ask his or her opinion of your product. You can also place a 50¢ or $1 rebate coupon inside your package. Call the people who send in the coupon to see what they like and don't like about the product.

Another tactic is to include a customer survey in each package. Offer customers $1 if they fill out and return the survey. This approach will save you the trouble of having to call people. Don't make the survey too long; ask a few pertinent questions that will help you gauge your product's future chances of success. If you don't understand some customers' answers, you still can call or write to those people for clarification. Following are some of the questions that should appear on your survey:

- *What features do you like about the product?* You can list all the features and leave space for people to check off those they like. Be sure to include an "other" category and space for comments.
- *Is there anything you* don't *like about the product?* People can check "yes" or "no." Leave space for explanations of what customers don't like.
- *Does the product work as you expected?* Again, allow for a yes or no answer and an explanation. If the product doesn't work as expected, the instructions may need revision, or users may not think the product works as well as you think it does.

- *Are there any improvements you would like to suggest?* Under the "yes" box, leave room for suggestions. Don't be discouraged if 25 to 50 percent of the respondents suggest some improvements. That rate is not unusual. Consider adopting any suggestions that are made by over 50 percent of those who reply.

- *How did you learn about the product?* Include boxes for: "saw it in the store," "heard about it from a friend," "recommended by store personnel," and "saw it in an ad." Include advertising even if you didn't advertise; you may have benefited from a similar product's advertising. If people see an ad and like that *type* of product, they may buy your product when they shop. It took me six months to realize that the little rabbit that keeps on drumming was in a commercial for Eveready batteries, not Duracell. You're in great shape when your product is clearly superior to one that's heavily advertised.

- *Were you looking for this type of product, or was your purchase made on impulse?* You'll have a better chance of long-term sales success if people are shopping for your type of product. For example, there is on the market a vinyl strip that replaces silicone sealant around the edges of a bathtub. People who buy that product should be out shopping for sealant. If the people who are buying the product are purchasing on impulse instead, the product is probably placed in the wrong part of the store. It's missing the people who are fixing their bathtubs on the same day they're shopping.

- *Did you buy this product instead of another one?* If so, what was the other product? You may be targeting to replace another product. If you get positive reinforcement from customers, you can use that as ammunition to place your product on the shelves right next to the targeted product.

- *How satisfied were you with the product?* Satisfied customers will spread the word about a product and possibly increase sales. If people aren't satisfied, your product may have a short sales life. Not only won't customers keep buying, but your distribution network will drop your product like a hot potato.

REEVALUATING THE KEY GO/NO-GO DECISIONS

As you go through the decisions this time, you need to be much tougher than you were the first time around. For instance, instead of an estimate that you can manufacture a product for a certain price, you'll need a firm price quote. You'll have to give reasons, based on your analysis, for each of your answers. Entrepreneurs usually don't like putting their products through tough tests, but hard-nosed reevaluation is essential—not to look for reasons to drop a product, but to protect against failure and loss of money. Give solid business answers to the 12 key go/no-go decisions now. I've added some comments to help you with your evaluations.

1. *Can potential customers quickly understand your product's benefit?*

2. *Is your product clearly different from other products in the market?*

3. *Does your product have a benefit people want?* I like to compare the sales I've made myself with the sales made by other people. If my sales efforts produce a much better result, then customers aren't grasping the product's benefits. Compare your sales to similar products' sales in the same store or at other sales locations. For example, if your product is placed next to a product you've targeted, and your product is outsold three- or four-to-one, your product probably doesn't merit a yes answer for the first three go/no-go decisions.

4. *Can your product be packaged effectively?* Some products might not sell because of their packages. This drawback should have shown up and been corrected in the first sales period. Or you may have found that, even with your best efforts, your product couldn't be packaged so that it would communicate your message. Your package might run into other problems: It takes up too much room; it's too easy to steal; it doesn't conveniently fit on the racks. Your point-of-purchase display may have too many units. Packages and displays must fit into a distribution network's requirements, as well as providing the consumer with necessary information.

5. *Is the market open?*

6. *Does a distribution network exist with promotion costs you can afford?* Did you find a distribution network that requires only minimal promotion? Was that market open to you? A distribution network evaluation is important. These questions are hard to answer unless you ask people whether they will continue their support. Many answers will be hidden from you until the initial evaluation. For example, a store owner might have some open shelf space, allow you to put your product in for a test, and sell your product well. But the owner may prefer to promote products that are advertised. Your product's stay on the shelf could be short-lived.

7. *Are your customers easy to target?* Your product should be in a store, catalog, direct mailer, magazine, or location where customers can easily find you. Targeting could become a problem if sales hover just above or just below a network's sales threshold. Terry M. had a device to stabilize a ladder on uneven terrain. When the product went into a hardware store, its sales were

about the same as another product designed to stabilize a ladder. But neither product sold well, because the store wasn't targeted at people who owned homes built on uneven terrain. The store owner was willing to carry only one product for stabilizing ladders, and Terry's product was out. You can determine whether your sales outlets are targeting your customers by comparing average monthly sales. If most products in the store sell 10 to 15 units per month and your product sells only 2 to 3, you might have a targeting problem. I've often thought I should open a store that sells supplies for product creators—small parts, casting materials, low-cost molding equipment, and so on. But product entrepreneurs are hard to locate. Not only are they spread throughout the country, but every year new people join the ranks and others stop trying. The market is too scattered to make it practical to open a store for inventors. This same phenomenon can occur with a product: Customers can be too hard to target.

8. *Can you afford to make your models, prototypes, and initial production runs?* If you can't, you won't make it through the initial sales period without a manufacturer's help.

9. *Can you find a contract manufacturer that's willing to absorb some of the start-up manufacturing costs?* I wouldn't proceed to the transitional sales period without a firm agreement, backed up with either a contract or a letter. You need a firm price for start-up costs and for per-unit manufacturing costs. The first step in the transitional sales period is to prepare a budget, a detailed statement of how much money you need to raise. You can't prepare a budget without a firm manufacturing agreement.

10. *Can you find insiders to help you?* Change is the only constant factor in new-product introductions. Insiders are no different from anyone else. Some insiders will stay interested and excited about a project; others will lose interest. Their reactions may be a gauge of their expectations: Have you exceeded or fallen well short of what an insider expected? Insiders' situations will change, and they may not be able to help you anymore. Keep in touch with your key contacts; know whether they're still willing to work with you.

11. *Does your product have a perceived value that's at least four times its manufacturing cost?* In the transitional period, you're no longer testing your product. Instead, you're taking the product onto the market to make money. You need a price equal to four times your manufacturing costs.

12. *Is the market size of your distribution network large enough to justify your time and expense?* Your initial sales period might have more narrowly defined your market. For example, your initial target

market might have been all those who use a product. Now it may be those who use it 10 to 15 times per year. You might also have discovered that you don't have quite the same distribution outlets you expected. Estimate your potential earnings again. Then decide whether you should proceed into the transitional period.

TACTICS FOR CORRECTING PROBLEMS

Suppose your product has not passed the go/no-go decisions. I know it's discouraging, but don't give up. You haven't spent much money, and you have plenty of time to correct your problems and reenter the first sales period. The evaluation isn't only to decide whether to drop a product; it's also to reveal whether you need to make adjustments before entering the transitional period. It's a rare product that doesn't need some adjustments. I said earlier that the first sales period could last from 3 to 15 months. Within that length of time, you can go back and start your sales over again. I also told you to prepare to sell only a limited number of units during the first sales period. That strategy pays off when you have to make adjustments, because you'll still have plenty of sales outlets to approach about taking your product.

Most of the problems entrepreneurs encounter are in one or more of the following areas: targeting, benefits, communication, costs, distribution, packaging, and promotion. Many of these problems can be resolved so that you can get your product back on track. In Chapter 10, I discussed methods of readjusting after the initial go/no-go decisions. This section offers advice based on the more accurate information you'll have after the initial sales period.

Targeting

Targeting the right audience is a problem, not only for new entrepreneurs, but for all marketers. Targeting refers to the tactic of identifying a specific type of market or customer for a product. For example, a new type of gardening tool might be targeted at gardeners who spend over ten hours a week working in their flower gardens. That's a specific market, and only four or five stores in a city might cater to that market.

Most product creators and marketers are afraid to target small markets. They want to appeal to *all* users so that they can sell more units. But two things happen when they appeal to larger markets. They don't sell enough units to satisfy the distribution networks, and their advertising fails to be cost-effective. The most discouraging result is that the products sell like losers.

What would have happened if the gardening product had been targeted at the specialty market? The four gardening stores would have been happy with the sales volume. The inventor could have purchased a mailing list from a gardening magazine and announced, in a mailing, what the new product was and where it could be bought. The entrepreneur could have attended gardening association meetings and trade shows and contacted potential buyers.

I can't know for sure whether an entrepreneur will succeed in a targeted market. But I do know that the chances of success increase greatly when the focus narrows to a smaller market.

What is your target market? Most product creators answer "teenagers," or "housewives," or some equally general category. You'll fail if you don't target your market more precisely than that. Serving a small niche market doesn't prevent you from making enough money. Many small markets can produce several million dollars in annual sales. As an example, Arthur Engstrom and Howard Hawkins have built Park Tool Company into a $5-million-a-year business by making tools for repairing bicycles.

Benefits

A benefit is what a product does for a customer. Saving time, making better-tasting coffee, or having easy-to-prepare dinners handy are all examples of benefits. Product creators have two problems with benefits: They don't tell people what their products' benefits are, and they don't find out what benefits their customers want.

Entrepreneurs don't clearly state their products' benefits because they wrongly assume that people will realize what they are.

Michael D. created a product he called a "toe jamb holder." The package stated: "Holds nails at a 45-degree angle." I asked what the benefit of the product was, and the answer was: "To get secure joints when putting up 2-by-4s at a 90-degree angle." Michael's product was helpful. When you're building a wall or a frame out of 2-by-4s, especially during remodeling projects, you sometimes can't hammer straight through one 2-by-4 into the end of another. When you are adding a new window to a house, for example, you need to frame in the top and bottom of the window. You can't hammer through the side of the vertical 2-by-4 into the horizontal 2-by-4 because a wall is in the way. Instead, a homeowner or carpenter has to hammer a nail in at a 45-degree angle to secure the frame. This job is somewhat difficult for a homeowner.

The product's benefit was that it simplified home repair by allowing any homeowner to make a secure toe jamb. I would have displayed on the package the product's name (toe jamb holder), the product's benefit statement (simplifies home repairs), and a picture of an application for which the product was useful. This combination would have been more effective than Michael's package, which simply stated: "toe jamb holder."

The second problem is that product creators don't find out what benefits customers want and then give them those benefits. In Chapter 7, I mentioned a product that reduces back strain when people rake or shovel. Does that benefit sound good to you? Maybe, at first glance. But do people with bad backs go out and shovel? Not often. People who use shovels want one benefit: Make the job easier.

Communication

Many product creators simply don't communicate effectively to their target markets. To remedy typical problems, I recommend telling potential customers what they want to know and having short, informative messages that make it clear why the product will work.

- *Tell customers what they want to know.* Products require specific information. Is an item dishwasher-safe, microwave-safe, flammable, or toxic if taken internally? Does it need operating instructions or specifications? Your product won't sell without the proper information. Check all of your competitors' packages to be sure you are offering all the necessary data.

- *Give short, informative messages.* At least half the product entrepreneurs I've worked with make the mistake of not offering clear information. One reason for the problem is that entrepreneurs know their products too well. They often omit some very valuable information because they assume people already know it. Another source of poor communications is that entrepreneurs don't realize that their information is confusing.

To check whether a product's instructions are clear, I give the package and instructions to people who've never seen the product, and then watch to see whether they can understand them. I let them have the package for only 10 or 15 seconds before I take it away. I can't ever remember a time when I didn't have to make at least two or three changes in a product's information.

Joe S. created a new board game that was a lot of fun to play, as long as Joe was playing. No one could understand the directions without Joe.

I was never able to get Joe to change the instructions. He thought they were clear enough, and the product is still sitting in his basement.

A final reason entrepreneurs don't have clear packaging and instructions is that they don't commit the necessary time. I've spent weeks trying to get one phrase that's exactly right for a package. Effective operating instructions can be particularly tough. I once worked for a month to develop instructions that a person could complete in less than a minute. The best method is to write out the instructions or message, then set a reasonable time for a person to understand them: 10 seconds for a package, or 45 seconds for operating instructions. Ask people to read the package or instructions and see whether they can understand them within the time limit.

Writing something that's simple to understand is difficult. I recommend that you get help from a freelance writer or a technical writer if you can't make the information simple enough on your own.

Costs

At times, you won't be able to change the fact that a product's perceived value is not more than four times its manufacturing cost. When that happens, I don't recommend that you proceed. Don't count on your costs coming down as your sales volume increases. That may happen; but your volume may never increase.

Instead, take corrective steps to get your costs down. Redesign your product so that it's cheaper to manufacture, look for another manufacturing source, or consider adding a feature or two to increase the product's value.

Another tactic is to transfer manufacturing overseas. This is a last-ditch strategy for a new entrepreneur. You'll need complete manufacturing documentation—engineering drawings, specifications, inspection standards, and so on—and they may have to be translated into another language.

To get low-cost products, you may also need to make a large down payment. You can find overseas manufacturers by looking at trade magazines, reading want ads in your local paper's business section, or researching the business-to-business Yellow Pages of major cities such as New York, Los Angeles, or Chicago.

Two other options are to look for domestic manufacturers out of your area and revisit some other local manufacturers. If you get a lower cost quote from another manufacturer, don't switch immediately. Moving a product from one manufacturer to another will cost you both time and money. Instead, take the new quote, along with evidence of your sales success, to your contract manufacturer. You may be able to negotiate a lower price.

You might want to consider adding a feature or two that will raise the perceived value of your product. A sunglasses manufacturer added a string so that the glasses wouldn't fall off and get lost or break when the wearer was participating in activities. The string probably cost 5¢, but it raised the product's perceived value by $1 to $2. My son Eric is 13 and he is rough on his glasses. My wife found a pair of glasses with a spring that allows the bows to be pulled out, away from the ears, without breaking the glasses. The spring probably costs $2 or $3, but the glasses cost an extra $30.

Office supplies such as date books or appointment calendars are sometimes similar products inside, but there is a big price difference between them, because one has a fancier cover. Products such as jewelry or perfume offer deluxe packages to add value.

Distribution

If a product will sell and you can prove it, a distribution network should be willing to handle the product, right? Unfortunately, the statement is not true. There is an oversupply of products for a distribution network to sell. Unless your product is an incredible seller, the distribution channel can get along without you. The two areas to focus on are your sales efforts and your distribution mechanics.

A distribution channel always starts with the manufacturer's salesperson, which more than likely happens to be you, the new-product entrepreneur. The go/no-go decisions are designed to help you find a product that can be sold, but that doesn't mean you'll end up with a product that will sell itself. You still have to get out and sell the product. If your product isn't selling, answer the following questions honestly.

- *Are you making a dedicated sales effort?* You have to spend a lot of time to make sales. You must be prepared to spend the time needed to develop a sales presentation and then call on enough people. I wouldn't consider it unusual if an entrepreneur took a week to get one or two stores to handle a new product. Store owners will often be out or too busy to talk to an unknown salesperson. Probably only one out of every four or five owners that you talk to will buy.

- *Do you have a sound sales strategy?* Do your contacts include an experienced salesperson? Ask him or her to review your strategy and make suggestions on how to improve it. I have sometimes spent two or three weeks preparing a sales strategy, along with the appropriate sales material, so don't expect to create an effective strategy in an evening. If you have no sales experience, I suggest that you take a course on selling or buy a sales strategy book at your local bookstore and do some self-teaching.

- *Do you have an effective follow-up system?* I estimate that at least half of all sales are made with a follow-up call or letter. Again, ask for help from a contact who has sales experience, or find a good book.

Distribution mechanics deals with order size, payment terms, order schedule, number of units per carton, advertising and promotional support, and so on. These little things, if done wrong, will kill your chances of selling a product. Because the mechanics of a distribution network is not always obvious, you need insiders, and you need to always ask people why they didn't buy.

Spearhead Industries of Eden Prairie, Minnesota, makes Halloween and Easter merchandise. Spearhead has to know which trade shows to attend, when it needs to contact stores, the date by which it must receive orders, what dates to ship by, the type of payment terms it needs, what size cartons to ship in, the best minimum order size, and the correct policy on returned merchandise—an incredible number of details for a new entrepreneur to iron out.

Packaging

I've covered packaging thoroughly in Chapter 7 and have mentioned it frequently throughout the book. If you've tried quite a few packages, consider hiring a marketing consultant to review your efforts. Developing an effective package often requires marketing experience. An expert can't solve every packaging problem, but there may be times when an expert can find a solution that will turn your product into a winner.

Promotion

A product might need promotion or advertising. I've said repeatedly that new-product entrepreneurs really can't afford to advertise their products; in fact, that's not always true. The one time you can afford to promote your product is when you have a small, targeted market that you can reach easily.

The secret of overcoming promotion problems is to shrink your target market until you can afford to reach it. You can expand to other markets after you have an established base.

Andy Bonnette makes crosses and statues that can be either placed on poles for processions or hung on a wall of a church. His market is Catholic churches in Minnesota and Iowa. His family has had the business for 30 years and is quite happy with the business's small volume. When Andy's father started out, he envisioned a worldwide market. But he couldn't afford to promote to that market.

Targeting a smaller market is similar to shrinking a market. I mention them separately because targeting usually refers to defining customers by what they do. Shrinking a market means limiting the geographic area you're selling to.

IS IT GO-GO TIME?

You won't be able to resolve every problem, but you should be able to resolve at least half of them. A normal pattern for most entrepreneurs, especially those who are introducing products for the first time, will be to resolve at least two or three problems and then reenter the first sales period before proceeding to the transitional period. Your evaluation should not be quick. Instead, take your time, and be sure that the considerable amount of money you're about to invest will be spent wisely.

13

LICENSING: NOW IS THE IDEAL TIME

Companies are interested in five points when licensing ideas:

- A bold vision—a product with large sales potential to help the company
- A product that fits the company's overall product strategy
- A clear path to producing a final design at a profitable cost
- Clear evidence that consumers want the product
- Clear evidence that a distribution channel will take the product

The most important step in licensing an idea is a bold vision. The company has to see that your product will make a difference, and the product has to be something better than ideas that the company has come up with on its own. Projecting this broad a vision is difficult with many products that might have single applications or are just not in glamorous fields. In many cases, companies will forgo ideas that they could successfully market because the products don't seem worth the trouble.

This chapter discusses the last four steps in the licensing process that was introduced in Chapter 5. Figure 13-1 lists the key steps to licensing an idea. But before starting on those steps, I want to explain how product creators can expand their chances of licensing ideas by taking a broader view of the licensing process, in which you put a product on the market with a company, whether it be through a license, distribution agreement, financ-

Figure 13-1   Key Steps to Licensing an Idea

1. Create the idea.
2. Research the market.
3. Decide on the type of company you want to approach.
4. Determine your basic positioning statement and marketing strategy.
5. Pick out the specific companies you want to approach.
6. Start making personal contacts with sales representatives and marketing personnel.
7. Decide when you need to get a patent.
8. Finish developing your idea—if necessary, start working to get an investor or partner. Apply for your patent, if appropriate.
9. Develop proof that your product is marketable.
10. Prepare your presentation materials.
11. Make your presentations to the appropriate companies.
12. Negotiate the contracts.

ing deal, or contract-manufacturing agreement with extended terms. Once you start to view licenses in this context, you'll be able to license smaller products for specialized applications and many other products that normally can't get the attention of manufacturers.

A BROADER VIEW OF LICENSING

Licensing is generally defined as allowing a manufacturer to produce your product idea in return for a royalty, which might be anywhere from 2 to 20 percent of sales. The advantage to the inventor is that he or she doesn't have to invest in getting the product onto the market and royalties from a big company's sales will probably be bigger than profits resulting from the efforts of an inventor's small company. The advantage to a company is that it gets a product with a minimal R&D investment.

One reason more ideas don't get licensed is that it's hard for companies to see how things will work out when they go from product ideas to products on the market. That's why you should develop prototypes and sell your own product if at all possible. You remove much of this doubt by actually making and selling a product. Another reason that companies won't take on inventions is that introducing your idea typically means that they have lost the opportunity to introduce ideas of their own. A final reason that companies won't license ideas is that they don't have the time or resources to introduce them. You can solve the last two problems by offering more licensing-type options to the manufacturer.

Kathy C., mentioned earlier in the book, is a good example of someone who used a broader view of licensing to get her product on the market. Kathy had developed a new type of polyethylene pipe-coupling device for the mining, pipeline, and construction trade. This product was intended for pipes with diameters from 2 to 18 inches and was expensive to manufacture and introduce. Overall, the product was an ideal candidate for licensing. Kathy made prototypes and sold a fair amount of product through a couple of trade shows.

Kathy had already identified a strong licensing candidate, a company that manufactured polypropylene pipe and accessories, and she had made contact with a regional sales and marketing manager of the company, who was interested in the product. But the company balked at the license because it had just completed an acquisition and was struggling to complete the assimilation process.

Rather than give up, Kathy worked with me to put the program back on track. We offered a series of approaches that would still let the manufacturer help us out. The approaches we took were as follows:

1. We offered to let the larger company buy 25 percent of Kathy's company in return for a an exclusive distribution agreement. The company declined the offer.

2. We offered to allow the manufacturer to buy the steel for the product and we would just pay an up-front charge for manufacturing. We also requested that the manufacturer guarantee the tooling cost on a per-piece basis. This would allow the tooling manufacturer to recoup his investment at $2.50 per part. The tooling company was willing to accept a guarantee from the big manufacturer, but not from Kathy. This arrangement would save a tremendous amount on Kathy's requirements for operating cash and up-front investments. The company was interested in this option, and it was still open when option number three was accepted.

3. We asked the company for an exclusive distribution agreement, worth $3 million dollars per year, for Kathy's products. The company wouldn't go for $3 million, but it did agree to $1 million. With that agreement, Kathy was able to get a bank loan and equity financing from investors to make the product. We also could have proceeded to a find a contract manufacturer who would agreed to make the product on very favorable terms, even as a joint-venture partner, on the basis of the contract.

Just a few months after the contract was signed, the manufacturer was already mentioning that after one year it would like to buy Kathy's company and switch over to a royalty/license agreement.

Inventors are drastically limiting their chances of taking products to market when they limit their options to traditional licensing agreements. The key to increasing your odds are, first, to find a manufacturer that is a good match for your product (see Chapter 5) and then be prepared to offer other options if it is not open to a licensing agreement. Some of the options you could offer include:

- Having the manufacturer be the exclusive distributor—with an agreement you should be able to get funding
- Getting the manufacturer to agree to make your product for you on extended payment terms (90 days) in return for a right of first refusal to buy or license the product
- Providing the money ($20 to $100,000) necessary to run a more extensive market test in return for the option to license the product once the test is over
- Getting the manufacturer to agree to help you market your product through its sales organization in return for 15 to 20 percent of your gross revenue
- Getting the manufacturer to agree to pay for your participation at a key trade show in return for an option to buy your product, based on the response at the trade show
- Getting the manufacturer to agree to fund a consultant (for $15,000 to $25,000), who would set up a distribution network

Your options in agreements are limited only by your creativity. The key point in licensing is that there is a huge gap between a manufacturer liking an idea and agreeing to license it. Your job is to fill that gap by coming up with creative options to make it easy for the manufacturer to take your product. In many cases, you'll be able to convince the manufacturer to supply you a small amount of funding to help you bridge the gap. It is easiest to get funding that is not a direct payment to you, such as allowing you to use part of a booth at a trade show, offering you extended terms for manufactured products, or permitting you to use company equipment or employees to help produce your products or prototypes.

STEP 9:* DEVELOPING PROOF THAT A PRODUCT IS MARKETABLE

Proof, of course, is a subjective term, and the only real proof that your product is marketable is that you've sold it for a year or two to a large mar-

---

* Steps 1 through 8 were covered in Chapter 5; they are the preliminary actions to take when considering whether to license a product.

ket. Even though you've sold a product in the past, there is no guarantee that it will sell in the future. But you can develop evidence to show that your product has a good chance of selling. I've presented here a list of the ways that you can build evidence to prove that your product will sell. I've broken the methods down into two categories: the first for products that can actually be made and sold by an underfinanced entrepreneur and the second for products whose expense or difficulty is too great for the inventor. The list is prioritized, starting with the best evidence for you to have and descending from there. Occasionally, you may have several items, rather than just one, which will bolster your case that the product will sell.

Tactics for Products That Can Be Built and Sold

1. *Have an established two- or three-year sales pattern in a broad market.*
2. *Have an established sales pattern in a smaller market*—either a geographically small market, such as North and South Carolina, or a small market channel, such as high-performance backpacking stores and catalogs.
3. *Have a distribution channel ready to go.* For example, you might present your product to a large company that is interested in selling but not licensing it. If the company will sign a letter of intent with you or an agreement to distribute your product, you can use that as leverage to get a smaller company to license the product from you. For example, Kathy could use her distribution agreement with an $800 million company to land a license for her pipe-coupling product with a $10 million company, which will be glad to have the business.

   Another way to utilize this tactic is to approach a large distributor or manufacturing-representative organization and offer exclusive distribution rights for your product in return for an up-front payment to help get the product produced. Most of the time, the company will turn you down. But some may be willing to distribute your product once you have it available. This commitment can then be used to set up a license with a small to midsize company.

   A final approach is to ask retailers if they would take your product once it's available. As an incentive to take your product, you could offer the retailer a one- or two-year exclusive and/or a discounted price. If you can get a purchase order or letter of commitment from the retailer, you can use it to help negotiate a license agreement with a small to midsize manufacturer. Having a distribution channel ready to go with you is a tactic you can use for all types of products, whether you can afford or have the expertise to introduce the idea.

4. *Have sold product in a market test through a small distribution network.* This could be sales through five or six retailers, or through a handful of distributors.

5. *Have sold products directly to consumers* at a state fair, flea market, or other type of trade show.

6. *Have managed to produce only a final product.* This is a weak position for the inventor. While you show that you can build a product, people will still wonder why you were unable to sell any products.

Tactics for Products That Can't Be Built and Sold

1. *Have a contract from a larger company to finish prototype development.* If you can get a large company to foot the bill for completing a stage of product development, you can use that as an incentive for a license from a manufacturer or industrial design house. These stages might include building a prototype or preproduction model, doing a small market test with a limited number of products, or even completing a market research study. If the larger company wants to eventually license the product you can work with an industrial design firm, and if the large company just wants to distribute your product, you can work with a smaller manufacturer.

2. *Have a firm distribution agreement in place.* (See number three above—have a distribution channel ready to go—for products you can manufacture and sell).

3. *Have orders in hand.* For retail products, this might mean orders from retailers or distributors. For industrial products, you might have orders from customers or commitments from manufacturers' representatives to handle the product.

 This tactic should be used more often than it is. If you have a picture or model of your product, you can get an order that includes the phrase "per the attached specifications." Attached to the order, include a product sheet listing specifications, or simply present the actual specifications, including dimensional details, mechanical and electrical requirements, and performance criteria. This tactic works best for industrial products. Customers in this market occasionally order custom-built industrial products or have to order products that have not yet been built. They are more receptive to ordering *new* products that have not yet been built. But the tactic can also work for unique consumer products.

 Another way to use this tactic is to obtain consumer orders from a trade show or magazine ad (preferably with a down payment) and then use those orders to entice a manufacturer into a licensing agreement.

4. *Have letters from a distribution channel or retailers that liked your product and would want to evaluate or purchase the product once it is available.* One way to do this is to have an advisory team of several members of a distribution channel. They would help you to contact distributors and get written commitments to look at your product. You can also get commitments without such an advisory board, though it is more difficult.

5. *Show that your product has been designed based on industry needs and input, and that it has been evaluated by a group of potential buyers.* This tactic works well for industrial products for which a need can be well documented and where the same need exists for a variety of customers. This tactic doesn't work as well for consumer products.

6. *Conduct interviews with 10 to 15 store owners or people in a distribution network.* This demonstrates, first, that there is a real need for your *type* of product and, second, that *your* product idea can fill that need. If you are going to use this tactic you should put together a standard interview form to use with every contact, which you can then show to potential licensees.

7. *Conduct consumer interviews.* These interviews should be based on consumers picking out or rating your product in relation to a choice of seven or eight other products. See Chapter 6 for details on setting up a survey.

Whatever you do, don't tell the manufacturer, "I have been around this business for years, and I know this product is going to be a big winner." If your product is so good, you should be able to develop convincing proof that it will sell. If you do that, you will increase your odds of getting a license, and you'll probably end up with a better royalty rate.

STEP 10: PREPARING PRESENTATION MATERIALS

Your goal when making a licensing presentation is to convince the company that your product can make an impact in its market—hopefully, a very big impact. The people to whom you make a presentation will have no idea what to expect, and they probably will come into your presentation with cynical attitudes regarding your ability to create a winning idea. The rules you need to follow for presentations are:

- Be dramatic, use theatrics, and have a real show.
- Keep the main presentation short—no more than 20 minutes.
- Be positive, and maintain a high degree of forward momentum throughout.
- Close with an option-oriented statement.

- Create a sense of urgency.
- Get some money.

What about all the statistics and data I've told you to gather? Don't you want to prove to the company how much work you've done by having an imposing statistical presentation? Only if you want to put the group to sleep. Hit only the high points, and make those points with charts and visual aids. What you should do is put all your backup into one or two three-ring binders. Make them available and refer to them if you field any questions referring to information they contain. Having the information will convince the company that you really know what you're doing.

Being Dramatic

I was showing a new dental chair, targeted at the midpriced market, to a group of executives and salespeople. The product wasn't as innovative as I would have liked, but it did have some new features. I set the room up in advance, with the new chair on a pedestal and the top two competitive chairs on the floor. All three of the chairs were draped. When people entered the room, they were immediately curious—people love suspense. Then I gave a little talk about the size of the market, and with great flair, I pulled the drape off a competitor's chair. The occupants of the room let out a sigh, and then realized it was not the new chair. Suspense kept building as I mentioned a couple of flaws in the competitor's chair. Then I uncovered the next competitive chair. By the time I undraped the new chair, the audience was totally concentrated, alert, and excited, and that new chair controlled 40 percent of its market within six months of its introduction. Without the dramatic presentation, the product would have started out as a big dud.

You need a dynamite opening with tremendous appeal. If you are not good at setting up a dramatic scene, ask someone who is involved in local theater or drama school to get you off to a great start. Even with an industrial product you can add pizzazz.

For an industrial drain product, which is as dull a product as you are going to get, the only thing in the room at the start of the presentation was a huge washtub. The presenter came out with his product in a black box. Then two big men came out with a large pail and poured 20 gallons of water through the drain in about 10 seconds—a very impressive display.

Another inventor had a video of about 20 kids laughing and scream-ing while using his product. An inventor of an easier-to-use electronic product videotaped a group of students trying (with great difficulty) to use a product that was currently used by most electricians. You have to stage that opening minute to literally stop the show. When making a pre-sentation, ask for a conference room that you are allowed to enter a half hour in advance. Set up the room and be prepared to forgo introductions until after your theatrics are over. People are heavily influenced by their first impressions, so make sure yours counts.

The Main Presentation

Back in Chapter 5, a presentation format was discussed. The idea was to do a presentation first to help you design a product that meets your goals and the market's needs. Now you need to polish your presentation so that it is informative and fast paced, and lasts less than 20 minutes.

After your presentation, you should make a dramatic statement about your product, explaining why the company would want to license it. Following the presentation for the dental chair, I said, "In 12 months the Advantage Chair will be the top-selling dental chair in America." This is your moment to state—powerfully—why the company should buy your product. Some other examples of power statements might include:

"the (*product name*) . . .

- . . . is the key to opening up the sporting goods store market to Company X's entire product line."
- . . . will put a huge dent in the stranglehold your top com-petitor, Company Y, has on the market."
- . . . will position the licensee as the technological leader in a market that is growing at a rate of over 400 percent per year."
- . . . will provide an immediate market entry into the boom-ing in-line skate market and can, within one year, be the fore-runner of a new market category."

You have caught the attention of the audience with your theatrics, and you want to bring home, in an equally convincing manner, the benefit that your product offers the company.

After your dramatic statement, pause and then walk to a new loca-tion in the room, the area where you will do your slide show or audiovisual presentation. Introduce yourself, and give a couple of brief background statements. If you've been working with an advisory group, I'd mention it now. For example, you could say:

My name is Don Took, I'm the inventor of the (*product name*). I've been involved in the hardware industry for five years, both as a manufacturers' representative and as a customer service representative. I've been helped on this project by two advisors, Bob S., an engineer with 15 years' experience at Randolph's Axe and Saw, and Jim P., a marketing manager at Bannigen's Hardware.

You are now ready to move ahead and follow the presentation format from Chapter 5. Everything you do should be visual. Try to use as many charts and visual aids as possible. For a 20-minute presentation, you should have about 40 slides. You might want to consider using a desktop publishing service to take your information and turn it into a snappy visual display.

Being Positive and Generating Momentum

Your job during the presentation is to keep everyone interested and alert. If you can keep people feeling upbeat, they'll feel upbeat about your product. The biggest problem inventors and entrepreneurs have during presentations is that they say way too much and beat every point to death. That is not necessary. Your only job is to get the audience excited about your product. Unless people are excited, you won't make a sale. There will be plenty of time later for sharing more details.

Consider an inventor who wants to share market research results with a potential licensee. This is the information she has available:

- An independent market research study detailing market size. The study includes twenty graphs and segment-by-segment analysis, including future trends.
- Results from interviews with eight manufacturers' sales representatives and fifteen retailers.
- Thirty-five consumer questionnaires and surveys.
- Eighteen magazine articles that discuss the need for this type of product.
- Anecdotal examples from four or five friends which illustrate the need for the product.
- Quotations and interviews from university professors regarding their evaluations of your product.
- Actual sales results.

If our inventor proceeded through all this information, it could take 10 to 15 minutes. But she needs to present it all in just 2 or 3 minutes, maximum. All she should offer in the presentation is:

- A slide showing the total market size and the market's projected growth rate. (The statistics source, which in this example is the research study, should be credited on the bottom of the slide.)
- Three slides of charts showing the overall results from the manufacturers' sales agents, retailers, and consumer surveys. The charts should show the percentage of people that liked your top two or three features, as well as the percentage that will buy the product. (More than 30 to 40 percent would be considered an outstanding ratio of people in a research group that would buy the product.)
- A slide stating that 18 magazine articles have been written on the topic. Include the names of any well-known magazines.
- A slide quoting two good one-line recommendations from university professors. Skip your anecdotal stories.
- A slide showing how many stores have sold your product and the number of projected reorders. If you've sold over $20,000 worth of product, you should list a total sales figure.

The comment I always hear from entrepreneurs is that they have a lot of strong information and they want to present it. They believe that presenting more information has somehow got to be better. A preferable way to look at it is that the short presentation gets across your point, which is that *the market likes your product*. Once you've made this point, anything else is counterproductive.

Close with an Option-Oriented Statement

I've already discussed several times in this chapter the need to have a more open approach to licensing in order to achieve your licensing goals. I recommend that you end your presentation with a broad statement about how much you want to work with the company. You might use a statement like this one:

> I firmly believe that your company is the best choice for my product. You have a strong market position, an established reputation as a leader in the industry, and the financial resources to effectively promote my product. I also believe my product offers your company an innovative solution to an industry problem that will help both your sales penetration and your company image. I'm prepared to work with your company in any number of ways to get the product introduced. I've listed on this slide some of the options you and I could consider.

Some of the many options you could offer are:

- Overseeing final product design through your partnership with an industrial design firm. Cost: $15,000. (*Note:* List the cost figure that is correct for your project.)
- Do additional market research with key companies or executives. Cost: $5,000.
- Conduct an additional market test in a specified market or store. Cost: $20,000.
- License the product outright for an up-front fee and ongoing royalty percentage.
- Sign an exclusive distribution agreement for the product. You can supply the product through an agreement with a contract manufacturer.
- Agree to a nonexclusive distribution agreement.
- Contract a manufacturing agreement coupled with an exclusive or nonexclusive distribution agreement.
- Supply a private-label product (a product with the manufacturer's name on it) for the manufacturer's exclusive distribution.

These options can be broken down into two basic approaches (in addition to a straight licensing agreement):

1. *You finish the product development.*   Your goal is to get the manufacturer to pay for the development cost in return for a first option on the contract or a right of first refusal. A first option on the contract means the manufacturer will have the first chance to buy your idea. Typically, the contract will include agreed-on terms such as up-front fees, royalty rates, and minimum royalty. For example, the contract might read, in effect, "ABC Company shall have the first right, for a period of 30 days after the completion of this step, to license the invention or new product at a 6 percent royalty rate, with a $20,000 up-front payment and a minimum royalty of $25,000 per year."

A right of first refusal generally means that, before you sign a contract with another company, you have to give the first company the rights to match the second company's contract terms. A right of first refusal is harder to get from a company because it doesn't specify any terms that both sides agreed to. Both of these types of contracts are complicated, and you should consult with an attorney before finalizing an agreement.

I personally like this approach because it helps both the inventor and the company. The inventor gets funding for the final, sometimes expensive, stages of product development. Without this help, the inventor may never get his or her product to a stage at which it can be licensed. The company gets a look at what might be a promising product for a $1,000 to $20,000 investment. That same look might cost the company up to $100,000—and maybe much more—if it tried to start a similar project on its own. The advantage of this type of proposal is that it gives a licensee a reasonably low-cost intermediate option so it can better determine if a product has strong market potential.

2. *You make the product and the company just distributes it.* Often you can set up an agreement like this with a buyout clause that would let the company buy out the product in one or two years for a fixed amount of money plus a royalty rate. In some instances, the company will agree only to sell the product, in which case you'll need to leverage that contract to sign a license agreement with a small to midsize company. In other instances, you may sell 25 to 50 percent of your company to your potential licensee in return for funding to set up your company. You would want to do this with a *benchmark progress program.* For example, the company might agree to pay $200,000 for 40 percent of your company. You will get the money at certain times in development. Your benchmark schedule might read as follows:

1. $10,000   At project initiation
2. $15,000   Upon completion of approved prototype
3. $15,000   After consumer market research studies
4. $25,000   After approval of initial preproduction models
5. $35,000   When production and delivery schedule is approved
6. $50,000   After approval of initial production run
7. $50,000   After production of 5,000 units

The benchmark funding system is good for both inventors and manufacturers. You get the money when you need it, and the company doesn't have to risk most of its money until you show meaningful progress toward producing your idea.

Another way to handle financing is to require money from the manufacturer in return for exclusive distribution rights or an option to buy the product. You won't be able to get as much money as you would if you sell part of the company, but you still should be able to get some money. Again, you can agree to take the money only after achieving certain benchmarks.

Creating a Sense of Urgency

I believe you lose leverage the longer a company evaluates an idea, so you should create a sense of urgency to move the company into a quick decision. You should offer a reasonable choice that won't scare off potential licensees.

Inventors and entrepreneurs sometimes create the most outlandish stories to explain the need to move ahead quickly. This simply makes them look unprofessional. Companies understand what is going on. Another approach inventors use is threatening potential licensees that they will find other manufacturers if the companies don't move quickly. This approach puts a rift between the company and the inventor.

The approach I recommend is simply to tell the company that you've been working on the idea for three years (or whatever the actual time is), you've spent a considerable amount of money on it, and you can't afford to wait around too long to put the product on the market. You can give the company two weeks to look at your product before you approach another company, but after that, the potential licensee will have to pay $2,500 for an exclusive look for an extra two weeks. It's a straightforward approach, and the $2,500 is not an unreasonable amount for a manufacturer to pay. You'll create some urgency on the part of the company without alienating it. The $2,500 is an arbitrary number. You can increase or decrease the amount, depending on how unique the product is and how big a market your product targets.

Get Some Money

When you get paid by a company—even if it's just $1,000 for a two-week extension on an exclusive look agreement or $5,000 for product design— you are bringing the company much closer to signing a licensing agreement. By paying the money, the company has already shown that it likes your product, and once money is paid, the company usually accepts that you have a good idea.

Thus, your goal, if you can't land an immediate license, is to get a small payment of some sort from the potential licensee. Some entrepreneurs like to project an image of strength when they ask for money, talking about how strong their products are and how they'll go to other manufacturers if the companies don't respond immediately. I don't like this approach, because it tries to bully people and typically hurts, rather than helps, the licensing process.

A much better approach is just to state that you've worked on the project for some time and aren't in a financial position to sustain a long delay in the project. You want to work with the company, but you do need a speedy decision. Both approaches really project the same message: You need a quick response or you'll have to go to another company. However, my approach is direct and simply asks for help.

Earlier in the chapter, I discussed getting a small up-front fee for a company to review your idea for more than two weeks or asking for money for more product development. Another tactic is to request a small amount of money for a specific marketing project that will offer a company more information about how well your product will do. Some examples of how to use this tactic are:

- Requesting $5,000 to attend an industry trade show
- Asking for $4,000 to place products at a small retail chain
- Suggesting splitting the cost of an $8,000 direct advertising campaign
- Requesting $1,500 to prepare sales materials to support two new representatives

A good way to get the company involved is to request in-kind services, such as time in the prototype shop, use of a shrink-wrap machine, or assistance in an audiovisual presentation. In-kind services don't require a cash outlay from the company to you, but they still are worth money to you. The important point for you is that they get the company involved in your project.

STEP 11: PRESENTING TO THE APPROPRIATE COMPANIES

Step 5 of the key steps to licensing a product covered selecting the types of companies you'd want to approach (see Chapter 5). I mentioned at that time that you should try to establish contacts that can help you get presentations with a company. Step 11 calls for you to actually get in the door to make a presentation. While having a contact is important, you still need to:

- Know the company's strategy
- Have the right overall approach
- State your case so you have the best chance of getting an appointment

Know the Company's Strategy

Rarely, if ever, will a company change its strategy or direction just to take on a new product. But it will be very responsive to a new product that helps it execute its strategy. In fact, most acquisitions of small companies by larger companies are made to help implement business strategies. You need to find companies with strategies that are a good match for your product. If you go to just any company in the market you'll not only be wasting your time, you'll also be lowering the value of your idea by shopping it around.

Some samples of business strategies are:

- To supply all the computer design needs for industrial design engineers
- To be the market leader in low-cost CD packages
- To dominate the gourmet frozen-food section in high-end supermarkets
- To provide value-priced garage doors to large home improvement retail chains

Most companies have readily available mission statements, but those are not business strategies. For example, the mission statement of a company that supplies mid- to low-priced home windows to contractors and home improvement stores includes phrases such as "high-quality products," "superior customer service," and "asset to the community." But the business strategy is to sell first to contractors of homes costing less than $175,000 and then to discount home improvement centers.

The business strategy segments you need to focus on are:

- What markets does a company target?
- What product segments is a company trying to either support or expand into?

For example, the window company's current product line might concentrate on double-paned windows for cold-weather climates, and its targeted product segment might be windows for three-season porches. This company would probably be interested in anything you can offer in three-season porch windows, but it probably won't be interested in anything else.

In Chapter 4, I discussed the importance of trade magazines. Those magazines will have publicity releases about new products, and you can often tell a company's business strategy just by knowing what other products a company is releasing.

The Right Overall Approach

A couple of twenty-year-old men spent the night in a diner working on a new idea. They did a few drawings, produced a short product description, and decided they were ready to start contacting companies. Next, they contacted four companies, identified themselves as inventors, and requested an appointment with the president of the company. They were shocked that no one would see them, even though their idea was a "guaranteed success."

Anyone can claim to be an inventor, whether he or she just had an idea last night or has been working on one for years. Many companies have an immediate resistance to those who call themselves inventors, and it can be tough to get in to see a company if this is how you present yourself.

Instead, you want to be a company. Incorporating as a Subchapter S company typically costs less than $250 (in some states it's only $50) and you can still use most, if not all, of your expenses to reduce your personal tax liability. Then you should get letterhead, business cards, and business envelopes printed with the name of your company.

Next, you should try to establish some longevity for your company. If your town has an entrepreneur's or new-venture club, you should join it. If at all possible, work at getting your company and its product focus listed in the group's directory. If your area doesn't have any entrepreneur organizations, join the local chamber of commerce.

Once you have applied for your patent, you should also send out press releases announcing your new product. Do this even if your product isn't ready. The press release might generate inquiries from interested parties. More important, it can be used later to help get an appointment with a company, as it will show you've been operating for awhile, and it will give the company the impression that your own company can and does develop new products.

The right approach to take is that you are a company, that you've been operating for a number of years, and that you want to discuss options for how you can work together to exploit a new market opportunity.

Setting Appointments

I've seen recommendations from other invention-marketing groups that say the best way to get an appointment is to tell companies that you have a great idea and, if they don't see you, you'll talk to someone else. I personally think that approach doesn't get you very far. First of all, the company doesn't believe you have a good idea just because you say so. Second, the company will probably think this approach is unprofessional. Finally, people just don't like to be pushed around. I am convinced that this "I've got a great product" approach is all wrong.

I discussed in Chapter 5 how to make contact with people at your targeted companies. Using those contacts to set up appointments is by far the best way to have an opportunity to present your product.

If you don't have a contact you should follow a sequence, similar to the following one, that will make the company interested in hearing what you have to say.

1. Call the company and ask for the marketing director. When you get the person—or, more likely, the secretary—ask for the person responsible for marketing your type of products. For example, for our window company you would ask, "Are you the person

responsible for marketing windows for three-season porches?" Always ask this question, even if you know you've reached the right person. It clarifies what you want to talk about.

2. State who you are and what your company does: "My name is Don Debelak, and I'm with a company called Minnesota Windows. We make products that help three-season porches capture and hold the heat from the sun in the fall and spring. Our products are designed to stretch out the time a three-season porch can be used." Naming your company second helps establish that you *are* a company and gives the person you called a general overview of what you are doing.

3. Verify the company's business strategy: "Is your company still targeting three-season porches as a growth-product line?" The person's answer will confirm that it is a company you should target. This question again helps the person frame the conversation: You want to talk about products for three-season porches. If the company's strategy isn't what you expect, you should probably just go on to the next company. You can end the conversation by saying, "Oh, that's too bad. I'm looking for a company that is targeting three-season porches. I've come across a product that is really bigger than my company can handle alone. Do you know anyone at another company that is promoting to the three-season porch market?" The contact might still want to talk to you about your product, which would be OK, or the person might give you a name to call. If you do contact a referral, be sure to mention that your initial contact suggested that you call.

4. If the company verifies its strategy, explain that you've developed a new product for its market that is too big for your company to distribute. Indicate that you want to have a chance to meet with company representatives to discuss, first, if they like the idea and, second, if you can find a mutually beneficial option for your two companies to work together.

5. The person will ask you what the product is. Don't give a direct answer to this question. Say, for example, "I can't do justice to the product with an explanation. I'd like to demonstrate the product to you in person. I can tell you that the product is designed to help capture heat from the sun so a three-season porch can be used longer into the fall and earlier in the spring. It can be built into or attach to a window. The product has been very popular with consumer focus groups, and I think you'll enjoy seeing it. I would like to set up a meeting so I can come in and demonstrate the idea and explore how we could work together. Would Monday or Tuesday of next week work for you?"

   You'll probably find that the first meeting won't be attended by every major decision maker. So, if the first group likes the idea, you need to set up another meeting, later in the day or the next day, to give a demonstration to additional important people. Whenever you have to travel, always schedule your return trip for one or two days after your appointment. Then you can tell your contact, "I'll be in town tomorrow; let's set up another demonstration then." Don't expect your initial contact to convince other people in the organization. Instead, set up two or, if necessary, three demonstrations.

STEP 12: NEGOTIATING THE CONTRACT

I don't like to talk in too much detail about negotiating a licensing contract, because you really should get a lawyer to assist you. But you should have some knowledge about the contract so you can intelligently discuss terms. In most agreements, the *licensee* is the company paying the royalty, and the *licensor* is the inventor or company to whom the idea belongs. The basic elements usually contained in the license include:

- The nature of the license, exclusive or nonexclusive
- A definition of what exactly is being licensed
- Geographic or market limitations
- Future inventions
- Term and termination of the agreement
- Right to audit
- Royalty rate, payment terms, and any up-front royalty payments
- Patent expenses
- Infringement by others
- Right to sublicense
- Patent assignment

Each of these terms is discussed in the following sections.

Nature of the License

You might license a product to just one company, which is an *exclusive license*. In some cases, especially with technology products, you might license a product to several manufacturers, which is a *nonexclusive license*. An example of nonexclusive licenses is VHS videotape technology, which is licensed to dozens of companies. New processes, such as a better way to strengthen plastic molds, might also have nonexclusive licenses. A *sole license* occurs when you license the product to just one company, while you retain the rights to manufacture and sell the product yourself.

One important point is that you can't grant someone exclusive rights unless you have a patent, copyright, or trademark. Those are the intellectual property rights as defined by U.S. law. If you don't have property rights, your agreement could have another name, such as a "marketing and manufacturing agreement." In your agreement you are disclosing your technology and trade secrets in return for a payment based on sales volume. You could also specify in the contract that you will grant exclusive rights to the company if a patent is issued.

Definition of the Product or Technology Being Licensed

This definition is typically listed in the paragraph in which you grant a license to the licensee. This is a very important paragraph. You want the license to be for the product and its subsequent variations, derivatives, and modifications. The licensee will try to define your product—probably just the specific product under current consideration—more precisely.

Geographical or Market Limitations

The license might be restricted to a specific market area, such as the United States, or it might be restricted to a market, such as sporting goods. For example, if your product combined two different fabrics for a unique feel or look, you might license it to a sporting goods company that could use it for its insulating value in underwear and you might license it to a children's clothing manufacturer for its unique look for blouses and dresses.

Future Inventions

The licensee might ask for the rights to future inventions or the right of first refusal of your future inventions. Typically you can have this clause removed. It is restricting to the inventor, and the company is not offering anything in return. If you are forced to keep the clause, accept only a right of first refusal and allow the company only a 30- to 60-day period in which to evaluate the idea before agreeing to release it back to you.

Term and Termination

The licensee usually tries to negotiate a set period or tie the license to the period of the patent or to the life of patent improvements in determining the life of a license agreement. You, as the licensor, want to benefit from a royalty for as long as the company sells the product. After all, the company's initial market position, which was developed based on your product idea, will help it sell the product long after the patent expires. As a licensor, you want the license to last as long as the product and any subsequent variations, derivations, or modifications are still being sold.

As a licensor, you should have the right to terminate the agreement for nonperformance. Usually this is tied to a minimum royalty payment per year. For example, the contract might state that the licensee has the right to terminate the agreement if yearly royalty payments are less than $50,000. You might agree to a three- or six-month advance notice clause to give the manufacturer a chance to liquidate its position before the license expires.

You should also have a clause in the contract to the effect that either party can terminate the agreement if the other party violates the terms and conditions of the contract.

Right to Audit

You need to include a clause indicating that you have the right to audit the books of the company to ensure that you are getting the correct royalty payments.

Royalty Payments

The three considerations in this section are up-front royalty payments, which may or not be advances against future sales; the royalty percentage based on net sales; and a minimum royalty payment over the life of the contract. The other royalty consideration is the minimum royalty payment, which I prefer to be in the termination clause.

License agreements are fully negotiable and there are no hard and fast rules that apply. Royalty percentages can run from 1 percent to 18 percent, and up-front fees can vary from less than $5,000 to millions of dollars. I recommend using the following general guidelines as a starting point for determining royalty rates:

1. A product that has a 50 percent manufacturing margin (manufacturing costs equal 50 percent of the manufacturer's selling price) should have a 5 to 6 percent royalty. The royalty rate should go up one to two percentage points for every 10 percent increase in margin. For example, a 60 percent margin product should have a royalty rate of 6 to 7 percent.

2. The up-front fee should be equal to 50 percent of the expected yearly royalty payment. I try to arrange it so that the up-front fee is not considered an advance against future royalty payments, but rather a separate fee. Typically, licensees will insist that the up-front payment be an advance.

You should also try to get a minimum for total royalty payments that is equal to twice the expected yearly payments. For example, if the company decides not to pursue your idea or if you terminate the contract for lack of performance, you can still receive the remainder of the minimum total royalty payment. Licensees will resist this clause, but you can sometimes have it included if the company is excited about your idea.

Patent Expenses

License agreements sometimes require licensors to pay for patent expenses. Be careful of this clause. If you have to pay for patents, be sure that includes only U.S. patents. Getting overseas patents could cost up to $100,000, and you'll want the licensee to pay for those.

In many cases, products will have only U.S. patents, although they are still sold overseas. This is one reason I don't like royalty payments to be tied to a patent. The licensee could claim that you are entitled to royalty payments only from markets in which you have a patent in force.

Infringement by Others

This clause specifies who is responsible for taking action against a person or company that infringes on the patent. You don't want to be responsible, as patent disputes are very expensive. The licensee also doesn't want to be responsible. I recommend that the clause not be included. If it is, the clause should just say that both parties will mutually agree to a course of action at the time the infringement is discovered.

Right to Sublicense

Often, the licensee will want the right to license the product to other manufacturers. Fifty-fifty is a typical split in a sublicense agreement, and often the licensee ends up being able to license at its discretion. This can be a good or bad clause for the inventor, depending on the situation. If the company licenses the product overseas or to new markets, the sublicense could earn income for the inventor that he or she never expected. But if the company just licenses the product to another company in the same industry, you could end up with only half of the royalty rate you expected.

A sublicense clause should read that the licensee cannot sublicense a product without your permission. The licensee should add that permission cannot unreasonably be withheld. Try to negotiate a clause saying that, in targeted markets, which you specify in the contract, you will split the royalties 75-25, with 75 percent to the inventor. In all other markets, you can split the royalties 50-50. This will prevent the company from quickly selling out your interests.

Patent Assignment

You don't need to assign a patent to a company in order for it to license a product from you. I don't recommend that you ever assign the patent rights except to your own company. Your ability to withdraw a patent for lack of performance is severely limited if you decide to assign patent rights.

CONCLUSIONS

You should never just start out thinking that you'll license an idea. First, it limits your options and, second, it often prevents you from doing the work that will increase your odds of getting a license. But licensing is a viable alternative, and one you should consider, even if you are planning on manufacturing and marketing your idea yourself.

14

THE TRANSITIONAL PERIOD: GROWING YOUR BUSINESS

After its second year of business, Pepin Heights Sparkling Cider had revenues of about $250,000. Its products are sold through bars, restaurants, delicatessens, and grocery stores in Minnesota. Pepin Heights is a good example of a company in the transitional sales period. It has a foothold in a regional market, its sales volume is large enough to give it stability and good credit, and it has a distribution network in place.

In the transitional period, a company moves from having a few sporadic sales to a steady, though small, ongoing business with an established distribution network and customer base. One key factor in this period is that the sales effort is no longer solely dependent on the product entrepreneur; instead, sales agents or stores generate sales volume.

I believe that this period is, by far, the most difficult time in the establishment of a business. I estimate that, out of ten entrepreneurs who start to sell a product, no more than one survives the transitional period.

A typical example is Norm H., who created a cleaning cloth that looked similar to a washrag but was capable of taking stains out of carpets, clothing, and furniture. The product sold for $3.99. Over a period of two years, Norm sold an impressive 5,000 units through drugstores. In addition to sales success, Norm received several testimonial letters from satisfied clients.

Norm appeared to be poised for a successful product introduction, but he couldn't persuade distributors to pick up the product, and his idea died. What happened to Norm? Part of the problem was that he never appeared to have a company; he seemed to be someone making a product in his basement. Another part of the problem was that Norm didn't have a sales strategy that would convince a distributor to carry the product. Norm's major problem, however, was that he always figured distributors would be coming to him, if he could get his product into a few stores. Norm had no idea how to take his product through the transitional period.

Norm is not alone. Most product entrepreneurs don't even know that a transitional period is needed. That's not really surprising; every day, established companies are moving straight from market-testing into nationwide distribution. Entrepreneurs feel they can do the same if they can get some investors or one lucky break.

I sometimes ask entrepreneurs what they'd do if they found investors. Typical answers are: "I'd put my product into production," "I'd be able to afford an advertising campaign," "I'd buy the tooling I need to lower my production cost," or "I'd hire a sales manager." The problem with all of these answers is that they don't address the total picture of what an entrepreneur has to do in the transitional period: advertising, promotion, distribution, manufacturing, administration, sales, and customer service. Entrepreneurs need investors, and they can all use lucky breaks, but they also need orderly plans for expanding their sales bases.

THE TRANSITIONAL PLAN

If you've followed the action steps I've outlined through the first 13 chapters, you'll have a fairly easy time with your transitional plan. Almost everything I've advocated is designed to prepare you for the transitional period. You have key insiders to help you set up a distribution network, and you know who your customers are, how they can be reached, and what benefits they want. You know how to package and promote your idea, and you know approximately how many units will sell in each sales outlet.

Why bother with a plan? There are three very good reasons:

1. *The plan details a one- to two-year action plan.* With a plan, you're more likely to do everything that's necessary, and you'll do it in the right order.
2. *The plan provides the details you'll need for a budget.* A product entrepreneur's plan will list all the costs of producing and selling a product, and these are the building blocks of budget numbers.
3. *The plan forces you to channel all your thoughts into a coherent strategy.* Product creators receive input from a thousand directions. Because

they pick up bits of data from everyone they talk to, their information is often inconsistent and contradictory. A plan helps turn this maze of information into a purposeful pathway toward success.

The transitional plan doesn't have to be particularly long. The beginning text, which provides an overview, shouldn't be more than 2 to 5 pages. The action plan should cover in detail the steps you'll be following over the next 12 to 18 months.

Your transitional plan should contain the following items, preferably in the following order:

1. Product description and benefits
2. Targeted customers
3. Targeted geographic market
4. Where the targeted customers buy
5. Market potential
6. Competition
7. Distribution plan
8. Current sales status
9. Detailed sales forecast
10. Promotional activities
11. Manufacturing overview
12. Start-up expenses
13. Action plan

In some respects, a transitional plan is simpler than a routine marketing plan: You don't have as much history or as many activities to detail. However, the detailed sales forecast is much harder, because you must explain where every sales dollar will come from. You can't say, "With the promotional program we have planned, we expect sales to increase 10 percent." Instead, you have to say, "I expect to gain three distributors [name them] next July. I have had initial talks with seven distributors in the area who indicated a strong interest in the product, and I expect purchase orders for one hundred units from at least three of the seven." Note that you need to name the distributors, and you need to have had discussions. Backup like this is essential to having any hope that your sales forecast will be accurate.

Let's look at the plan's elements one by one.

Product Description and Benefits

State succinctly what the product is, why you decided to develop it, its features and benefits, its sales proposition, and any known deficiencies.

I've covered the first three points earlier. A sales proposition is a *short, clear* description of why people should buy the product. Examples are: "cuts weeding time 30 percent"; "cleans up bathroom clutter"; "reduces back strain by 50 percent"; "hot, new fad item"; "improves testing accuracy by 80 percent"; "great conversation piece"; "totally new taste".

Pointing out product deficiencies is a task that product entrepreneurs don't enjoy doing. They don't like to acknowledge that their products may not be perfect. Every product has its flaws, and those flaws can have varying impact on your plan. Your product might have to be displayed on a counter or special apparatus because it doesn't package well enough to stand on a stock shelf. Or you might want to sell through distributors because of service and installation requirements. Or a product's benefit might be apparent only to an older audience. You can adjust for flaws if you know what they are. You should list not only what the flaws are but what you're doing to overcome them. For example, if you acknowledge that consumers need a product demonstration, your plan might call for demonstrators at stores every other weekend.

Targeted Customers: Who Are They?

To whom is your product going to be sold? As I've been telling you throughout the book, an entrepreneur has to focus on a small, easy-to-reach market.

In the 1980s, Len and Lisa Brown decided to go on a two-year horse-back-riding adventure. Len and Lisa didn't last two years, but they learned that a traditional saddle gives a horse a very sore back. Len created his Ortho-flex saddle, which has a suspension made of sheet plastics and other synthetic materials. Len and Lisa's first sales efforts were directed to Western riders. The product didn't sell, primarily because the target market was too broad.

The couple decided to concentrate on the endurance-rider market, which is composed of people who compete in 24-hour horse races. This market is focused and easy to reach. The riders could be contacted through lists of entries in endurance races, and the market had its own magazine, Trail Blazer. *Five years after focusing on a small market, the Browns have branched out to Western riders and now have a million-dollar business.*

Your transitional plan has to be specific, and it has to be able to make an impact on targeted customers. You need to list a series of activities that (1) can be accomplished and (2) will repeatedly reach target customers. For example, consider the Pepin Heights Cider Company, which I mentioned at the start of the chapter. Its plan could involve sales through ten restaurants; a display card, promoting the cider, for each table; a point-of-purchase display listing the ten restaurants, to be used at participating delicatessens; and a promotional flyer sent to each of the restaurants' mailing lists. These actions make sense because they connect directly to the targeted customers—people who frequent certain mid- to high-priced restaurants—and they communicate the same message to those people frequently enough to be effective. I strongly believe that entrepreneurs won't be able to reach their target audience unless it's small.

Targeted Geographic Market

In addition to limiting the type of customers you're going to appeal to, you should limit the area of the market you're trying to serve. For example, the apple cider company's target market was Minneapolis.

Where the Targeted Customers Buy

Customers buy most products through a wide variety of outlets. Focus your efforts and choose only one or two outlets to work with.

Use a market analysis chart to support your choice of a certain distribution network. The chart reviews the market size, as well as various sales outlets and their distribution networks. It offers comments pertinent to the level of promotional support required, and it summarizes any previous discussions with the network. Figure 14-1 is a market analysis for a hair-crimping iron.

After you present the chart, include a paragraph on why you chose a particular network. For example, an entrepreneur marketing the hair-crimping iron might decide to sign an exclusive one-year sales agreement with a metro-based department store because of the favorable sales publicity from a co-op advertising program.

Market Potential

In this section, you should include sales potential for the next year, market potential of the targeted market, and market potential of the total market.

- *Next year's sales.* This number comes right from your market analysis chart. The market size for the hair-crimping iron is 30,000 units in the metro market. The locally based department store has 15 percent of the market, or 4,500 units. The sales potential of the product, based on input from the store's buyer, is 20 percent of what the store sells, or 900 units.

Figure 14-1 Target Market Analysis

Product category:	Hair styling	
Product description:	New type of crimping iron for introducing waves in women's hair	
Market size, U.S.:	Approximately 2 million units per year	
Market size, metro:	1.5% of U.S. market or 30,000 units per year	
Unit sales distribution:	Drugstore chains	30%
	Independent drugstores	10
	Discount stores	30
	Mail order	5
	Department stores, metro-based	15
	Department stores, non-metro-based	10

Market Comments:

1. Drugstore chains: Sold direct or through rack jobbers. Chains prefer either a well-known or a well-advertised product. Required promotional support is too expensive at this time.

2. Independent drugstores: Sold through a buying cooperative or rack jobbers. Independents have expressed interest in the product, provided it has an appealing point-of-purchase display, primarily because they are not able to purchase the top-selling crimping products.

3. Discount stores: Can be sold either directly or through a distributor. Stores prefer a brand-name product, but they will handle a small manufacturer if its pricing is substantially lower than competitive products'. The chains prefer to purchase on a regional or national basis.

4. Mail order: Most catalogs are headquartered outside of metro, which makes a sale difficult. In addition, mail order is just a small part of the market, and it's preferable to develop sales momentum at the retail level.

5. Department stores, metro-based: Sold either directly or through distributors. Stores have expressed interest in an exclusive sales agreement, as long as a co-op advertising program is included. One store has promised to prominently display the product in return for the exclusive agreement. *(Continued)*

Figure 14-1   *Continued*

> **6.** Department stores, non-metro-based: Sold either directly or through distributors. Meetings with buyers have been difficult because of the distance involved. Early talks indicate that the stores will support only a brand-name product.

- *Potential of the targeted market.* You should be able to penetrate new retail outlets every year. Go back to your market analysis chart for an estimate of the sales potential of the targeted market. For the hair-crimping product, the local market took 30,000 units per year. Based on the first sales period and estimates from local buyers or insiders, an entrepreneur might estimate a 15 percent market share, or a sales potential of 4,500 units.

- *Potential of the entire market.* I personally hate making this estimate. The number is usually meaningless because nationwide sales can't be reliably projected based on a local market. However, everyone wants to know the product's "true" sales potential. Take the market number from the market analysis and multiply it by your projected market share. For example, the sales potential for the hair-crimping iron would be 2 million times 15 percent, or 300,000 units. This is the number of units you may be able to sell after being in business five to ten years.

If you are not able to obtain a total market size number, try to find another product to use as a sales base. For example, Product Y might be the top-selling crimping iron, at 1.2 million units per year. Your estimates could then be based on selling 20 percent of Product Y's volume. Base your percentage of sales either on actual results from the first sales period or on insider or buyer estimates.

Competition

When introducing a product, an entrepreneur typically is offering an item that fills a void or need, is the next logical step in the evolution of a product line, or takes advantage of an opportunity. For example, a box for feminine hygiene supplies meets the need for an all-inclusive container for such items. An easier-to-use wind-surfing board is a natural extension of a product line. T-shirts with Desert Shield and Desert Storm emblems took advantage of a marketing opportunity.

Base your section on competition on one of these three points so that people can understand the logic of a product's introduction. Explain the competition and tell why your product fills a void, is a logical extension, or capitalizes on an opportunity.

Product feature charts or function comparison charts are helpful in illustrating how a product is different. Figure 14-2 is a comparison chart for a new rake. *Consumer Reports* magazine is a good source for samples of product comparison charts.

Distribution Plan

So far, your plan has explained who your targeted customers are, what type of outlets you'll cultivate, and what the distribution network is for those outlets. For example, suppose you're selling to walleye-fishing enthusiasts in Minnesota, through bait-and-tackle shops as well as a small chain of three discount stores. Sales to bait-and-tackle shops are typically made through fishing distributors, and sales to the discount store chain are through a manufacturers' representative.

You've already presented the framework for the distribution plan. Now you need to add the necessary details: the actual distributors, manufacturers, representatives, or other sales network components involved in selling the product. If you have a key contact who will help, mention that person in your discussion. Figure 14-3 is an example of a distribution plan for the fishing product.

Figure 14-2 Competitive Product Chart

Product category:	Rakes
Production description:	A rake with two rows of tines; greatly decreases raking time. Every other tine on this rake is an inch shorter than the longer tines. The rake ends up with two rows of raking tines when the tines are bent at a 60-degree raking angle.
Competition:	Traditional bamboo, metal, and plastic rakes.

Product	Price	Speed	Dethatching Capabilities	Anti-clogging	Ease of Use	Effectiveness
Bamboo rake	$4.95	Poor	Fair	Some	Good	Poor
Plastic rake	6.95	Fair	Poor	No	Fair	Fair
Metal rake	8.95	Good	Good	No	Fair	Good
New rake	12.95	Excellent	Excellent	Minimal	Good	Excellent

Figure 14-3   Sample Distribution Plan: Walleye Lures

Distribution Network: Two distributors—Minnesota Fishing and Lures and Lures and Jigs—will sell to bait-and-tackle shops, and Peterson's Manufacturers' Representatives will sell to Merlin's Discount Stores.

Minnesota Fishing has a line of 11 products that it sells through 41 bait-and-tackle shops in Minnesota. The company's sales manager has been a consultant on the project for six months, and he feels he will be able to place the product in half of those stores next year.

Lures and Jigs carries a line of 24 fishing products that it sells to 117 stores in central Minnesota. One of the company's salespeople has field-tested the product for over a year. He thinks that he can place the product in 24 stores next year.

Peterson's Manufacturers' Representatives: The owner of this company has close ties with a small chain of discount stores. He currently sells 14 products to the chain. The owner has agreed to sell the fishing lure provided we offer him a 20 percent commission and offer the chain 60-day terms and guaranteed sales.

Current Sales Status

Give a brief overview of where your product is selling. List each outlet and the approximate number of units that it sells per month. Detail how many units have been sold by manufacturers' representatives or distributors.

Your goal in this section is to show that your product has had some initial sales success. Mention any trade shows or fairs you have attended. State not only what your sales were, but also what the sales were at booths around yours. Include, as an attachment, your sales comparison chart (see Chapter 12).

Detailed Sales Forecast

New entrepreneurs are absolutely horrible at sales forecasting. To them—in fact, to most people—a sales forecast might start with 100 units the first month, move to 120 units the second month, and then proceed nicely up to 220 to 250 units per month by year's end. I wish sales could build that smoothly, but they don't. If a fishing store buys a product in April, it might buy again in May, but, more probably, it won't order again until the next year. A fishing product might have 90 percent of its sales in a 2- to 3-month period. Entrepreneurs sometimes make another faulty assumption: If three stores order one month, then four stores will order the next month. New products often have a burst of sales in the beginning, when stores bring in their initial stocking orders. Those initial stores are usually "friendly"; the product creator has a friend or helpful contact there. After that initial burst, sales can be hard to come by. When you do your sales forecast, list each customer and when it is expected to buy.

Your sales forecast is the most important part of your budget. Not only does it drive your revenue, but it also provides the information you need to prepare manufacturing and promotional budgets. A combined sales/revenue forecast for the fishing product is shown in Figure 14-4. Sales occur when a unit is sold; revenue occurs when payment is received. You need to know when sales will occur so that you can plan production. You need to know when you'll receive revenue so that you can determine cash flow requirements.

Notice several points about the forecast. There is a considerable difference between when you make the sale and when you collect the money; neither sales nor revenue shows a consistent pattern; and the sales in the transitional period's first year aren't very high.

Promotional Activities

List, month by month, every activity, from point-of-purchase displays to television advertising, that you plan for the next year. This list will tell you how much money is needed and provide an action plan to follow.

Figure 14-5 shows what the fishing entrepreneur's promotional list might look like. This schedule budgets $4,000 for promotion against a sales budget of $11,200—not bad, considering that the product is still becoming established. You have to promote your product if you expect to sell it.

The costs listed are extremely low. You won't get these prices by walking into a TV station and saying you want to buy some ads. You'll have to call every cable station in your sales area and ask for discounts. Tell each TV ad salesperson that you're an entrepreneur with a new product and that you're trying to save money. Promise to run more ads if the product is successful. Be willing to take undesirable time at a discount, provided it will reach your target audience.

Concentrate on a market in which you can afford to run your ad in at least 25 to 50 spots; you'll need the repetition to convey your message to consumers. No one will see all 25 runs, but if you advertise that much, some people might see the ad 5 times.

Be sure that the timing of the promotional programs ties in with your sales forecast. For example, the discount stores will want to have an ad campaign to promote the product when it first comes into the stores. Your

Figure 14-4   Forecast of Sales and Revenues: 12-Month Projection

	Jan.	*Feb.*	*Mar.*	*Apr.*	*May*	*June*
Sales units (returns)	0	300[1]	600	4,800	210	100
Revenues[2]	0	0	$600	$1,200	$600	$420
	July	*Aug.*	*Sept.*	*Oct.*	*Nov.*	*Dec.*
Sales units (returns)	100	0	0	(300)	(300)	(100)
Revenues[2]	$200	$200	$9,000	0	$(600)	$(600)

Fishing Widget
Sales and Revenues

Sales Explanation:

February

Distributor X has 6 stores that will buy early.[3]

Distributor Y has 4 stores that will buy early.

April

Distributor X will have 4 stores buy.

Distributor Y will have 6 stores buy.

Each large store[4] will purchase 1,500 units.

June–August

Small number of reorders expected to restock shelves.

November

Product returns.

March

Distributor X will have 10 stores buy.

Distributor Y will have 10 stores buy.

May

Distributor X will add 3 stores.

Distributor Y will add 4 stores.

October

Product returns. Payment within 30 days of return.

December

Product returns.

Notes:

1. Small fishing stores are projected (based on the first sales period) at 30 units per store. Each large store is projected to buy 1,500 units based on the buyers' preliminary estimates of 1,500 to 2,000 units based on 90-day dating, guaranteed sales, and a television ad campaign.

2. Based on an average selling price of $2. Payment expected in 30 days from small stores. *(Continued)*

Figure 14-4 *Continued*

3. Sales projections are based on half of Distributors X and Y's customers purchasing. This is consistent with the results of the first sales period and with the distributors' own sales projections.

4. Five large discount chains have indicated they would buy 1,500 to 2,000 units each. The plan calls for selling only three of the five stores. [List the names of the stores.]

promotion budget should show a campaign in the month when the discount stores buy. The fishing entrepreneur needs to have ads running in April and May to coincide with the discount stores' April purchase.

Manufacturing Overview

This section explains how you plan to have the product manufactured and contains a manufacturing budget.

Manufacturing Plan

Figure 14-6 shows a month-by-month manufacturing plan. According to the sales forecast, the fishing entrepreneur needs to manufacture 6,110 units. The cost to produce the units in a garage is 73¢. The costs from

Figure 14-5 Schedule of Promotional Activities: Fishing Widgets

Month	Activity	Cost
January	Print 250 11"-by-14" point-of-purchase displays emphasizing the product's benefits and the fact that the product is new.	$ 400
March	Produce a 15-second TV commercial for April and May TV spots.	400
April	Run 100 ads on cable-TV fishing shows carried by small cable systems in northern Minnesota.	1,500
May	Run 100 ads on cable TV in northern Minnesota.	1,500
June	Prepare 100 point-of-purchase cards with a $1 instant-rebate coupon offer, to help clear out remaining store inventory.	200

Figure 14-6   Manufacturing Plan: Fishing Widgets

August	Order packaging artwork.
	Order inventory to build 1,500 units. *Note:* Shipment lead time is 12 weeks.
September	Order inventory to produce 1,500 units.
October	Order inventory to produce 1,500 units.
	Order packaging supplies for 6,500 units.
November	Order inventory to produce 1,500 units.
December	Hire a part-time worker for the December–March period.
	Produce 1,500 units.
	Order supplies to produce 500 units.
January	Produce 1,500 units.
February	Produce 1,500 units.
March	Produce 1,500 units.
April	Produce 500 units.
May	Rework product returns.
June	Rework product returns.
July	Determine manufacturing plan for next season.

a contract manufacturer are: 95¢ for up to 5,000 units; 75¢ for up to 10,000 units; and 67¢ for over 20,000 units. Packaging adds 12¢ to each unit's cost, no matter how it's produced.

Both manufacturing options should be explained so that potential investors can see that the units produced in a garage will end up costing about the same as if they were made by the contract manufacturer. The entrepreneur should make the product in a garage, rather than invest $3,000 to $4,000 in inventory.

Manufacturing Budget

The first step in preparing a budget is to list when you need to produce your product. Refer to your sales forecast and your production capability. If you need 4,800 units to ship in April and you can produce only 1,500 units per month, then you need to start producing four months before April, or in December.

Work backward from your production schedule to determine when you need to order supplies and when you'll have to pay for them. A supplier might have a 12-week lead time; if you need to start production in December, you'll need to order supplies in September. You may have to pay for supplies 30 to 60 days after shipment, or give cash on delivery, or make a 50 percent deposit before a supplier will accept your order. Include in your budget not only when you must place the order, but also when you'll have to pay for it.

Another expense to include is packaging. Again, what are your lead times and payment terms? Packaging costs almost always have dramatic price drops; for example, 1,000 units might cost 45¢ each, and 5,000 units might cost 22¢ each. New entrepreneurs tend to buy large quantities to "save" money. Don't do that. Your goal is to preserve working capital. Figure 14-7 shows the fishing entrepreneur's manufacturing budget. Study it along with the manufacturing plan (Figure 14-6). With a part-time helper, 1,500 units per month can be produced; without a helper, 500 units can be produced. As you can see from the plan, a product entrepreneur has to be planning 3 to 6 months ahead and has to faithfully execute every action item.

Figure 14-7 Manufacturing Budget: Fishing Widgets

Month	Comments	Month	Comments
August		*January*	
$1,000	Artwork	$450	Pay 75% on shipment
150	25% prepayment for supplies	500	Labor
$1,150		$950	
September		*February*	
$150	Prepayment for supplies	$450	Pay 75% on shipment
$150		500	Labor
		$950	
October		*March*	
$150	Prepayment	$450	Pay 75% on shipment
300	Half of charge for package	500	Labor
$450		$950	
November		*April*	
$150	Prepayment	$150	Pay 75% on shipment
450	Pay 75% on shipment	$150	
$600			
December			
$50	Prepayment		
450	Pay 75% on shipment		
500	Labor		
300	Payment for last half of package		
$1,300			

Start-up Expenses

These expenses can be quite numerous. Beyond tooling costs, they include product liability insurance, incorporation costs, manufacturing and office supplies, logo design, moving expenses, engineering documentation, legal fees for partnership or contract manufacturing agreements, telephone, rent deposits, and so on. You should have a fairly good estimate of your major costs, such as tooling. But you may overlook many of the small, miscellaneous expenses. If at all possible, ask another entrepreneur (suggested by your local chamber of commerce or named in magazine and newspaper articles) what his or her unexpected start-up expenses were. An example of start-up expenses for the fishing product is shown in Figure 14-8.

$1,600! And the product is being produced in a basement! None of the purchases is a major item; that's the nature of start-up costs. They're small, but the dollar total sneaks up on entrepreneurs.

Action Plan

In this section, you combine all of the actions you plan to take through the transitional sales period: marketing, manufacturing, and any other activity. Figure 14-9 gives an example.

Investors love action plans because they like to know whether things are going as expected. In your first few months, it may appear that nothing is happening. Your investors may panic. They'll be reassured if you can show that you're right on the action plan's schedule. And if you're not on target? You can expect to have upset investors. The action plan gives you and your investors a guide for tracking your performance. It

Figure 14-8   Start-up Expenses: Fishing Widget

1.	Two additional manufacturing fixtures	$ 400
2.	Incorporation costs	125
3.	Company name registration	225
4.	Business phone deposit	250
5.	Stationery, invoices, statements, bills-of-lading forms, and business cards	275
6.	Miscellaneous manufacturing and cleaning supplies	150
7.	Shrink-wrap equipment	175
	Total	$1,600

Figure 14-9 Action Plan: Fishing Widgets

August	Order packaging artwork.
	Order inventory to build 1,500 units. Confirm shipment lead time is 12 weeks.
September	Order inventory to product 1,500 units.
	Order manufacturing fixtures.
October	Order inventory to product 1,500 units.
	Order packaging supplies for 6,500 units.
	Order stationery, invoices, etc.
	Start procedures for incorporating and filing for company name registration. Obtain any necessary local licenses.
November	Order inventory for 1,500 units.
	Start development of a point-of-purchase display.
	Order miscellaneous office, manufacturing, and cleaning supplies.
	Order shrink-wrap machinery.
December	Put down deposit for business phone.
	Hire a part-time worker for the December–March period.
	Produce 1,500 units.
	Order inventory to produce 500 units.
January	Produce 1,500 units.
	Order 250 point-of-purchase displays. *Note:* Order extra point-of-purchase displays to replace those that will get damaged.
February	Produce 1,500 units.
	Develop the concept for the 15-second TV commercial.
	Find low-cost producer to put together TV ad.
March	Produce 1,500 units.
	Produce 15-second TV commercial.
April	Produce 500 units.
	Run 100 ads on cable-TV shows carried by small cable systems in northern Minnesota.
May	Rework product returns.
	Develop point-of-purchase display to help clear out inventory. *(Continued)*

Figure 14-9   *Continued*

June	Rework product returns.
	Print point-of-purchase return coupons.
July	Determine manufacturing plan for the next year.

will help to keep you on schedule. Without a plan, dates can slip by without any action occurring.

The Budget

Refer to Figure 14-10 as you read the next few paragraphs. There are four key points that you should note:

1. The highest cumulative profit/loss amount is in May, a loss of $10,650. To survive the first year, the company needs, either from the entrepreneur's resources or those of investors, an additional $10,650.

2. The year shows a loss of $2,630. Many entrepreneurs don't want to show losses. What appears to be the only area that can be cut back? Promotion. Cutting promotion is exactly what most people do, and it's a mistake. Without promotion, stores won't carry your product. You need point-of-purchase displays, selling boards for distributors, and co-op advertising programs if you are to move out of the first sales period.

3. The monthly profit/loss figure acts like a scorecard; it tells how you're doing. In May, after nine months of operations, if you show a cumulative loss of $10,650, your investors won't say: "What's going on?" Instead they'll say: "Ah yes, you're right on budget."

4. The budget is strictly on a cash basis. Don't consider any other accounting method. Project when you'll receive the cash and when you'll spend it.

Your budget gives you a basis for putting a value on your business. The budgeted sales revenue for the year is $11,000. A new, growing company is worth about three to five times its current sales volume. Fishing Widgets is worth about $30,000 to $50,000. A 20 percent share in the business should sell for about $10,000.

Your transitional plan and budget are important documents in your entrepreneurial path to success. Every step I've introduced has been

Figure 14-10 Budget: Fishing Widgets

	Aug.	Sept.	Oct.	Nov.	Dec.	Jan.	Feb.	Mar.	Apr.
Sales (units)	—	—	—	—	—	—	—	600	4,800
Production (units)	—	—	—	—	1,500	1,500	1,500	1,500	500
Revenue	—	—	—	—	—	—	—	$600	$1,200
Expenses									
Manufacturing									
Supplies	$1,150	$150	$450	$600	$800	$450	$450	$450	150
Labor	—	—	—	—	500	500	500	500	—
Overhead	—	—	—	—	—	—	—	—	—
Promotional	—	—	—	—	—	400	—	400	1,500
Start-up	—	400	625	325	250	50	50	50	50
Other	50	50	50	50	50	50	50	50	50
Total expenses	1,200	600	1,125	975	1,600	1,400	1,000	1,400	1,700
Profit/loss	(1,200)	(600)	(1,125)	(975)	(1,600)	(1,400)	(1,500)	(800)	(500)

	May	June	July	Aug.	Sept.	Oct.	Nov.	Dec.
Sales (units)	210	100	100	—	—	(300)	(300)	(100)
Production (units)	—	—	—	—	—	—	—	—
Revenue	$600	$420	$200	$200	$9,000	—	$(600)	$(600)
Expenses								
Manufacturing								
Supplies	—	—	—	—	—	—	—	—

(Continued)

Figure 14-10 Continued

	May	June	July	Aug.	Sept.	Oct.	Nov.	Dec.
Labor	—	—	—	—	—	—	—	—
Overhead	—	—	—	—	—	—	—	—
Promotional	1,500	200	—	—	—	—	—	—
Start-up	—	—	—	—	—	—	—	—
Other	50	50	50	50	50	$50	50	50
Total expenses	1,550	250	50	50	50	50	50	50
Profit/Loss	(950)	170	150	150	8,900	(50)	(650)	(650)
Cumulative profit/Loss	(10,650)	(10,480)	(10,330)	(10,180)	(1,280)	(1,330)	(1,980)	(2,630)

designed to help you create a workable transitional plan. For most new-product entrepreneurs, however, things don't always go smoothly.

PROBLEM-SOLVING TACTICS

New-product entrepreneurs typically face the serious problems of not enough money, not enough sales, and/or manufacturing costs that are too high. Frequently, the first two problems are tied together: An entrepreneur doesn't have enough money to promote his or her product and, consequently, sales are too low. Fortunately, a wide variety of tactics can be used to overcome these problems.

Find a Smaller Market

The rallying call of every financially pinched inventor seems to be: "I need some investors." The true cry should be: "I need a smaller market." The goal of the transitional period is to become established in *a part of* the market. Being established means that consumers have heard of your product and you have a fair number of sales outlets carrying it. Whether the market is a town with 75,000 people or a metro area with 2 million people, what matters is that you choose a market in which you can afford the promotion costs.

You are much better off away from the standard consumer market. Turn your product into a specialty consumer or industrial item; these markets have much lower promotional costs.

Jim McCoy created a great-tasting ice cream, which he marketed under the name McConnell's. Can you imagine a worse product for a new entrepreneur? Think of the packaging, distribution, and advertising expenses involved in reaching consumers. Because the product was difficult to market, Jim repositioned it as a premium ice cream for restaurants. He made the sales calls himself and was able to persuade 60 restaurants to start buying his product.

Enlist More Insiders to Help You

Insiders can take pressure off you in the transition period by placing a product in key stores, finding cooperative distributors, and generally endorsing the product. Their support can cut your promotional requirements because sales outlets may be willing to help you, even if you don't have a strong promotional program.

If you're having trouble getting enough help from insiders, increase your attendance at trade shows, association meetings, and chamber of commerce gatherings. One or two contacts isn't enough. More inside contacts will give you more opportunities for lining up investors.

Arrange Exclusive Agreements

Earlier in the book, I mentioned the value of an *exclusive,* a sales agreement in which you promise to sell a product through only one outlet. Most exclusive agreements are for one year, but they can be for periods of from six months to five years and may even be permanent. An exclusive is a powerful tool for both an entrepreneur and the customer. The entrepreneur receives the benefit of having a distributor or store that wants to promote a product. The benefit to a store or distributor is that it will be the only place where a product can be purchased. A chain of stores called the Museum Shops carries only museum replicas that no other stores stock. That strategy makes the Museum Shops special places to visit. People go out of their way to shop there. Think of the ads you've seen that end with "available at Macy's," or "available only at Macy's." Exclusivity is a strong sales tool if a product is unique and advertises well.

Most entrepreneurs hate exclusive agreements because they cut a product's sales potential. However, as you saw from the first budget of the fishing inventor, the main concern is to get a product established, and I know of no better way to do that than by signing an exclusive agreement with an important sales outlet.

The exclusive helps you in two ways:

1. You might be able to get by with a lower promotional budget because the sales outlet might promote the product.
2. When the outlet has an interest in promoting a product, your sales should rise because you'll receive better shelf space.

An exclusive is worth something to an outlet only if your product is recognized as being unique. Use all your market research findings when trying to sell an exclusive. A disadvantage of an exclusive is that the sales outlet will pressure you for a lower price. I recommend that you grin and bear it. Next year, when the exclusive is over, you can say: "This product was carried, and heavily advertised, by Sales Outlet X last year."

You can take an exclusive one step further by offering a contest or other promotion. For example, you could have a drawing for a free weekend, or dinner for two, or a $250 savings bond, or some other prize, available at only one store. This is an especially strong tactic when you want to place a large point-of-purchase display in an outlet.

Sell through Co-op Advertising Programs

When you see a full-page newspaper ad for a sporting goods store promoting Head Skis, for example, you are probably looking at a co-op advertising campaign. Half the cost of the ad is paid by the store, which is promoting a sale. The other half is paid by Head Skis, which receives favorable exposure in the paper. Co-op ads are also run on radio and television.

Co-op advertising offers an entrepreneur a lot of advantages. If you give a sales outlet a discount in the form of a co-op advertising program, you get a promotional benefit from a price reduction. For example, rather than giving a 15 percent discount on a hardware item, you could offer to pay for half of a newspaper ad.

The name of your product becomes associated with a big store. As XYZ Product Entrepreneurs, no one knows who you are. If you're advertised by a large retailer, your product gains tremendous credibility, which will help all your other promotional efforts. Co-op ads also give you leverage when you sell a product to other customers. Businesspeople, as a rule, don't like to be trendsetters; they like to jump on the bandwagon of a winning product. Once you have a few co-op ads to show, you'll find other outlets more receptive to a sales presentation.

The big disadvantage of co-op advertising is that ads are expensive, and you have to go along with the rates negotiated by the retailer. Always put a top-dollar limit on a co-op program. For example, you might agree to a 15 percent co-op advertising allowance, with the total not to exceed $500. Personally, I like co-op programs. I believe that they deliver a lot of exposure for their cost and offer entrepreneurs long-term sales benefits. Be sure to sign up for a co-op program if you get a chance to run one with a big sales outlet.

Offer Guaranteed Sales

Your offer will mean that you'll take back anything a store doesn't sell. This clause is very bad for entrepreneurs, but you will probably have a tough time getting around guaranteed sales. Most outlets receive those terms from even some large suppliers. This is one of the reasons for proving that a product can sell in the first sales period. You don't want to ship some large orders, only to end up taking the product back and issuing a refund.

Check with your insiders to see whether guaranteed sales are a requirement in a market. If they are, resign yourself to them, but always specify a date when you'll take unsold products back. For instance, the fishing product should be on the store shelves at least four months before it is taken back. If you have to take guaranteed sales, ask for prepaid orders. Small convenience stores, drugstores, and variety stores are accustomed to having to pay for small orders up front.

Guaranteed sales hurt when products are returned and you can't afford refunds. Put aside at least 10 percent of your sales volume to handle returns.

Ask for Deposits

Entrepreneurs should ask for deposits—or even full payment—a lot more often than they do. You aren't going to check a distributor's or store's credit rating when you get a $250 order. Instead, ask for a 50 percent deposit with the order. In that way, you won't lose money if the account doesn't pay. You can get deposits from large companies if you offer a corresponding discount. For example, you can offer a 5 percent discount with a 25 percent deposit and an 8 percent discount with a 50 percent deposit. Deposits can be an ideal negotiating tool if a large potential customer is pushing for a lower price. Offer a discount, but only if the company will give you at least a 25 percent deposit.

Deposits are common for nonconsumer products sold to companies. For example, Skyline Displays of Burnsville, Minnesota, sells a booth that companies can use at trade shows. The booth's benefit is that it can fold up into a little container and be carried to and from each show. Prices range from $1,500 to $3,000, depending on size. Skyline was started by a couple of partners in a garage. From the beginning, the company always insisted on a 50 percent deposit with every order. Today, after ten years of operations, Skyline has $40 million in sales and still demands a deposit.

Collecting money is an enormous problem for product entrepreneurs. Most businesses in the United States are short of cash. Most eventually pay their bills, but slowly. When a business is strapped for money, it first pays suppliers whose products or services it needs to keep operating. A convenience store will pay its soft drink suppliers, to keep stock of a product that's important to its customers. Because new-product entrepreneurs rarely have key items that businesses need to keep ordering, their invoices fall to the bottom of the pile. For this reason, I always prefer to sell through distributors. I may have to give up a percentage of profit, but the distributor will be a better bill collector than I am.

Allow Cash Discounts

Your discount might be 10 percent off for payment on delivery, or 10 percent off for cash with an order, or an 8 percent discount if an account is paid in 10 days. These are all forms of cash discounts. They will greatly speed up payment and remove some of the financial pressure on an entrepreneur.

Another way of collecting money right away is to factor your receivables. Commercial finance companies and some banks will buy receivables (invoices that show how much customers owe) for discounts ranging from 5 to 10 percent of the receivables' value. For example, if a large retailer owes you $10,000, the factoring organization might give you $9,200 for the receivable. It then becomes the organization's job to collect the $10,000.

Negotiate with Contract Manufacturers

Earlier in the book, I said that contract manufacturers have a lot to gain by working with product creators. They get increased production and profits and they have little risk. As the product's creator, you are in a favorable position to try and push more costs back on the contract manufacturer. Absorption of product liability costs, six-month payment terms, collection help, and outright loans are all possible if you can make a strong enough case that your product will succeed. You should have ample evidence of your product's potential from the first-period sales evaluation and the transitional plan. If your current contract manufacturer won't help you, look for another one that will.

At times, your manufacturing cost will end up being too high. For example, your costs might total $1.25 for a product that has a perceived value of only $2.00. Address this problem immediately, and don't proceed until your costs are back to an acceptable level. In my experience, manufacturing problems never go away; they only get worse.

Join Other Product Creators, or Sell through Another Manufacturer

I've mentioned both of these tactics before, but they're worth repeating because they illustrate the value of a broader product line. When you run a co-op ad with a retailer, the retailer wants its name spotlighted. It doesn't care whether you list one, two, or three products. By joining products into a line, you can cut your promotional costs in half. The same principle applies to the costs of sales calls, trade shows, and virtually any other promotional expense.

Joining forces with another entrepreneur or company makes it easier to have *workable* promotional programs. Most promotional programs are based on a percentage discount, such as a 10 percent discount on sales given as a straight discount or as a co-op advertising discount. A 10 percent discount on a $400 order is only $40—not a very exciting amount.

For the program to be effective, your 10 percent credit has to amount to something. If two or three entrepreneurs joined as a unit can raise the sales level to $2,000 to $3,000, the promotional money will look more attractive. Substantially more benefit can come from placing a product with a company that sells 10 to 15 other products. (See Chapter 7.)

This tactic can be used backward: You can become a distributor for other products. In that way, you can offer a broader product line, one product of which happens to be yours.

Brian H. once talked to me about marketing a fishing product that was primarily geared toward deep-sea fishing charter boats. The product didn't generate enough volume by itself to justify the promotional cost. I found another entrepreneur who had a product geared to the same market, and I might have been able to market the two products together if I could have worked out a favorable deal.

DREAMING POSSIBLE DREAMS

The first sales period proves that a product can sell. In the transitional period, you show that a product can become established in a small market. You are now ready to enter the next phase of a business: selling the product through a much larger part of the market.

Some entrepreneurs' ideas are one- or two-year phenomena. The slap bracelets that sold millions of units in the fall of 1990 weren't on the market in 1992. Entrepreneurs like to go for broke (one of the most appropriate phrases in the language) and plunge into national exposure in one short swoop. I don't agree with that philosophy, though it works for some people. I like to think that I'm selling a series of new products, not widget X. I'm not concerned if I can take the first product only so far in the market. I've built up contacts and I'm going to do a lot better with my next product.

At the beginning of the chapter, I mentioned Pepin Heights Sparkling Cider. Its first-year transitional plan was short and simple. The company ran a joint promotion program with a radio station, had a booth at some fairs attended by upper-income people, placed its product in about a dozen restaurants, and sold the product off the shelves of several delicatessens. It was not the most exciting plan, but it worked because it had limited, achievable goals. The plan began to establish name recognition in a small, targeted market, and it set up a distribution network that placed orders each and every month. By setting up the same type of simple, achievable goals, you can keep your sales volume growing.

15

CHECKLISTS FOR
A SMOOTH-RUNNING
COMPANY

Once you've established the transitional phase of your business, I recommend that you go through a series of checklists one last time before expanding sales. You will be an operating company at this point, and you'll have sales, accounting, marketing, manufacturing, advertising, and administration tasks to accomplish at this point. You are much better off preparing to handle these tasks before you start, rather than waiting to resolve them after you're in business.

The purpose of this chapter is to provide you a series of checklists to use to ensure you have most, and hopefully all, of the necessary large and small tasks completed before starting. Some of the items on the checklists may not be applicable to your business. Always check to be sure, as you'd hate to have your business shut down because you overlooked a minor detail. There are five checklists in this chapter:

1. Eight Factors That Determine Success
2. Financial Considerations
3. Sales and Marketing Support
4. Administrative Tasks
5. Manufacturing Coordination

FACTORS FOR SUCCESS

The first four points on Checklist 15-1, concerning product benefits, manufacturing, distribution, and industry insiders, are covered in the initial go/no-go decisions discussed in Chapters 6 through 10. Reviewing these points now is just a final check that you haven't lost sight of the basic functions of your business. You can't operate successfully without a strong business base.

The last four points all relate to momentum, which is crucial for success. People will be glad to jump on your bandwagon when your introduction looks like a major success. To generate that momentum, you need to have the groundwork laid to support continual expansion of your business.

FINDING ENOUGH CAPITAL

Bootstrapping refers to a great American tradition in which people with very little money fund their entire businesses with only the profits of their

Checklist 15-1   Eight Factors That Determine Success

	Completed	
	Yes	No
1. Have you defined a narrow, easy-to-reach target market?	___	___
2. Have you signed an operating manufacturing partner or a contract manufacturer?	___	___
3. Have you located a distribution network looking for your type of product?	___	___
4. Do you have an advisory group of experienced industry professionals?	___	___
5. Have you found enough money to support your introduction, and do you have access to additional funds if needed?	___	___
6. Have you presigned enough sales representation to support your sales goals?	___	___
7. Do potential customers immediately understand your benefit statement, and is it important to them?	___	___
8. Does your product package motivate potential buyers to pick up your product and look at it?	___	___

companies. They may borrow funds, but they don't sell any part of their companies to investors. While the image of a bootstrapping entrepreneur certainly is appealing, I usually don't recommend that you rely solely on the profits you generate for funding. If you do, your growth will be limited and you will have trouble generating market momentum.

I prefer to think of new-product introductions as a series of leveraging tactics. First, you leverage your knowledge of the customer by concentrating your product design on features that will motivate prospects to buy your product. Second, you leverage your selling efforts through the use of industry experts and by finding a distribution channel that will support your product. Third, you leverage your limited manufacturing expertise by combining with a manufacturing partner or by signing an agreement with a contract manufacturer. And finally, you leverage your money, by generating additional funding, primarily from friends, industry insiders, contract manufacturing partners, private investors, distributors, and other vendors.

Chapters 2 and 17 deal exclusively with financing. Chapter 2 covers financing a product's start-up phase and transition plan, and Chapter 17 deals with financing a company that is ready for its rapid-growth stage. These chapters explain how to raise the money you'll need to succeed.

The one point I'd like to add here is that, most of the time, entrepreneurs run out of money before they finish a phase of their introductions. For example, they may finish 80 percent of the start-up phase and then not have any more money. When this happens, you need to be able to go back to your original investors for money to finish the phase. They should be able to give you money quickly so you can keep your momentum. If you need outside investors, you may be looking at a delay of several months in order to find someone with money and then convince him or her to invest.

Brad, for example, raised $45,000 to take his project through the transitional sales period. But after 12 months he ran out of money. To new investors, Brad looked like a shaky investment. He had taken $45,000 and hadn't been able to complete a successful transition period. Original investors, on the other hand, will look at Brad's project in a completely different light. They'll be thinking, "I've invested $10,000 and Brad's made considerable progress. Now Brad needs $2,000 more from me or he will have to fold the project. I'd rather invest $2,000 and see how things work out than just lose the $10,000." Once investors are in a project, they will almost always keep investing when you need them to, as long as you continue to show progress in your introduction.

Getting more money from original investors is a tactic that will work only when you have investors with more money to invest. If your Aunt Millie invests her $20,000 life savings, she won't have more money to offer you. This is why you want to have four or five investors and why you want to ask them for only a small original investment.

You will be judged by investors and other businesspeople primarily on how well you handle money. Checklist 15-2 will help you look like a winner.

PRESIGNING SALES REPRESENTATION

You should have at least one or two sales representatives ready to begin selling for you immediately so your sales will start strong. The only prob-

Checklist 15-2   Financial Considerations

	Completed	
	Yes	No
1. Do you have enough money on hand to survive the transition phase of your business?	___	___
2. Do you have a monthly budget to follow?	___	___
3. Have you negotiated terms and lines of credit with your suppliers sufficient to support your sales goals?	___	___
Note: Explain to your vendors in advance the amount of credit you may need. Otherwise, you may not have enough money available to support your sales goals.		
4. Do your documents, including board minutes, clearly state the number of shares each shareholder owns? (The documents also need to support any stock you are receiving for the work you're doing without pay.)	___	___
5. Do you have a detailed list of any personal obligations you may have that are related to the business? This could include credit card debts, vehicle debt, or personal guarantees you've made for rent on phone services. Detail how these will be paid back if the company is to pay the debt. Make sure your investors know of these obligations before they invest.	___	___

lem is that most new-product entrepreneurs don't have any money to hire salespeople. The two most ideal situations for you are to find either manufacturers' representatives who will sell your product and to whom you can pay a commission or retired sales representatives who would be willing to work on a part-time basis. Once your sales efforts are producing results, you will be able to add more sales power.

Manufacturers' Representatives

Representatives generally don't want to handle small, one-line companies, because they just won't be able to make enough money from their products. Two ways to line up representatives in advance are to use them early, in your advisory group of insiders, and to have them involved as investors. Representatives involved in either of these two ways will be willing to help you set up an initial sales network.

If you can't get a representative involved in your business early, you can usually find one or two by showing that your idea has big potential and by offering one of them a chance to come on board as a sales manager once the business takes off.

You can get the names of representatives in your area by attending trade shows (see Chapter 4) and by requesting literature from trade magazines and then talking to the representatives whose names come with the literature. Once you have the names of some representatives, pick out five or six who are top salespeople and approach them with the following points:

- You are a new company that needs sales agents.
- You currently plan on getting a few investors for a regional sales effort and then, in a year or two, you plan a large stock sale to achieve national distribution.
- You will be hiring a national sales manager from your sales agent network, and whoever wins the job will have an opportunity to have stock options in a fast-growing firm.

The best representatives for you to find are those who have just a few products in their lines. They will be looking for more products and might be interested in having a chance to jump on board a company, earlier in its life, that might go on to a be a large successful operation.

Part-Time Sales Representatives

You may be able to locate a retired sales representative who will be willing to work part-time for a commission. Typically a retired salesperson will have strong relationships with 10 to 15 stores where they can place your product. The retired sales representative probably won't call on any extra stores, but a product can start to generate momentum just by being placed in five to ten stores.

Your insider group may know of retired salespeople who might work with you. Otherwise, you can check association membership lists for retired salespeople or simply ask retailers if they know of any. You should be able to find sales representatives and/or part-time salespeople if you start looking for them at the onset of your project and if you start net-working at trade shows and association meetings.

THE BENEFIT MUST BE CLEAR

Inventors and, in fact, most small business people know their products so well, including all of their features and benefits, that they lose their ability to explain their ideas simply. Here is an explanation from an inventor of the Dish-Net:

> The Dish-Net is made of temperature-resistant netting and plastic that allows it to be used in any dishwasher, no matter how hot the water is. The stretch factor of the netting allows it to go in any-size dishwasher, and the netting will hold its shape even after 500 washings. The product just slips over the end of the dishwasher rack and holds in place plastic cups and small plastic items so they don't turn over or fall down into the hot-water heating element.

When you give that much information, people will lose sight of your product's true benefit, which is, in this example, that the product holds plastic cups and utensils in place in a dishwasher. This product's name, the Dish-Net, also doesn't reflect the product's purpose well. The end result is that prospects don't understand the product when they glance at it on a supermarket shelf.

People have to be able to look at your product and know in five seconds what it does and what its benefit is. Chapter 7 covers the topic of whether consumers will buy. You should double-check the go/no-go decisions in that chapter. But I also like to take four products—three products selling now and the product being evaluated—and then show the products to eight to ten people for only ten seconds. Then I ask them to list all of the products they can remember. I believe the package and name need to be reworked unless 80 percent or more of the people can remember my new product.

Your success depends on sales, and your sales require support. Figure 15-3 will help you ensure that your sales are launched with strong support.

Checklist 15-3   Sales and Marketing Support

	Completed	
	Yes	No
1. Do you have easy-to-understand price sheets ready?	⎯⎯	⎯⎯
2. Do you have a promotional flyer for mailings?	⎯⎯	⎯⎯
3. Do you have samples for salespeople?	⎯⎯	⎯⎯
4. Have you prepared a targeted list of customers that you will approach in the first 60 days?	⎯⎯	⎯⎯
5. Do you have a point-of-purchase display or other display materials?	⎯⎯	⎯⎯
6. Have you decided if you'll put units out on consignment or offer guaranteed sales?	⎯⎯	⎯⎯
7. Have you set your delivery terms—for example, one-week delivery?	⎯⎯	⎯⎯
8. Have you developed a sales procedure and sales script for your representatives to follow initially?	⎯⎯	⎯⎯
9. Do you have a testimonial list of satisfied users?	⎯⎯	⎯⎯

ARE YOU MOTIVATING BUYERS?

People have to pick up your product and look at it before they buy it. If you have an industrial product, prospects must think your idea is worth investigating. Your package (or, with industrial products, your brochure) offers a benefit to prospects. If your benefit offer is compelling, people will pick up the package or the product brochure and read more.

If you have a consumer product, you can take it to a flea market with three or four other products that are already on the market. Then just count how many people pick up and look at each package. You can even include in this experiment two or three of your own packaging ideas. You will be surprised at the different responses you'll get from different packages.

ADMINISTRATIVE CONCERNS

Entrepreneurs by their nature are not detail oriented. Checklist 15-4 covers some commonly overlooked details to which you need to attend in order to meet your new corporate responsibilities. Most of the points in Checklist 15-4 are self-explanatory, except for number 7, concerning board

Checklist 15-4   Administrative Tasks

	Completed	
	Yes	No
1. Have you created a legal structure for your firm and registered its operation with your state?	——	——
2. Do you have all the necessary licenses and permits? Check with your local city hall.	——	——
3. Do you have the liability and accident insurance you need?	——	——
4. Have you completed manufacturing, sales, and marketing plans for the next year?	——	——
5. Have you set up a bookkeeping system to record sales, income, expenses, accounts payable, and accounts receivable?	——	——
6. Have you determined how to handle payroll records, tax reports, and tax payments?	——	——
7. Have you started your corporation properly? Do you hold periodic meetings with your board of directors or officers and take minutes of these meetings?	——	——
8. Do you know what financial reports you'll need to prepare for your investors?	——	——
9. Do you have a dedicated business phone line and the capability to accept faxes?	——	——
10. Do you have all the necessary forms to hire new employees, and do you have a form explaining personnel policies for employees?	——	——

meetings. Once you incorporate (which you should do with investors), you need to hold board meetings, which may be attended by yourself and the company's other officers to approve significant actions such as stock sales. Check with an attorney or the small business development center in your area for assistance. Most books on incorporating a business will outline the general rules for company meetings, and your state's secretary of commerce should be able to provide you with state regulations.

MANUFACTURING CONSIDERATIONS

New-product entrepreneurs typically run into two big problems when they start marketing a new product. The first is that they don't figure out their costs accurately. They leave out items such as scrap and incoming freight, forget to account for all of their manufacturing overhead, or over-estimate the amount of production one worker can do. I highly recom-mend that you have all of your costs reviewed by an accountant. Be sure the accountant you choose works for other manufacturing companies and is familiar with cost accounting procedures. Without this help, your pric-ing could be off up to 20 to 30 percent.

The second problem entrepreneurs have is that they don't set up procedures to handle quality problems. Inevitably, at some point, parts from various vendors won't work together as designed. Then someone has to determine what happened and decide who is responsible. You can avert this problem somewhat by establishing firm specifications and qual-ity control procedures for each component. But problems can still arise,

Checklist 15-5 Manufacturing Coordination

	Completed Yes	No
1. Have you established performance requirements and detailed specifications for the product and all its components?	——	——
2. Do you have firm commitments on price and availability of raw materials, processing hardware, and required components?	——	——
3. Do you have a contract with a manufacturer to produce your product or is your own facility fully operational?	——	——
4. Have you confirmed your manufacturing procedure with a pilot-plant run?	——	——
5. Have you finalized manufacturing costs based on an actual production run?	——	——
6. Have you had your production costs verified by an accounting firm?	——	——
7. Have you arranged for sufficient space for both raw-material and finished-goods inventory?	——	——
8. Have you included your shipping boxes in both your manufacturing costs and procedures?	——	——
9. Do you have a quality control inspection process in place?	——	——
10. Have you clarified with your vendors who is responsible for handling quality problems?	——	——

even when every component is within specifications. Unless you have an extensive manufacturing background, your contract manufacturer should be responsible for final product quality. Either the contract you sign or your purchase order should state that the manufacturer is responsible for delivering a quality final product. The manufacturer should also be responsible for inspection and approval of incoming component parts.

Sales momentum can be stopped cold by manufacturing delays. Checklist 15-5 outlines the points you must cover to be sure you can ship products on schedule.

16

THE BUSINESS PLAN: TURNING INTO AN OPERATING COMPANY

Some readers may be surprised that discussion of the business plan doesn't appear until Chapter 16. I know that many other books emphasize that preparing a business plan is the *first* thing to do when starting a business. I don't think a new-product entrepreneur can say that he or she is ready to start a business until after the transitional period.

A business plan has two purposes: to raise money and to prepare an operating plan. These are the objectives of the transitional plan. The difference is that a transitional plan is for a small market, and it is geared only to raise enough money to show that a product can penetrate a small market. A typical transitional plan won't show much, if any, profit. A business plan is designed to expand sales to a larger market in which a product's sales will increase to a level at which they generate profits.

A business plan is usually not a one-time event. You'll normally do one right after the transitional period, when you're ready to expand to a larger market. But you might need to expand in three or four stages before your company is penetrating the entire market. As you approach each expansion, do a revised business plan.

A business plan is a well-known action item. A transitional plan is a new concept that I firmly believe in. Most product entrepreneurs face a tremendous leap from the development stage (making a prototype and conducting some research) to the business plan stage (setting up a full-fledged operating company). Only businesspeople with proven records of success can risk that leap. Most new-product entrepreneurs approach the end of the development stage and then watch their efforts die because they don't have the momentum needed to carry them across to the business plan stage.

The small entrepreneurs that I've seen succeed have invariably found a middle ground, a stage between development and the business plan, where they have proven that their product can support a profitable company. Most of these people didn't necessarily plan a transition period; they fell into it because they were short on money, or because of the nature of their products, or because it was a toehold when they were scrambling for places to sell their products.

There are more similarities than differences between a transitional plan and a business plan. I prefer to separate them because of their different goals and the different amounts of money entrepreneurs are trying to raise in each stage.

Let me mention again that the purpose of this book is to help you establish a product in a market. Many other books offer specific information about business plans and raising money. This chapter's overview of the business plan will help you to understand its importance and its place in a product's introduction cycle. When you're ready to write your own business plan, you may want to look for a book that's devoted entirely to the subject.

BUSINESS PLAN MYTHS

Recently, more than ten university classes on the subject of business plans were offered during one term in the Twin Cities area. Bookstores routinely carry three or four (and sometimes many more) books on how to write an effective business plan. Business magazines run articles on business plans at least every few issues. As a result, most entrepreneurs have begun to regard the business plan as *THE Document* that determines whether a business will succeed or fail.

Business plans are now elevated to a status that they definitely don't deserve. They're important, but they have become overrated. The key to attracting investors is not how good the plan is, but rather how good the company behind the plan is.

Myth 1: Business Plans Are All-Important

A business plan is a reflection of how the plan's author believes a company is operating now and will grow in the future. That's all the plan is and says. Most investors, if they like what a plan has to say about a product, will still want a thorough evaluation of the product.

For investors, an evaluation is essential. A business plan provides some operating details, but it doesn't show any underlying weaknesses that a business might have. For example, a business plan might list product costs that are correctly broken out as raw material costs, production costs, packaging costs, and so on. On the surface, the company may seem to have costs under control. But the product costs may not be reliable at all. An important supplier may not be able to meet a surge in demand without raising prices. A contract manufacturer might have quoted a low price to receive initial orders; after one year, its own plan may call for raising prices 15 to 25 percent. The product cost might include a 5 percent scrap rate for both product returns and manufacturing defects; the actual scrap rate may be 15 percent.

Investors are always worried about unseen problems. Until a company is actually running, an investor can't be sure of how many unexpected problems the company will encounter. I think it's imperative to establish a business's basic functions before doing a business plan. It's not time yet to hire people for each projected position. You may still be doing most of the work yourself, but you should be producing and selling products.

Most advice regarding business plans does not recommend that you have ongoing operations before writing a plan. My advice is different because product creators have a much more difficult time raising money than do other entrepreneurs. There are three reasons for the resistance they encounter:

1. Product creators do not have successful companies to use as comparisons. If I'm going to open up a new restaurant in Omaha and there is a successful one just like it in St. Louis, I should have a good chance of finding financing. Investors would have confidence in my venture because someone else has already proven that such a business can work. Product entrepreneurs are introducing products that have never been on the market before.
2. Product creators tend to be short on management experience; they are usually people who think about new ideas and take time to tinker around with them. This type of person is rarely found among business managers. In contrast, most other entrepreneurs have track records of management success.
3. Product entrepreneurs have a high failure rate. Investors and bankers, who know that, are leery of any investments in new manufacturing ventures.

The all-important element is to make sure the basic operations of a company are thought out, documented, and proven.

Myth 2: Every Business Always Needs a Business Plan

Some product entrepreneurs establish a product in a small niche market during the transitional sales period. Then, either because they can't find financing or because they're happy with their small sales volume, they increase their sales slowly every year.

Earlier, I mentioned Scott Turner, the inventor of specialized semiconductor inspection equipment. Over seven years, Scott built his business up to annual sales of $1 million. He was in a small niche market, but he could have expanded and gone after other markets. He decided that his small business, with only 12 employees, was just right for him. He never borrowed any money, and he never had a business plan until he decided, after 14 years, to buy his own building.

What would have happened to Scott if he had decided to expand into a broader market? Immediately, he would have faced increasing competition. He wouldn't have been able to adapt his product readily to the specific needs of his niche market. He would have had to cope with intricate financial problems, an increasing number of employees, and a loss of control of his business. To Scott, it wasn't a pretty picture. On the downside, Scott's earning power was limited in the smaller market.

Some experts recommend writing a business plan because it offers an operating budget. I certainly agree that you need a budget. But, as I showed in the discussion of the transitional plan (Chapter 14), a budget can be generated from sales, marketing, and production plans, and these documents are much easier to prepare than a business plan.

Myth 3: A Business Plan Guarantees That You'll Find Financing

---

I don't want to belabor this point; I've covered it earlier. Instead, let me update you on Jamie Leach and her husband, a couple that seemingly did everything right, but still couldn't get financing. Their product, the Wiggle Wrap, is a cloth-and-Velcro restraint that keeps babies in high chairs. Jamie and her husband sold 8 percent of their company to private investors to raise money during their initial and transitional sales periods. They had some start-up sales success and eventually increased sales to $1,000 a month, at which point they needed more financing. Unable to obtain any money from conven-

tional sources, they had to factor their receivables. The Leaches kept increasing sales, using factoring as their financing tool, until sales hit $20,000 to $25,000 per month. At this point, they were rejected again for conventional financing because they didn't have any equipment or real estate to pledge as collateral.

IMPORTANT POINTS

Business plans are typically 10 to 30 pages long; some are even longer. You can increase your chances of receiving a favorable response to a plan if you can (truthfully) stress these facts:

- All your sales efforts to date have been for market research.
- Your current equity position is favorable.
- Your product has already had some limited market penetration.
- You need a specific amount of money.

Market Research

"Last year, Product X was successfully introduced with sales in excess of $45,000. This year, if this plan is implemented, sales should exceed $2 million." How does that sound to you? $45,000 to $2 million in one year! That's almost impossible.

"Last year, I completed the final phase of market research on Product X, successfully selling $45,000 of the product in a limited area. Based on those market research sales, Product X should sell $2 million with a full-scale marketing effort in Illinois, Wisconsin, and Iowa." That projection sounds a lot more believable; the product creator was careful to perform extensive market research. Still, he or she must be an entrepreneurial genius to be able to sell $45,000 during a market test.

Be careful when you're calculating your sales projection. If you sold $45,000 with earlier sales efforts, what makes you think you can increase sales to $2 million? No matter how much explanation you give, that growth seems out of line. When you say you've done market research, people will assume that you had a limited advertising and promotion budget. They'll be more receptive to your notion that a "real" marketing program will increase sales tremendously.

I don't think you're misrepresenting your business by calling the transitional period a market research phase. You are establishing, in a test market, that a product will sell through a distribution network. That qualifies as market research by almost anyone's definition.

Equity: How Much Money Do You Have Now?

The Leaches had trouble raising money because they didn't have any *collateral* (another term for money). The Leaches were out of cash. As I discussed in Chapter 2, almost no one will lend money to someone who is broke.

At least 80 percent of all product entrepreneurs don't try to raise money until they've spent all of their own. How much money an entrepreneur is investing is one of the first queries an investor will have. If you have reserved cash, be sure to point that out. Include a funding history in your business plan. Show how you've spent your money to date and how much money you have available for future expansion.

Figure 16-1 shows the funding history for a hardware product. Note that the entrepreneur lists funds available from personal assets ("from inventor"). These funds could include cash from a home equity line of credit, credit cards, and personal savings. (You don't have to indicate that your available funds are primarily from credit sources. All that is important is the amount that you're personally responsible for repaying.)

Compare that funding history with a report in which an entrepreneur tells how he and two investors have spent $100,000 on their product and are now looking for additional capital to market the product. To investors, the first entrepreneur has been prudent, managed the product well, and controlled expenditures—and, most important, the entrepreneur still has money to invest in the product. Those same investors will sense that the second entrepreneur has simply run out of money and is now looking for someone who can bail out the project.

Don't put the funding history in the plan itself, as it is more detail than investors want to see. Instead, put it into the appendix, where people seriously investigating your business opportunity can find it.

Strong Operating Position

Three points are crucial in this area: management, cost control, and sales reliability.

Management

To an investor, you're not a strong manager until you've taken a product successfully onto the market. Because most new entrepreneurs haven't done that, they have to lean for support on their insiders. Your management team will look strongest if some insiders are investors, mem-

Figure 16-1   Funding History: Hardware Widgets

Original funds invested by inventor: $5,000

	Budget	Actual Costs	Revenue	Net Cost	Funds Left
Product's preliminary stages: prototypes, market research, initial sales period, etc.	$4,500	$3,800	$600	$3,200	$1,800
Funding prior to transitional sales period:					
From inventor $10,000					
From inside investor 5,000					
Total $15,000					
Transitional period: initial penetration of Rochester, MN market (or market test in Rochester, MN)	$6,000	$19,200	$10,000	$9,200	$7,600*
Funding for market expansion throughout Minnesota and Wisconsin:					
From inventor $10,000					
From original investor 5,000					
From new investor 15,000					
Total $27,500					
Total funding required to expand throughout Minnesota and Wisconsin, including manufacturing, marketing, and cash flow requirements			$60,000		
Funding to be provided by inventor and investors			$27,500		
Additional financing required			32,500		
Total			$60,000		

*$7,600 cash reserve to continue to be used for operating cash.

bers of the board of directors, or members of an advisory council. An advisory council might meet once every three months to offer input regarding the activities of the business.

Cost Control

This element is crucial to any company's success. All types of hidden expenses seem to rise up and swallow profits. Installation of phone lines, sales training expenses, unemployment insurance, property and equipment maintenance, incoming freight charges, and office supplies are all potential sources of totally unexpected charges. The best way to show that you have a good handle on costs is to be in operation for a year or so, even if you've spent the time on market testing. By actually operating, you'll know what the miscellaneous charges are because you'll be paying them.

Sales Reliability

Will you really sell the units listed in a plan? I've prepared dozens of sales forecasts for new products, and I can tell you from hard experience that sales are never easy, no matter how wonderful the product is. Potential entrepreneurs are taking wild guesses when they estimate sales for a product that's never been sold. After completing your transitional sales period, you will have *actual sales* to base your forecast on. Your investors can have a certain degree of confidence that you'll reach your budgeted sales levels.

How Much Money Is Needed

You must state why you need the money and how much the investor is going to obtain for his or her contribution. For their Wiggle Wrap product, the Leaches might need $50,000 for operating cash so that they can stop selling their receivables. Investors might receive 10 percent ownership of a company in exchange for financing the additional growth that will improve operating margins.

Telling people how much money you need and why you need it may seem like a simple task, but you'll find it's surprisingly easy to write a 30-page document that never states plainly what you're looking for.

THE BUSINESS PLAN FORMAT

Business plans can vary in format, to represent a particular product or situation. Make any changes that are needed to stress the points listed in the previous section. At a minimum, your business plan should have the following sections:

1. Executive summary
2. Product and market information
3. Activities to date
4. Strengths and weaknesses
5. Company operations
6. Management team
7. Funding requirements

8. Business pro forma
9. Action time line
10. Formal offer

Executive Summary

Keep this section to no more than two to three pages that tell:

- What you're doing (you're introducing product X)
- What your sales proposition is (why people will buy your product)
- Why you feel your product will be successful (you sold $X,000 of product during your initial market test)
- How much money you need ($25,000)
- Why you need the money (to expand into a larger market)
- What your expected sales are for both the first and second expansions (you expect initial sales of $1 million to grow to $10 million in the second expansion period)

A short executive summary for my tire-cutter venture (see Chapter 1) might have read as follows:

ETC Corporation has introduced a tire-cutting device that separates a tire's treads and sidewalls. The result is that old tires are easier to store and ship and a tire's high-quality tread can be recycled. Twenty-five units were sold at $99 each through a tire equipment distributor, during an initial market test. ETC Corporation currently needs an additional $30,000 to support sales in eight midwestern states. Based on initial market tests, sales in the eight-state area should be $85,000 per year. Once the product is sold nationally, sales are expected to reach $400,000 per year.

Product Information

You can use the same information and format that you used for the first six points in your transitional plan (see Chapter 15). As a quick review, those six points are product description, targeted customers, targeted geographic area, where targeted customers buy, market potential, and competition.

Activities to Date

Include in this section a brief review of your accomplishments, a sales and profit summary, an explanation of your distribution strategy, and a summary of how you're currently manufacturing the product.

Entrepreneurs sometimes have long delays in their product introduction efforts. These delays are frowned on by investors and bankers, who prefer to see continuous progress. If you've kept up your momentum, include a timetable that shows how your product is building on its past success. If you have had long delays, either don't mention them or, if they eventually had a positive effect, explain why they occurred.

Strengths and Weaknesses

You'll be covering the product's strong and weak points in the product information section. In this section, describe strengths such as a favorable attitude across the distribution network or an advantageous manufacturing arrangement; weaknesses might include difficulty in locating good salespeople or the business's requirement for strong seasonal promotions.

Every business has obstacles to overcome, many of which have nothing to do with whether a product has merit. The lottery pen I discussed earlier had several problems. It had to be sold at lottery sale locations (bars, convenience stores, hotels, legion halls, and a variety of other installations). The market was scattered and I couldn't find any distributors or rack jobbers that sold to the entire market. Another problem was that retailers needed to see the point-of-purchase display before they would buy pens. There was no easy way to set up a sales force for a short, one-time promotion. My solution was to concentrate on convenience stores, where I reached about 20 percent of the market.

Don't feel bad if you have problems; everybody has them. What's important is to show that you've figured out how to solve them. Your company's operations should be designed at least partially around your product's strengths and weaknesses.

Company Operations

Don't make this section longer than one or two pages. Review the following areas: sales strategy, distribution network, promotional plans, manufacturing plans, and administration plans. I've given a considerable amount of space throughout the book to the first four points. Like most entrepreneurs, I tend to overlook administration plans. Billing, collecting, taking orders, paying bills, handling legal affairs, and keeping the books are tasks that take a tremendous amount of time and effort and are a big part of a company's success. They may require one or two clerical people as well as professional legal and accounting consultation.

Management Team

Management is a part of a company's operations, but potential investors consider it important enough to deserve a separate section. Earlier in the book, I talked about how to make a favorable impression with a management team. Management and money are probably the only true go/no-go decisions that an investor or lender makes. If the management isn't sound, no one will invest. Sound management will overcome a host of problems.

Funding Requirements

Why do you need money, how much do you need, and where will it come from? Give details; don't announce that it's needed to "penetrate a target market." Instead, develop a list of major expenses such as:

1. Promotional programs $15,000
   - 100 TV ads
   - Point-of-purchase displays
   - Attendance at three major trade shows
2. Manufacturing expenses   35,000
   - Inventory to support sales
   - Packaging equipment
   - Two pieces of machining equipment
3. General and administrative   20,000
   - Office supplies
   - Rent deposit
   - Computer and other office equipment
   - Professional services (lawyer and accountant fees)
4. Operating cash   20,000
            Total $90,000

To explain where the necessary money will come from, the funding history (see Figure 16-1) is an excellent tool that can be adapted to show how much money you plan on investing and how much money you need from outside sources.

Business Pro Forma

This section is really your budget for the next 12 to 18 months. The pro forma should contain, at a minimum, the entries shown in Figure 16-2.

Figure 16-2   Business Pro Forma

	Jan.	Feb.	Mar.	Apr.	May
Sales					
Cost of goods sold					
Gross profit					
Marketing expenses					
Administrative expenses					
Other expenses					
Total expenses					
Operating profit					

To demonstrate the reliability of your sales forecast, include a sales chart similar to the one in the transitional plan (Chapter 14). You should also include a cash flow chart. I've created a model, shown in Figure 16-3.

Action Time Line

Investors look for two time lines: a tight one for the action steps in your initial market and a very loose one for expanding into the entire market. The time lines for initial operations don't have to be as specific as the transitional period's time lines, but they should list major advertising, sales, and manufacturing efforts. Your time line for further expansion can be stated as a number of years or a specific future date, such as 1999. You

Figure 16-3   Cash Flow Chart

	Jan.	Feb.	Mar.	Apr.	May
Starting cash					
Revenue					
Materials and labor					
Marketing expenses					
Major purchases					
Other expenses					
Total spending					
Cash flow					
Ending cash					

don't have to be precise, because you can't know how market conditions might change.

Besides your targeted time for your next expansion, investors will also want to know how much additional investment will be needed. You won't be able to give a precise estimate, but you should provide a ballpark figure. For example, you might state that your current expansion, which will raise annual sales to $1 million in the Upper Midwest, will require an investment of $200,000. In three years, when you will expand again to sell throughout the entire United States, you will require an additional $1 million investment. Provide a backup chart that itemizes what the additional money will be used for. For instance, to sell to the entire market, you might need to hire a sales manager and four new salespeople, run a national ad campaign, and increase operating cash by $250,000.

Formal Offer

What are you offering potential investors? This is a very difficult area for most entrepreneurs. They believe their products are *worth* millions because of their sales potential; however, they might *have* ongoing sales of less than $50,000 per year and fixed assets of less than $5,000. That's why I favor starting off with the formula given in Chapter 9: A new, growing business is worth about twice its projected sales volume for the next year.

The funding chart (page 285) details how much money you need and how much money you need from investors. The next step is to briefly state your offer. If your company expects to have $50,000 in sales next year, then you might offer an investor a 10 percent share of the company in return for a $10,000 investment. If you want to borrow money from a bank, ask for a loan for a specific period of time—for example, a $10,000 loan for three years.

FINANCING

A review of potential financing sources is covered in Chapters 2 and 17. Offered here is a quick review of the three-step approach most product creators take to obtain funds for their sales expansions.

First, they contribute, from their own resources, about 10 to 25 percent of the money they need to expand. In Chapter 2, I warned that you need money to raise money. Perhaps money projects an image of success, or shows people that an entrepreneur is a prudent money manager, or assures investors and lenders that, if they lose money, then the entrepreneur will lose money, too. The fact is that you need to put up some of your own cash. Plan on having money available from personal assets or from credit cards or other loans.

The second financing step is to raise from investors another 15 to 35 percent of the money needed for expansion. Potential investors include family members, friends, insiders or salespeople in your chosen market, community leaders anxious to help a new business, suppliers, and your contract manufacturer.

Another way to find an investor is to take on a working partner. Many product creators ask where they'll ever find working partners. Retired or laid-off managers can be ideal working partners. Not only can they provide money, but they also may have a great deal of experience in running a company. Many of these managers who are having a hard time finding jobs are searching for opportunities to join up-and-coming companies. Advertise for potential working partners in the Sunday paper under Business Opportunities. State that a new manufacturing company, with a successful product (mention its sales potential), is looking for a working partner. Add that you prefer a partner with experience in, for example, marketing hardware products. I've received five to ten qualified responses per ad when I've run ads similar to this one:

> New manufacturing company looking for working partner. Dental product has completed successful market test and is ready for sales expansion. Need individual with sales/marketing experience to help product reach its $1 million potential.

After you've lined up funding for 25 to 50 percent of your financial requirements, the last step is to apply to a bank, commercial finance company, or government agency for a loan. You should be able to borrow the money if you have a strong business plan and if investors have purchased a share of your company.

Before you even start your business plan, get copies of loan applications used by banks, commercial finance companies, and government agencies. You'll be able to tell how much financial information needs to be included in your business plan. Banks and government agencies almost always have information packages for business loans.

You can learn which banks are making small business loans by calling the chamber of commerce or individual banks. Commercial finance companies are listed in the Yellow Pages under either their own headings or the heading for factoring companies. Trade shows for small businesses and ads in local business papers are other information sources. For information on government loans, contact the nearest Small Business Administration office or your state's small business assistance agency.

17

FINANCING THE GROWING BUSINESS

Raising money for a new business is almost a full-time task. Most presidents of rapidly growing companies spend over 50 percent of their time raising money. Most small entrepreneurs are unsuccessful raising money, and their companies fold or just barely keep operating. I am amused by most articles I read about financing, because they make it sound as if raising money is as easy as going to a bank to apply for a credit card. Raising money for your company is hard work, and it can be completed only with careful planning.

There are six critical steps to follow when seeking financing:

1. Understand the available financing options.
2. Know which options are available to your type of product.
3. Determine which options to pursue at various phases of your company's growth.
4. Make yourself known to financing sources well in advance of needing money.
5. Prepare your business for financing.
6. Approach multiple sources of financing.

I don't mean to imply that there is just one tried-and-true method for raising money. That's definitely not the case. Each successful entrepreneur has a slightly—and, in some cases, dramatically—different financing story. The six steps do represent the basic strategy that will give you your best chance to raise money.

STEP 1: UNDERSTAND THE FINANCING OPTIONS

There are many ways to finance a business, each one with its own benefits and drawbacks. Some of the more glamorous methods, such as using venture capital, apply to few companies. Other methods, such as royalty financing or joint-venture financing from infomercial producers, are new and relatively unknown. Some traditional sources of money, such as banks, are offering far less money than entrepreneurs need, while other sources of money—such as community-based lending, commercial finance companies that buy receivables, and "angel" financing—are playing increasingly important roles.

I've arranged the most common forms of financing *alphabetically,* not in order of best to worst. The best place to find more detailed information about any single method of financing is your local Small Business Administration (SBA) office or small business development center. The SBA will have offices in the largest city in your state and the people there can direct you to the office closest to your home. Your local chamber of commerce can also tell you where any local business assistance offices are.

Bank Financing

Banks do give out loans, but they typically aren't a good source for new companies. First, they want you to be able to collateralize the loan, which means you have to have assets, personal and business, that the bank can claim if you can't make payments. Banks also require restrictive covenants on loans, which are terms and conditions that you have to meet in order to meet the terms of the loan agreement. Restrictive covenants can dictate how much cash you need to keep, what your ratio of current assets to current liabilities must be, and even how high your inventory levels must stay. These are very tough terms for a product entrepreneur to follow without severely restricting his or her business's growth.

The four main types of loans that banks offer are:

- *Installment loans,* on which the business makes monthly payments over a certain number of years
- *Term loans,* with which the entire loan is paid off after a predetermined term (usually one, two, or five years)
- *Asset-based loans,* which might be for inventory or equipment
- *Revolving lines of credit,* which business can draw upon when cash is low and then pay off when cash flow is high

Bridge Financing

When companies are raising money, either through private or public offerings, they are often short of money and will borrow to bridge the time period until they receive financing. Companies in good financial positions can borrow bridge financing from banks; others may borrow from their brokerage houses that are handling the placement or offering. Companies may also borrow from private sources.

When you sell stock, you need to obey state and federal regulations, and you have to offer the same stock price to everyone. Big investors, on the other hand, like to get special deals for their investments. One way to get around this problem is to offer early investors a chance to take part of the bridge loan. Very young companies with little sales history may also offer warrants to people giving bridge financing. The warrant will allow the investor to buy stock anytime within three years at the price of the offering. The final deal will be a bridge loan, typically at 8 to 12 percent interest with one share of warrants for every dollar of bridge loan. If an investor lends the company $50,000 and the company raises the money it's seeking, the investor will get the bridge loan back and still have warrants for 50,000 shares.

Brokers

There are financial brokers in the market that can help you get money. Some of these are stock brokerage houses and others are independent businesspeople. Writing about brokers always scares me because, although most are honest, so many are dishonest and offer no real value to new companies. Product entrepreneurs are vulnerable to fraud because they are desperate to raise money. Entrepreneurs want to believe that someone will raise money for them. And they have five to ten thousand dollars to pay someone to raise hundreds of thousands of dollars. Far too often, the people who promise easy money really mean easy money for themselves. Before proceeding, be sure to check references closely and find out just who the broker has helped recently. Reputable brokers will also be very wary about doing business with you. They should check you out for several weeks before deciding to proceed with a stock offering.

Community-Based Lending

As people have moved out of rural towns and into cities, states, rural counties, and rural cities have started economic development agencies to lure jobs back. This funding may be in the form of loans from local banks, low- or no-interest loans from the city or county, tax-increment financing (an advance on the property taxes you'll pay in the future), and even outright grants. What the community wants in return is jobs or job possibilities.

This funding source will take on projects turned down by other lending sources. The best way for a new entrepreneur to utilize this is in conjunction with a manufacturer already in the area. For example, if you have an arrangement with a contract or joint-venture manufacturer in a rural area, the two of you can ask for funding for the new equipment you need to produce your product. You have a good chance of picking up funding if your project will add to the number of jobs in the community.

Distribution-Channel Financing

You can receive up-front money for signing a distribution agreement with a larger company. You might sign an exclusive agreement with a distributor or another manufacturer, you could assign rights to your product or your technology for a certain industry to another company, or you might negotiate an exclusive agreement for a certain territory. Sometimes you can arrange for a flat up-front fee, and other times you can arrange for an up-front fee that you'll pay back by offering the company a discount (say 10 percent) for one year. The advantage of distribution-channel financing is that it is really not financing—it's revenue. You don't have to pay it back, and you don't have to give away equity.

This is a powerful option that is used far too infrequently by product entrepreneurs. I personally like this option because it helps keep entrepreneurs focused on activities that will make them money. A typical example of how this works is when an entrepreneur is talking to a large distributor who states, "I really like your idea, but I think it needs a few changes." Most entrepreneurs run off to make the product changes and then reapproach the distributor, which may or may not result in a sale.

A better option is to respond, "Thanks for your input. Maybe we could take your idea and make it pay off for both our companies. For a small advance, I could make those changes for you, and, in return, offer you an exclusive agreement in your territory for two years. Is that something you'd like to pursue?" Some distributors aren't seriously interested in your product and they'll say no. Other distributors, who like your product, may say yes. You get two benefits from this approach: first, you weed out weak prospects for selling your product and, second, you may be able to collect an advance that could help finance your company.

Another way to use this strategy is when you talk to a company in another industry. If that company thinks your product could be adapted for its industry, you can say, "That's great. We could work in several ways to get the product on the market. We could set up a codevelopment project to produce models and prototypes so we can see if the idea is feasible. I can provide the expertise and supervision, but you would need to fund the project. A second option would be that your people could detail exactly what product you want, and I'll build it for you. Once I get the drawings, I'll be able to give you a quote. A final option is that you could just license my idea for your industry." Again, you'll identify who is interested in your idea and who is just a curiosity seeker.

A third benefit of this type of fund-raising is that it helps you attract other investors. You add a tremendous amount of credibility to the potential success of your product idea when you can say that company X has invested $40,000 to codevelop your product idea for another market.

Initial Public Offerings (IPOs)

This refers to a stage in which you sell stock in your company and that stock is freely traded. When you sell stock to a few individuals or have a private-placement stock offering, you'll also have investors and stock offerings, but the stock will not be publicly traded, and you will not be considered a public company.

The advantage of an IPO, or any subsequent stock offerings, is that you can raise large sums of money—anywhere from $3 to $200 million. The disadvantages are that it is hard to do an IPO unless you have an established sales base of several million dollars or a high potential product in a hot market such as telecommunications or surgical medical devices. Legal fees to go public can exceed $100,000 and you'll have to follow strict securities laws.

Invoice Financing (Factoring)

Invoice financing is another form of asset-based lending. A receivable refers to an unpaid invoice. For example, if you ship a customer a product and the customer has 30 days to pay, that unpaid invoice is a receivable. You can turn receivables into funding in two ways. First, you can borrow against the receivables, with the receivables as collateral. The second method is factoring, whereby a company will buy your receivables for a price discounted off the face value of the receivables. You might for instance, sell your receivables for an 8 percent discount off their face value.

Invoice financing used to be considered financing of the last resort. The biggest problem was that companies often needed to allow factoring companies to collect invoices from the customer. This gave customers the view that the company was in financial trouble. A more common practice today is to have invoices sent to a lock box, which is a new remit-to address controlled by the finance company.

Most invoice-receivable financing is handled by business-oriented finance companies. You can usually find a list of five to ten commercial finance companies in the Yellow Pages of your local phone book under Financing.

Inventory Financing

Inventory financing can be used when you are rapidly expanding your sales level, have a large contract to deliver, need to purchase a large inventory for seasonal sales, or can purchase materials at an advantageous price or time. Typically, you can have about 50 percent of your inventory financed. The best sources are finance and factoring firms or commercial banks. You will often find ads for factoring firms in the business section of your local newspaper or in regional business magazines.

Joint-Venture Financing

If your product is successful, quite a few people will make money from it. Distributors will benefit, your contract manufacturers will make money, and your raw-material vendors will increase their sales. When you need money to finance your business, why not approach these businesses, as they stand to gain the most by your success. You can sign a joint-venture agreement with one of these companies, by which they will own 20 or 25 percent of your business in return for an initial investment. You could also just take on the company as an investor, but companies prefer to say they are joint-venture partners.

Joint-venture agreements with manufacturers or distributors are usually the easiest form of financing to obtain, especially for a product in a stable industry. Devee Philpot, for example, created the Junk Drawer Organizer. This is a very nice product and it does fairly well, but it has a top potential of maybe $2.5 million to $3.0 million. That's not enough potential to really get an investor excited, and Devee didn't have the collateral she needed to get a bank loan. But to a plastics manufacturer with sales of $15 million, an extra $2 million in sales is an attractive piece of business. The manufacturer is your best choice for financing when you have a solid, but not spectacular, product.

Private Funding Sources

Funding can be received through four types of private sources: family and friends, people working on your project, "angel" investors, and professional investors.

Family and Friends

Most product entrepreneurs start with at least some investment from family and friends. This money is often essential to get a company started. Many product entrepreneurs are sloppy with their documentation when taking on family investors. This is a very bad idea, which can result in ill feelings later on. Instead, take the time and spend the money to have a subscription agreement drawn up. This is an agreement that explains the details of the offering and should clearly state that the investors' money is at risk and could be lost. A lawyer can draw this agreement up or you can look for a sample in a book on legal forms.

You must be careful anytime you sell stock. People (including your family and friends) can sue you for misrepresenting an investment. A subscription agreement will greatly reduce this risk. You should also recommend that friends and family members seek the advice of an accountant or attorney before investing.

One last point concerning investors that are friends or family is that they usually don't want to be long-term investors. You should offer an exit scenario, such as a buy-sell agreement provision, once you receive additional financing. This agreement simply states that you will agree to purchase back your investors' shares when you receive a predetermined amount (say, $100,000) of additional financing. Usually, you would agree to buy the stock back at whatever price new investors were paying at the time.

One clever way to buy out a shareholder is through a note at the time of financing. As an example, assume you've sold a relative shares at 40¢ per share when you started your business and now, two years later, you are going to sell stock at $1.50 per share. You can arrange to sell your relative's stock (provided he or she wants to sell) to a new investor on a three- or four-year note with 10 percent interest for $1.50 per share. The security for the loan would be the shares of stock that your relative is selling. This is a good deal for your relative, as he or she can sell the stock for a 300 percent gain. The investor also gets a good deal, being able to increase his or her number of shares for just over the cost of interest. If the stock doesn't do well, the investor can stop making payments and your relative will get the stock back. But the relative will have collected at least six to nine months' worth of payments and probably recouped most, if not all, of the original investment.

People Working on Your Project

Insiders, vendors, prototype builders, advisors, sales agents, and contract manufacturing people can also be approached for investments in a manner similar to that you took with family and friends. The best way to get this type of investment is to make the investment smaller and ensure that many people invest. People will be motivated to purchase stock when you tell them you are going to raise $50,000 with $5,000 investments from ten people—and you tell them that you already have seven investors on board.

"Angel" Investors

These are individuals who might give you $25,000 to help your project but do not regularly invest in new companies. These could be doctors, dentists, small business people, successful salespeople, or anyone else with money. These investors are generally used after a project has been developed to the point where you have some evidence that the idea could succeed.

Angel investors want you to succeed, and they generally invest to help you out—they don't drive the hard bargain you get when you deal with someone who invests regularly in new companies. Angels are best approached when you have a specific purpose for the money. For example, you may want the money to attend the industry's largest trade show or to finance an initial production run to supply samples and demonstration units for your sales force. You should make it clear that the investor will be helping to fund an activity that will directly relate to your success.

You can find angel investors everywhere. Your best bet is to start networking in your town early in your project. Associations, chambers of commerce, and church groups are all places where you can find investors. I know one inventor who sent invitations for a breakfast meeting to doctors, dentists, and small business people in his local town. There he would explain his company and ask for an investment. His meetings raised $125,000 to promote his business. If you keep a notebook of everyone you talk to about your product, you should have plenty of people to approach. Be sure to contact an attorney or small business development center before starting your campaign to be sure you are following all relevant security laws.

Private Investors

In most cities of any size, there are individuals who regularly (at least once a year) invest in small companies or product entrepreneurs. These investors are sophisticated, drive a hard bargain, and expect a large return—usually within three to five years. They invest in companies with ambitious growth plans and with an exit strategy—usually an IPO or buyout—within the first three to five years.

These investors play crucial roles in the development of fast-growing companies. Family, friends, vendors, sales representatives, and your contract manufacturer will get your company started. But if the company succeeds at that time, it may need another $1 million to $3 million to grow to the size you need for going public or attracting venture capital. Private investors can be crucial in financing this gap.

These investors are looking for a big return, rather than just being interested in helping you, and they will check your company out very closely before investing. Unless a product entrepreneur has already gone through a funding process, he or she is going to need help negotiating this phase. Check with other new start-ups in your area and ask what consultants, accountants, or other contacts they used to help them raise money. You can find names of companies that tried to raise money at your state secretary of commerce's office. Most major stock offerings are done with a legal document called a *private-placement memorandum*. This document must be registered with a state office, and a record of the registration dates by the company is a matter of public record.

Once you find the names of companies to contact, just call them and ask for assistance. People at these companies know what you are going through and will often be very helpful. You'll avoid many mistakes if you can convince the president or marketing director to review your business plan and investor presentation.

Often, other companies that have raised money will be willing to share the names of investors with you when you talk to them. Another source of private investors is the members of the boards of directors for private and public small companies (their names can be found at the library or secretary of state's office). Board members are often large investors, and they may have extensive lists of contacts.

You can find other names by contacting major accounting firms and mentioning to them that you will need financing in the next few months. Ask if they have any clients who would be interested in seeing a business plan. Another good source of leads is to check past issues of your newspaper's business section for the names of executives who have just sold their companies or retired. Networking at entrepreneur clubs or other relevant association events is another way to find potential investors.

Royalty Financing

This is a new method of financing that works almost in the opposite way that a license does. A company or investor gives you an up-front fee in return for a royalty percentage on your sales. For example, a company might give you $100,000 in up-front cash in return for 8 percent of your monthly sales revenue. If you sell $100,000 in a month, you'll have to pay the investor $8,000.

This method of financing has several drawbacks: You must pay the royalty fee even when you are losing money, the licensing fee may lower your profit margin to an unacceptable level, and the royalty arrangement may make additional financing or mergers impractical. The advantages to royalty financing are that you don't have a large fixed loan payment every month, and you don't dilute your equity. Check with your local entrepreneur group or small business development center to see if there is a royalty financing company in your town.

Sales/Leaseback

Another method of asset-based lending is to sell your equipment or real estate and then lease it back. Real estate is typically sold to an investor, who is then happy to lease your property back to you. You can contact an equipment-leasing company that can arrange to buy and then lease your equipment. Banks and finance companies are also willing to offer asset-based loans on equipment.

SCOR Public Offering Program

The Securities and Exchange Commission (SEC) has introduced a new program that allows you to raise up to $1 million with much less paperwork (and much lower legal fees) than an initial public offering. This program has the potential of being a tremendous option for entrepreneurs.

Before the introduction of Small Corporation Offering Registration (SCOR), the only viable stock option other than IPOs for an entrepreneur was to have a private placement, which is an offering of stock that is not publicly traded. Private placements frequently are used for raising $500,000 to $3 million. Unfortunately, private placements have many restrictions, which make them difficult to use except for companies in very high growth markets. Those restrictions include the following:

- Securities purchased in a private placement are subject to numerous resale restrictions.
- You can't advertise or solicit investors via standard marketing methods such as advertising or direct-mail programs. Your investors have to be through networking contacts.
- Private placements allow you to sell to only 35 nonaccredited investors. The rest must be accredited, which means either they have earned more than $200,000 over the last two years or they are worth in excess of a million dollars.

The problem with private placements is that you are forced to rely on a pool of sophisticated private investors, who want great returns and big markets. Entrepreneurs with solid products in slow-growing markets have a difficult time attracting accredited investors. With the SCOR program, entrepreneurs don't have these same restrictions. They can advertise for investors, take on as many nonaccredited investors as they'd like, and allow investors to resell their stock without any restrictions.

The SCOR program is an option you should look into. SCOR should be particularly effective in the future, with the increase in the number of users of public forums such as the Internet and the emergence of national financial databases such as DataMerge (1-800-580-1188). The SCOR program is very new, and not much money has been raised through it yet. Be sure to check with an attorney to be sure you are meeting all security regulations before soliciting investors.

Secondary Public Offerings

This is a public offering subsequent to an initial public offering. For example, you may raise $5 million in an IPO in January and another $10 million in the secondary offering in September.

Small Business Administration Loans

Most small businesses can't meet the tight requirements of traditional bank loans. The Small Business Administration has several lending programs, which make it easier for a small business to borrow money. The SBA doesn't lend money directly to you; instead, it guarantees part of a bank's loan to your business. But don't think of the SBA as an easy place to borrow money. Its requirements may be looser than those of banks, but it still has requirements that you must meet. The main advantage of SBA—and, often, of bank loans—is that you can get long repayment terms—from 10 to 25 years—which makes payment terms affordable.

The SBA offers several types of loan programs. The 7A Loan Guarantee program will guarantee 80 percent of loans up to $100,000 and 75 percent on loans over $100,000. The SBA Low-Document Program is available for loans of less than $100,000 and guarantees 80 percent of the loan amount. Despite its name, this loan requires almost the same amount of paperwork, especially for start-up businesses. The advantage of the loan is that the approval of credit is based, at least in part, on the character of the business owner and does not require full collateral coverage. Another loan program is the SBA 504, which will lend money for fixed assets with as little as 10 percent down.

Small Business Investment Companies

Congress has authorized Small Business Investment Companies (SBICs), which are financial institutions created to make equity capital and long-term credit (at least five years) available to small independent businesses. In return for making a commitment to small businesses, the SBICs are eligible for government-backed funds. I personally have not found that these funds are much different from standard venture-capital funds. SBICs look for investments with very high potential returns in glamour industries.

Specialized Small Business Investment Companies (SSBICs), on the other hand, have been very helpful. SSBICs make all their investments with socially or economically disadvantaged entrepreneurs. In many cases, SSBICs have provided funding to companies that otherwise had no access to financial sources. You can get a list of SBICs and SSBICs by sending $10 to:

National Association of Small Business Investment Companies
1199 N. Fairfax Street
Suite 200
Alexandria, VA 22314

Venture Capitalists

These are firms that invest in companies with very high growth potential, frequently by purchasing equity. Typically, venture capitalists want to see firms have the potential of increasing sales to $20 million in three to five years. They also want an exit strategy in three to five years, so they can liquidate their investments. Most often, the exit strategy is a public offering, after which the capitalists can sell their stock.

The two most important features venture capitalists look for are a top management team and a company in a high-growth industry. A survey by Coopers & Lybrand (Fifth Annual Economic Impact of Venture Capital Study, 1995) found that venture capitalists invest (at the proportions listed) in the following businesses, all of which are among the fastest-growing businesses in the United States:

Biotechnology	28%
Software	14%
Medical communications	14%
Semiconductors	12%
Medical devices	12%
Health care services	5%

Venture capitalists are often called "vulture capitalists" or other derogatory terms because occasionally they will take over a firm and kick a founder out. That does sound ruthless, but the venture capitalists are really just meeting the needs of their customers, who are very wealthy individuals, pension funds, insurance companies, and other large institutional investors. These people give money to venture capitalists with the expectations of high risk, but also of high-potential investments. So when a company's sales are leveling off or not growing fast enough, the company has to expect the venture capitalists to push to get sales moving or to replace the management team. Venture capitalists aren't just afraid of losing their money, they're afraid that you won't grow fast enough to meet their customers' expectations.

One of the myths inventors have is that venture capitalists invest in brand-new companies. Well, sometimes they do, but mostly they don't. The average age of companies that attract venture-capital investments is 4.8 years. Most venture-capital investments are large—between $500,000 and

$5 million, though some venture capitalists will invest as little as $100,000. Venture capitalists are listed in *Pratt's Guide to Venture Capital Sources** which is available at many larger libraries. You can also obtain a directory of investment-capital clubs, which are groups of private investors that invest in young companies, by sending $9.95 to:

> International Venture Capital Institute
> P.O. Box 1333
> Stamford, CT 06094

STEP 2: KNOW THE OPTIONS AVAILABLE FOR YOUR PRODUCT

I like to separate companies into three categories:

- Fast-growth companies in rapidly expanding markets
- Strongly differentiated products in well-defined, easy-to-reach markets
- Strongly differentiated products in fragmented markets

Well-defined markets are ones in which the distribution channels and customers are easy to identify. Golf products are an example. Most of the market is sold through pro shops on golf courses or specialized golf shops like Nevada Bob's. Another example is guitar accessories, which are sold primarily through specialized guitar stores. Fragmented markets have widely varying distribution channels with hard-to-locate customers—for example, picture frames can be sold almost anywhere, and companies have trouble predicting just who will purchase such a product in any given year. Figure 17-1 lists the type of financing companies can get for each type of product.

Fast-Growth Products in Expanding Markets

Venture capitalists and many wealthy investors are only looking for products that can grow at rates in excess of 100 percent per year. The good news is that you have an excellent chance to attract investors if you have a product with that type of growth potential. The bad news is that those investors will push you on ? rapid expansion path that will increase the value of their stock 500 to ֽ 0 percent within three to five years. That means you probably won't make a profit for two to three years, because you need to constantly push to expand your business. It's not unusual for

---

* Published annually by Venture Economics, a division of Securities Data Publishing, Inc., 40 W. 51st St., New York, NY 10019, 1-800-455-5844.

Figure 17-1   Financing Options

Fast-Growth Products in Expanding Markets	Products in Well-Defined Markets	Products in Fragmented Markets
Venture capitalists	Joint-venture financing	Community financing
Wealthy private investors	Wealthy private investors	Joint-venture financing
Public offerings	Community financing	Distribution fees
Distributor and licensing fees	Asset-based loans	Asset-based loans
Angel investors	Angel investors	SCOR offerings
	Public offerings	Angel investors
	SCOR offerings	SBA loans
	SBA loans	

companies seeking venture capital to show growth from $1 million to $30 million inside of five years. If you don't generate the type of growth that the capitalists want, they might just kick you out.

While the road to rapid growth looks great, the fact is that you need to be a good manager, with extensive experience in order to get this type of high-risk capital. If you don't have that experience, you should treat your product as a differentiated one in either a well-defined or fragmented market.

Strongly Differentiated Product in a Well-Defined Market

When investors, venture capitalists, and manufacturers consider financing your venture, they always start wanting you to identify your target customer. That's because many potential investors believe that you have an easier time making money off certain profitable target customer groups. For example, you might have a software package that facilitates computer networking of financial and marketing data. Investors generally believe that entrepreneur companies will probably be more profitable targeting large corporations rather than small companies, because big companies can buy multiple units, have more money to spend, and have computer resource people who will understand your product. Small companies, on the other hand, might need only one unit, require an education effort on your part, and not have enough money to make an immediate purchase.

Investors and potential manufacturer-partners like well-defined target markets because they can clearly see how the product might be successfully introduced. With a fragmented market, it is much more difficult for people to see the end because exactly how you will finally proceed to market may be confusing.

I personally believe that joint-venture funding from a manufacturer is the best, and often the easiest, financing to get for a strongly differentiated product in a well-defined market. The manufacturer's owners will see the value of your business to their product line and will understand quickly the economics of rapidly raising the volume of products produced by their plant. This financing might not always be cash, but it could include providing operating capital with delayed billings or not charging inventory costs until a product is produced.

I did not recommend manufacturing/joint-venture financing with fast-growth companies because most manufacturers are simply not prepared for the rapid growth investors want. For example, recall the Junk Drawer Organizer. Our $15 million manufacturer likes a product that can add $2 million to its sales base. That volume is significant without being overwhelming. But what if I had a product that could grow to $200 million? Typically, the manufacturer won't be willing to expand rapidly enough to keep venture capitalists happy and won't be able to finance the rapid growth on its own. But the manufacturer is an ideal financing vehicle for every other type of product.

Once you get a manufacturer to support you by picking up at least part of the investment, you will be in a strong position to get other investors and asset-based loans from either the SBA or banks. Companies in a rapid-growth mode rarely get in a collateral position (which means you have assets to offer as security for a loan) to attract loans. But slower-growth companies may get into a collateral position from which they can borrow money. You can get help deciding on when to apply for bank financing from your accountant or your local small business development center. Your bank also might be willing to help you if it is oriented toward small business. SCOR offerings will help this type of business if you use the manufacturer's financing once you get a sales base of $250,000 to $750,000.

Strongly Differentiated Product in a Fragmented Market

When you are serving a fragmented market, it is more difficult to show convincingly how the path you plan to follow will be successful. This makes it more difficult to get a financing or cooperative manufacturer. Three avenues are still open to you, including community financing, SBA loans, and distribution fees.

Throughout the book, I've told you that you should work with a contract manufacturer. I still recommend this. However, you can do this with financing in a community even if it is not where the manufacturer is located. You can set up a final assembly or packaging operation, requiring several workers, at a plant in the community. You can then have your manufacturer set up production for you and ship you the components you need for final assembly. Thus, the manufacturer helps you set up, and, once you have some outside financing, it may be willing to invest additional money.

Fragmented markets are also markets where you can pick up distribution fees and contracts. For example, consider an entrepreneur offering a new style of picture frame. She might choose, as her target distribution channel, photography stores, and her product might be an upscale offering in that market. This entrepreneur could also approach companies selling to home improvement stores, offering to private-label a product for that market or license a lower-value version of her product. She could then get upfront fees and a royalty rate that could help support her efforts in other markets. The entrepreneur could take the same approach with companies that sell primarily to large discounters such as Wal-Mart or Kmart.

This strategy is much less work than trying to license a product outright. You have a much stronger position once you start selling a product yourself, and your position is even better if the manufacturer thinks you might be able to sell to the market on your own.

Angel investors, SBA and bank loans, commercial finance company asset-based loans, and SCOR offerings are all possible once you have developed some support from other investors. This has yet to be proven, but I believe SCOR offerings will be particularly valuable for entrepreneurs moving to smaller communities. Once you get some sales and production started, you can have a SCOR offering to members of the community, who might invest small amounts of money. If the community gets behind your company, you might get 30 to 50 investors to put up $5,000 to $10,000 each to fund your business. This is really not a practical option under the nonaccredited investment restrictions of private placements.

STEP 3: DETERMINE WHICH OPTIONS TO PURSUE FOR VARIOUS PHASES OF FINANCING

There are three major phases of financing: the start-up phase, which runs through the initial sales period; the second phase, which takes you through the transitional period to the point at which you have a solid market presence; and, finally, your expansion phase. All three phases of a new business are risky, and the first two are extremely risky. On the positive side, new products offer more leverage to an investor than any other business does. You can invest $1,000 in a new product and make it worth $100,000 in three to five years.

Start-up Funding

Getting your product far enough along may take only $15,000, but that can be a difficult $15,000 to raise. You need to rely on your own savings, investments from friends and relatives, and people you know in the industry. Until you can get a prototype, you probably won't get far raising money from a manufacturer, and there are few alternative places to turn.

Most inventors take the wrong investor approach in this period. They are selling their ideas, and they tend to pitch the ideas to death. What you are really selling is a dream—a chance to be in on the ground floor of a company that could have rapid growth. This is a chance that people want, as evidenced by the millions of people starting their own businesses at home or participating in multilevel marketing (MLM) programs. And it's a chance very few people get due to securities regulations. Investing in the new company of a friend or relative is about the only chance the average person will ever have for a big payday.

Product entrepreneurs also tend to use the word *I* way too much when approaching early investors. Remember that you are selling a *team concept* and you want people to join the group that is introducing a new product. Someone once told me the story about two stonecutters who were asked what they were doing. The first said, "I'm cutting stone into blocks." The second one replied, "I'm on a team building a cathedral." The second stonecutter would be a lot more motivated than the first. That's the same outlook you need to convey to investors.

Before you approach any investors, be sure to map out your company's entire plan, with a projected timetable, from a starting prototype to a test market to a transitional period to a rapid-growth phase. Let the people see where you intend to go and what type of sales you expect to have. Tell them that, as early investors, they will be buying stock at a much lower price than any other investors.

The best people for you to approach first are salespeople or business owners. Both of these groups are risk takers. They take chances in their own businesses, and they won't be scared by the risky nature of a new business. Once you have your first one or two investors, it is much easier to find additional people to help finance your business.

Second-Phase Financing

You may need between $25,000 and $75,000 to complete this phase for a simple product, and from $200,000 into the millions to complete it for more complicated or technical products. If you need $100,000 or less for this phase, your best sources of financing are, again, friends and family; people in the industry such as distributors, salespeople, and retailers; angel investors; and joint-venture manufacturing partners. You can take these investors on without a private-placement memorandum or formal stock offering, but you still want to get an attorney to help you with a subscription agreement.

If you need between $100,000 and $250,000, you might need to take on additional angel and industry investors, get more help from your manufacturer, and apply for low-documentation SBA loans. You should always explore SBA loans if you have assets you need to purchase for the transitional period. Your best approach in this period is to generate investments of $50,000 to $100,000 prior to applying for a bank loan.

One mistake new entrepreneurs make is to not quantify assistance they may be getting from a manufacturer. For example, if a manufacturer is giving you an in-kind investment when it offers you 60-day terms from the day it finishes production, this could reduce your capital requirements for operating cash anywhere from $20,000 to $50,000. Or the manufacturer might give you space to work in its plant or free use of its equipment. Again, this is worth a considerable amount of money to you.

Very few people like to be the first investor into a project. They prefer other people to invest first, as it gives them more confidence that they are making the right decision. Treating the manufacturer's commitment as an up-front fee or investment will help secure other investors.

For investments over $250,000, you probably will need either a private-placement memorandum, a SCOR offering, or a significant manufacturing/joint-venture agreement. With investments of over $250,000, you enter a whole different world. This is more money than you can typically get from small investors and it puts you into the domain of accredited investors. These investors have hundreds of opportunities to invest in small companies like yours, and they might just invest in one or two opportunities per year. It is very hard to get these private investors to fund you when you don't have a successful sales history. You need to pick up investments, first, from people who know the industry and then you need significant support from a joint-venture or distribution partner before you can succeed with accredited investors.

Another option at this phase is community-based funding, provided you are offering job opportunities. You are better off waiting till phase three for community financing, because you'll be able to attract offers from several communities and raise more money. But if you are having trouble raising the money at the second stage, community funding is an option. SBA low-document loans are another option here, but funding can be difficult to get because you won't be able to generate significant profits in the transitional, or second, sales period.

Rapid-Growth Financing

You might be raising anywhere from $150,000 to $5 million, or even much more, for this phase of financing. All types of funding are possible during this stage, but private placements, IPOs, SCOR offerings, and bank or SBA loans are the most popular, because they have the potential of raising the most money.

STEP 4: MAKE YOURSELF KNOWN IN THE COMMUNITY BEFORE YOU NEED MONEY

People have to believe you'll succeed before they invest. No matter how good your presentation and product are, people will still want to track your success for at least a few months before investing. That small delay gives investors a better idea of how you are progressing and what type of momentum your project has. Since you want people to invest when you need to raise the money, you need to become known by potential investors before you need to raise money.

The key is to look for contacts early and network as much as possible. *Networking* is sort of an overused term, and I know it gives some people a queasy feeling. But it can be quite easy to do if you follow a few simple rules:

1. Network everywhere. All you have to do is ask people where they work and what they do. Keep a note card on every potential contact. You'll be amazed at how many of the people you meet who will have the potential to help you.

2. Tell people what you're doing—starting a new company with a great new product that provides a terrific customer benefit. Then mention that, right now, you are putting together a team of people to help you introduce the product. Most people will suggest possible contacts, if they know of any. Then contact those people. Be sure not to tell people you are an inventor (*translation:* potential crackpot). Tell them instead that you are an entrepreneur (*translation:* savvy businessperson). If people seem interested in your idea, ask them if you can give them periodic updates on how your company is doing. Tell them you don't need investors now, but you might in the future.

3. Attend any related gathering you can—fund-raising presentations, trade association meetings, chamber of commerce events, business roundtables, and civic and charity events. Be sure to network with accountants and lawyers at these meetings. They almost always have contacts with angel and wealthy investors.

4. Ask two questions of potential contacts. The first question should be related to the person's business. My favorite is simply: "How have you made your business stand out from the competition?" Ask follow-up questions as they come up, but focus on the main question. The second question is: "Could I call you sometime in the future to ask you questions?"

5. Take advantage of government resources. Talk to small business development centers and other similar groups. They may know some contacts, plus they will be able to help you contact other

investors. They will also help you identify banks friendly to small business at which you can open an account. Be sure to make presentations at venture-capital conferences whenever possible and have trade booths set up at the conference just to make people aware of your upcoming opportunity.

6. Get familiar with the securities documents in your state and the information that is available to the public. Often, you can get the names of early-stage investors in other companies from public stock registration requirements.

7. Put out a newsletter or short update every three months for everyone on your list. Make it clear that you don't have an investment opportunity now, but you will in six months, and that you will keep people posted on new activities.

8. If at all possible, publish press releases in trade magazines about your new product or approach local papers to run a story on your activities.

STEP 5: PREPARE YOUR BUSINESS FOR FINANCING

I can't count how many times I've had someone tell me, "I need $50,000 to get my product on the market." I usually ask, "What do you have for me to look at regarding your stock sale?" The answer typically is: "Nothing, but I can tell you all about it. What would you like to know?" Well, that is not a response that is going to get you very far.

Six strong business factors are necessary in order to have a real chance at raising money:

1. A strong management team
2. Solid business controls
3. A stock subscription agreement
4. Significant results to date
5. Clear information on how you will spend the money
6. A long-range plan, even if only in outline form, showing the expansion path you expect the company to follow

Strong Management Team

Managing a new company is difficult, and investors believe a management team is all-important. For rapid-phase financing, you need an experienced team in place. For first- and second-stage financing, you may not have your management in place, but you need a team of top-notch advisors, preferably from your target industry, who are invested in your company.

Solid Business Controls

Do you do a financial report at the end of each month? Do you prepare monthly budgets and inventory reports and cash flow statements? Investors expect you to have your management and financial control functions in place, and they expect you to have an accountant or bookkeeper overlooking your affairs. You also should be posting minutes of your officers' meetings, which determine items such as issuing new stock, setting salaries, or approving major expenditures. New-product entrepreneurs almost always think these controls are not worth the trouble, but they are. Without them, you could easily run through the investor's money without showing much progress.

Stock Subscription Agreement

Don't approach an investor unless you know how many shares of stock the company has issued, how many shares are currently owned, what the current value of the company is, how much product you are selling, and for what price. You need to do this with an attorney. Subscription agreements are common, and it shouldn't be too expensive for an attorney to help you. You need to have these documents in place or investors will think you're inexperienced.

Solid Success to Date

If you are to succeed in the future, you should have been able to succeed in the past. Show investors the results you've achieved. When you are starting out, this might be only a research study, a patent search, or interviews with insiders. But show momentum and progress in a meaningful way. Sales results are best, but progress on technical, distribution, or manufacturing fronts can be almost as important.

What the Money Will Do

What you do with the money is usually referred to as "use of proceeds." People aren't interested in each actual expense item, but rather what you will be able to accomplish. For example, you might be finishing a prototype so you can do further market testing, or you intend to use the money to put product into 18 stores. The purpose for which you need the money should be significant, and it should help the company take a major step toward a product introduction.

A Long-Range Plan

If you are going for third-phase financing, you'll need a business plan. For second-phase financing, you'll need either a business plan or a transition plan. for early-stage investments, you can often just use an outline of your product plans, including your transitional and long-term plans. For example for a new miniblind company, you might use a form such as the one shown in Figure 17-2.

STEP 6: APPROACH MULTIPLE SOURCES OF FINANCING

You'll have a sky-high closing rate if you can get one out of twenty investors to invest in your company. Other financing options can also require many trips to a company's headquarters, many presentations, and many turndowns. So don't pin your hopes on just one or two options. You need to go after as many opportunities as you can, with as much planning and enthusiasm as you can muster. Presidents of new companies may give three to four financing presentations each and every week for over a year to get the funding they need. This isn't a reflection of the quality of your investment opportunity but, instead, of the number of small companies trying to raise money at any given time.

Figure 17-2   Long-Range Plan for Early-Stage Product

Product:	New-style miniblind with richer fabric for upscale homes.
Distribution Channel:	Individual drapery and blind suppliers that provide custom window coverings for upscale neighborhoods.
Initial Product Test:	Two local providers will test products for two months. Number of consumers expected to be approached is 22.
Transition (or Second-Stage) Period:	Sales throughout the Richmond and Norfolk, Virginia, areas. Expected number of dealers is 25.
National Coverage:	Sales throughout nation. Expected number of dealers is 800. Expected annual sales is $12 million per year.

CONCLUSION

At the beginning of the chapter, I mentioned that financing is very hard work—which it is. Most successful entrepreneurs take three to four times as long to raise money as they originally expected, and many, many entrepreneurs never raise money. But every year new companies are formed and funded. Prepare yourself for the task that lies ahead of you, and you'll have a good chance to succeed.

CONCLUSION

EXHILARATING TIMES: YOU TOO CAN BE SUCCESSFUL

John Naughton was selling lounge chairs at the Iowa State Fair when a dentist came up and asked him whether he could make one of those chairs work in a dental office. John and his brother went to work modifying the lounge chair and eventually introduced the first reclining dental chair. John's company, Dental-Ez, sold as many as 7,000 dental chairs per year.

John's path to success wasn't easy. He took a year to develop the product, and he sold only 10 chairs the following year. But John did succeed: He had a product that was unique, he had the help of dentists who really wanted the product, he entered a market that had only three large distributors, and he was able to cut his development costs by modifying an existing product.

Susan Anderson created a line of kits for cleaning dust and lint out of computers. She started her line with $20,000 of borrowed money and now sells $250,000 a year. The secrets to her success were a small niche market, an easy-to-make product, and experience in the computer field.

I believe that almost anyone, with the proper desire, can be a new-product entrepreneur. The secret to success is to control the introduction process. To do that, follow the guidelines in this book. Not every product can be a winner, but you can find the winners if you learn to evaluate ideas without spending too much time or money.

Ken Hakuta made $10 million from his Wacky Wall Walkers, little plastic spiders that crawl down a wall. Bob Ayers found an investor to help him introduce a line of rocking wheelchairs. Eldon Jones built a $3.1 million company based on his design for a dump-truck hoist. With less than $1,000, Keith Kendall started a line of fashion clothing, now selling $400,000 annually. Domingo Tan invested 10 years of his time before receiving an order for 25,000 of his Instant Car Koolers. King Gillette was a salesman who had a flight of inspiration while shaving on a train. Estée Lauder started out toting jars of home-brewed "magic potion" to local beauty shops. William Hewlett and David Packard started out in a garage with only $538.

Most entrepreneurs I talk to are either sky-high with optimism after a few successes, or down low with depression from a series of rejections. I don't want you to be at either extreme. Know exactly where you stand during the entire introduction process. Know how to capitalize on your product's positive points and how to work around its negative points. (See box, p. 251.)

Few experiences are as exhilarating as working on an idea, molding it based on market input, and then selling it as a final product to a customer. I know several entrepreneurs who couldn't sleep past 4:00 A.M. because they were too excited about their ideas. Product creators will also start to be enveloped in the mystique of power that successful businesspeople have. Graham Lovelady was a repairman at a dental dealer—a pretty low notch on the totem pole. He never forgot the first time he walked in to meet with the dealer hierarchy, some of whom hardly knew his name, and then walked out with his first large order. His self-confidence from that encounter helped push him to build a $5 million business.

How are you going to get a product on the market? Your number-one action has to be to find the right idea. Keep referring to the five key criteria that determine whether a product can be introduced by an under-financed entrepreneur. These criteria will help you to quickly scan ideas when you are searching for one that might succeed:

1. Will the product be easy to distribute?
2. Is the product's technology simple? Can the entrepreneur build the necessary models and prototypes?
3. Do potential customers perceive the product to be unique?
4. Is the product's benefit obvious?
5. Can the product be sold at four to five times its manufacturing cost?

ENTREPRENEURS NEED MENTAL TOUGHNESS

This book has covered all the steps you need to take to put a product on the market. Entrepreneurs fail to sell their products 70 to 80 percent of the time. That doesn't mean that their products fail; even the most successful salespeople typically sell a product only 20 to 30 percent of the time. But entrepreneurs spend most of their time facing rejection. Many people are surprised to learn that product creators who spend $20,000 or more on a product may drop it after a minimal sales effort. That doesn't surprise me at all. A person has to have a tremendous amount of mental toughness to avoid being discouraged by repeated rejection.

When a person creates a product, it becomes his or her "baby." Someone who doesn't buy an entrepreneur's product isn't necessarily saying that the product is a bad idea. The person might not have the money, might not need the product, might need another product instead, or might be saving for another purchase. Some entrepreneurs have a hard time accepting those possibilities. Instead, they look at turndowns as personal defeats.

I put successful product entrepreneurs into two categories. At the top of my list are people with a strong belief that their products have potential, who keep pursuing their ideas against all odds. I once worked for an inventor who quit his job and worked on a product 70 to 100 hours a week, for four years, before he produced any revenue. Besides incredible commitment, he had a tremendous amount of mental toughness. The other category consists of people who are lucky enough to get immediate positive reinforcement for their ideas. Dr. Robert Cade, a faculty member of the University of Florida, developed Gatorade for the football team. Other schools wanted to know what the drink was, and the product started selling. You can't count on being lucky, so you should try to join those who believe in their ideas and keep pursuing them against all odds.

People who want to introduce products know that they must make a commitment of time, money, and energy. They may not know that they must be mentally prepared to face rejection of their ideas. To succeed, entrepreneurs have to realize that there are few products that *most* of the market will buy. To succeed, they have to avoid becoming discouraged and keep plugging away to capture their part of the market.

When you find a product that looks like it has a chance, learn everything you can about its market. You can't succeed without knowing the process by which products are bought and sold, the distributors that control the market, and the typical discounts and promotions that manufacturers offer. With this knowledge, you will make a professional presentation to your key contacts, and you will avoid making costly mistakes.

After you have a product and the necessary knowledge, the next action step is to proceed cautiously, following the step-by-step introduction process outlined in this book. No entrepreneur can know whether a product will succeed until it is on the market and selling. An entrepreneur's primary goal in an introduction cycle is to preserve cash—a goal that can be attained only by moving cautiously.

The last action step is to work hard. Introducing a new product is not an easy path to instant riches. It calls for an expenditure of plenty of time and effort.

Every month, someone walks into my office with an idea and an attitude of "Here I am; make me rich." Success doesn't happen that way. No one will help someone who is not willing to invest any personal time or money.

There are no magic formulas or secret techniques that will turn your product into a success. But if you find the right idea and learn how to introduce it, you can get your million-dollar idea onto the market.

John Naughton once sold contour lounge chairs at the Iowa State Fair. Today, he lives in a large home, retired after a very successful business career. You can join John as a success story. Work smart, and work hard.

APPENDIX

SAMPLE PATENT
DOCUMENTS

Sample Patent Disclosure (Partial)

The United States of America

The Commissioner of Patents and Trademarks

Has received an application for a patent for a new and useful invention. The title and description of the invention are enclosed. The requirements of law have been complied with, and it has been determined that a patent on the invention shall be granted under the law.

Therefore, this

United States Patent

Grants to the person or persons having title to this patent the right to exclude others from making, using or selling the invention throughout the United States of America for the term of seventeen years from the date of this patent, subject to the payment of maintenance fees as provided by law.

Acting Commissioner of Patents and Trademarks

Attest

United States Patent [19]

Klawitter

[11] **Patent Number:** **4,896,879**

[45] **Date of Patent:** **Jan. 30, 1990**

[54] **ADJUSTABLE WEIGHT DEVICE FOR HUMAN JOINT OR MUSCLE EXERCISE**

[76] Inventor: **Ronald J. Klawitter,** 321 Fifth St., West, Hector, Minn. 55342

[21] Appl. No.: **212,564**

[22] Filed: **Jan. 28, 1988**

[51] Int. Cl. A63B 21/12
[52] U.S. Cl. 272/119; 272/DIG. 4; 272/96
[58] Field of Search 272/96, 130, 119, 143, 272/145, 122; 128/25.3

[56] **References Cited**

U.S. PATENT DOCUMENTS

D. 271,408	11/1983	Bauer	D21/197
2,114,790	4/1938	Venables	272/57
2,214,052	9/1940	Good	272/57
2,689,127	9/1954	Silverton et al.	272/145 X
2,849,237	8/1958	Sinuthis	272/119
3,231,270	1/1966	Winer	272/84
3,380,447	4/1968	Martin	272/145 X
3,406,968	10/1968	Mason	272/119
4,079,932	3/1978	Schuetz	272/122 X
4,357,009	11/1982	Baker	272/96
4,575,074	3/1986	Damraoski	272/119
4,602,784	7/1986	Budden et al.	272/119
4,621,808	11/1986	Orchard et al.	272/119
4,650,183	3/1987	McIntyre	128/25 B X

Primary Examiner—Richard J. Apley
Assistant Examiner—H. Flaxman
Attorney, Agent, or Firm—Kinney & Lange

[57] **ABSTRACT**

An adjustable boot-shaped weight for exercising a human joint or muscle group, such as a knee, by strapping onto the foot and filling the container with liquid or other flowable material in the hollow body of the device. The ball of the foot extends beyond the base of the container, and the concave leg support partially surrounds the back portion of the leg while extending above the ankle to prevent slipping. The retainers over the instep and the lower leg keep the leg in place while the lining provides comfort for the user.

5 Claims, 2 Drawing Sheets

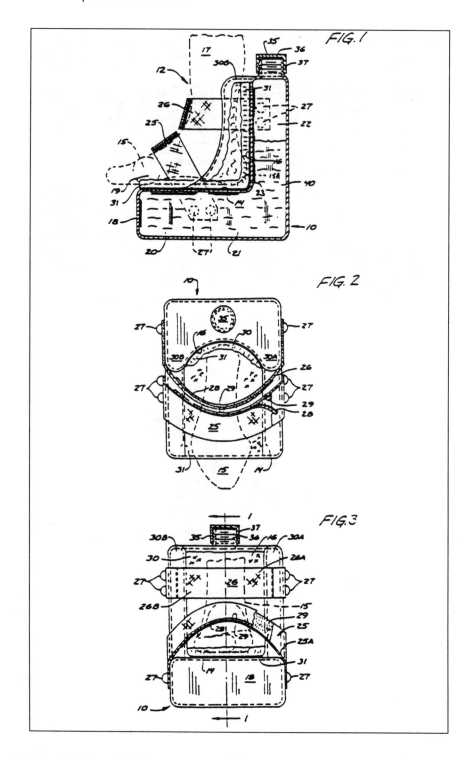

FIG. 1

FIG. 2

FIG. 3

SUMMARY OF THE INVENTION

An adjustable weight device for exercising a human leg joint or muscle group, such as a knee, comprises a container having at least one material holding compartment in the hollow body of the device. A first surface of the container is adapted to engage the bottom of the foot of a user, and a second surface extends upwardly at substantially right angles to the first surface. The surfaces support the leg and foot and hold them while exercising. The ball of the foot extends beyond the base of the container and the first surface so the toes are not constrained. The leg support is concave and partially surrounds the back portion of the leg. Preferably, the container is a hollow, molded hard plastic body which, as shown, has a single top opening with a threaded neck that could be closed by a screw-on cap, or a friction-cap type closing.

The foot is positioned on the device and retainers are provided for strapping the foot firmly onto the user to prevent slipping. The retainers placed over the instep and the lower leg keep the weight in place. A lining is provided for comfort of the user, if desired. The use of retainers in two places prevents the apparatus from slipping around and being uncomfortable. The retainers can be straps employing Velcro hook and loop fasteners or with plastic snap-type buckles on an adjustable length band, attached by cap screws to the device. Plastic gripping straps could be molded as part of the container.

The container can be filled with water, for example, or with dry particulate material such as sand, salt or gravel, or other liquids, to increase the weight. A typical size would weigh up to in the range of 19 pounds when filled. Varying the amount of liquid would provide a range of loads to be carried by the user capable of being changed to reflect the wearer's needs. The preferred amount of weight will vary with the physical condition of the individual and with the particular exercise being performed.

An exercise for strengthening muscle groups in the leg could be lifting the foot with the device outwardly and upwardly while sitting with the leg swinging freely from the knee. Another exercise could be done while sitting with the lower leg swinging freely and lifting from the thigh muscle, keeping the lower leg substantially at right angles to the floor plane to exercise the muscle groups in the upper leg and hip joint.

BRIEF DESCRIPTION OF THE DRAWINGS

FIG. 1 is a vertical sectional view of an adjustable weight device for human joint or muscle group exercise shown engaged on the foot of a user;

FIG. 2 is a top plan view of the device of FIG. 1; and

FIG. 3 is a front elevational view of FIG. 1.

DETAILED DESCRIPTION OF THE PREFERRED EMBODIMENTS

Referring to the drawings, in FIG. 1, an adjustable weight device for exercising human joints or muscle groups is indicated generally at 10, and is supported on a foot and lower leg region shown generally at 12. The weight device comprises a first surface 14 substantially perpendicular to a second surface 16 which extends upwardly from the first surface 14. Surface 14 supports the foot 15 and is designed to engage the foot no farther then the ball 19 of the foot 15. The surface area 16 which extends upwardly from the surface 14 supports the lower leg 17. The device 10 comprises a hollow, molded plastic container 18 which has at least one compartment 20 defined therein. The container is preferably constructed from a rigid or semirigid, molded plastic. The compartment 20 has a first section 21 and a second section 22 defined on the interior of the device 10.

As shown in FIG. 2, a concave shape 30 of upward surface 16 is formed to provide wall portions 30A and 30B which partially surround the back portion of the leg of the user. A heel 15A of the user seats back at junction region 23 of first and second surfaces 14 and 16, shown best in FIG. 1.

First fastening means 25, comprising strap sections 25A and 25B, fits over the instep of the foot 15. Second fastening means 26 comprises strap sections 26A and 26B that fit around the forward portion of the lower leg 17. The fasteners secure the general leg region 12 and foot 15 against the surfaces 14 and 16 and prevent slippage.

The fastening means 25 and 26 comprise adjustable straps having ends of the respective strap sections fixed on the container side walls with cap screws 27 or other suitable fasteners. The ends of fastener sections 25A, 25B and 26A, 26B are held together by means such as hook and loop fastener (VELCRO) straps 28, 29 or snap type buckles so that the straps can be fitted as desired or required, as shown in FIG. 3. The fixed ends of the strap sections 25A, 25B, and 26A, 26B can be attached to the container 18 with adhesives or other fasteners.

A cushioning liner 31 is supported on the first and second surfaces 14, 16 between the foot area 15 and the lower leg 17 of the user and the container 10. This liner is preferably an absorbent pad that provides comfort or reduces slippage of the foot, for example, sheepskin or other absorbent and soft materials. Foam of various types could be used, and no pad has to be used. The foot can rest on the plastic surface 14.

A single access opening 35 with a threaded neck 36 is closed by a cap 37 as best shown in FIG. 3. The cap could also be a type of friction cap that would allow easy access, and would be attached to the device by a loop to prevent losing the cap while adjusting the weight by pouring liquid in or out.

The walls of the container preferably are not flexible, but retain a distinct shape so the container keeps the weight from shifting excessively. While some liquid flow back and forth will occur in the container, the secure support from the fastening means and the use of the liner 31 will prevent slipping between the foot and the container.

The shortened length of surface 14 permits toe movement and also fits a wide foot size range. The outer shape can be varied as desired, of course, but the support of the foot and leg is important.

The device is easily portable, easily made, and easily used, as well as being reliable because of its simple construction and readily available weight adjustment. Water can be filled in from a tap to add weight and the compartment 20 can be filled with granular solid materials, if desired. Sand, salt, gravel, lead or steel shot can be used, if desired. The filling is shown at 40. This adjustable weight device for human joint or muscle group exercise is designed for convenient installation and removal from the body.

Although the present invention has been described with reference to the preferred embodiments, workers skilled in the art will recognize that changes may be made in form and detail without departing from the spirit and scope of the invention. Normal knee therapy would be to lift weights, beginning at approximately 3 lbs., and continuing gradually upwards to 20 lbs.

What is claimed is:

1. A foot and lower leg mounted exercise device for exercising a human knee under external weight comprising:

a substantially rigid L-shaped container having a base section and an upright section joined together and at least one compartment defined on the interior thereof, and an access opening to the compartment at an upper portion of the upright section;

foot and lower leg support surface means formed on such container defining a first surface on an upper side of the base section and adapted to engage the bottom of the foot of a user and support such foot along the instep region, and a second surface joining the first surface and formed on the upright section extending upwardly and substantially at right angles to the first surface to be adjacent and in contact with the calf of the leg of a user when a foot of a user is supported on the first surface, the compartment including a first compartment portion below the first surface and a second compartment portion to the rear of the second surface, the second compartment portion extending upwardly along substantially the entire upright section;

a first adjustable strap fastener mounted on the first section and adapted to be positioned over an instep of a user above the first surface; and

a second adjustable strap fastener mounted on the upright section and positioned for engaging and encircling a lower leg of a user and extending outwardly from the second surface, whereby the container can be filled with a variable amount of liquid including the compartment portion extending up-

wardly along the upright section of the container for adjusting the total weight carried for exercise, and wherein the ankle of a user is retained in substantially one position for such exercise when the container is in place on a user with the fastener means fastened to support such foot and lower leg.

2. A foot mounted variable weight exerciser comprising a substantially rigid L-shaped container having a base section and an upright section rigidly molded together and defining a liquid tight compartment on the interior thereof, the compartment including compartment portions substantially coextensive with both the base and upright sections, and an opening to the compartment for filling liquid into the compartment and removing liquid from the compartment;

foot and lower leg support surfaces formed on the respective base and upright sections of such container, including a first surface on an upper side of the base section and adapted to be engaged by the bottom of a foot of a user and support such foot, the container having sufficient rigidity to support the weight of a user, and an upright surface joining the first surface and formed on the upright section and extending upwardly and substantially at right angles.

Sample Issued Patent

United States Patent [19]

Chisholm

[11] **Patent Number: Des. 290,787**

[45] **Date of Patent: ￭￭ Jul. 14, 1987**

[54] **COMBINATION PHOTOGRAPHIC FRAME AND CLOCK**

[76] Inventor: Dell T. Chisholm, 1010 Fairmount Ave., St. Paul, Minn. 55105

[**] Term: 14 Years

[21] Appl. No.: 483,213

[22] Filed: Apr. 8, 1983

[52] U.S. Cl. D6/301; D10/2

[58] Field of Search .... D6/300–303, D6/309–312, 314; D10/2; 40/152, 152.1, 158 R, 154; D10/122–126, 127

[56] **References Cited**

U.S. PATENT DOCUMENTS

D. 3,396	3/1869	Sadler	D6/302
D. 31,165	7/1899	Sules	D6/300
D. 118,026	12/1939	Scott	D10/127 X
D. 129,998	10/1941	Lamothe	D10/2
D. 213,843	4/1969	Summers	D10/123
D. 245,833	9/1977	Dyssaat	D10/125
D. 247,612	3/1978	Lucich	D10/2

Primary Examiner—Bernard Ansher
Assistant Examiner—Terry Pfeffer
Attorney, Agent, or Firm—Thomas B. Tate

[57] **CLAIM**

The ornamental design for a combination photographic frame and clock, as shown.

DESCRIPTION

FIG. 1 is a top, front left side perspective view of a combination photographic frame and clock showing my new design.

FIG. 2 is a left side elevational view thereof.

FIG. 3 is a right rear perspective view thereof.

FIG. 4 is a top plan view thereof.

FIG. 5 is a bottom plan view thereof.

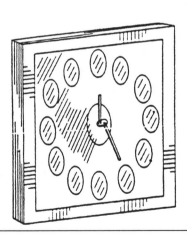

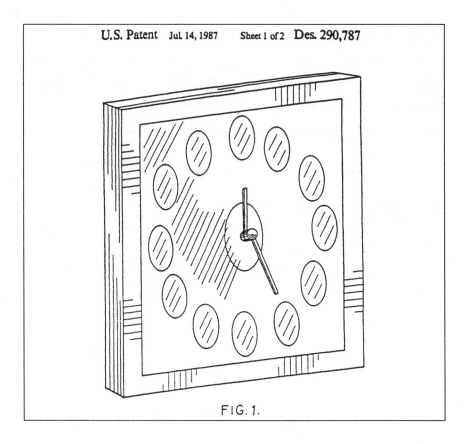

FIG. 1.

STATEMENT OF CONFIDENTIALITY AND NONUSE

I, _____ , agree that I'm only reviewing the product idea, _____ , created by _____ for one or more of the following purposes: providing market research information; offering price quotes; reviewing the idea for future sales opportunities; evaluation for a joint venture or partnership agreement; recommending advertising, packaging, or marketing strategies; any other review or evaluation purpose.

I, _____ , agree not to use any exclusive information obtained from the idea's creator, _____ , concerning the idea, _____ , except as specified under a future agreement or contract.

Inventor

Name_____

Address_____

_____

Phone Number_____

Contact

Name_____

Company_____

Address_____

_____

Phone Number_____

Signature_____

Date_____

Signature_____

Date_____

GLOSSARY

accredited investors: Investors who made over $200,000 annually for the past two years and have the expectation of making $200,000 next year, or they need to have net assets of over $1 million. Nonaccredited investors don't meet these requirements.

amortize: Turning a large payment into a series of smaller payments. For example, if a $10,000 tooling charge is amortized into the cost of a product, an inventor pays off part of the $10,000 cost on every production run.

back orders: Orders that are not shipped on time. For example, if normal delivery is two weeks and an order can't be shipped for eight weeks, the order would be identified as a back order.

blister pack: A piece of clear, hard, molded plastic that is glued to a paperboard backing. A popular package, especially for small toys.

brand name: Any well-known product or company name. Examples are Pillsbury, Betty Crocker, Mr. Coffee, Toro, and Sony.

bridge financing: Financing to cover the period during which a company is raising money. Typically, a loan with the possibility of an extra bonus of stock warrants or options.

cannibalizing: The practice of taking one product apart so that its parts can be used to make another product.

card pack: A package containing, usually, 15 to 120 postcards advertising products or services, which is mailed to a target market.

cavity: A part of a mold that can produce one unit. Injection-molded parts are usually produced from two-, four-, or six-cavity molds, which means that two, four, or six products are manufactured at once.

clip art: Black-and-white drawings of people, places, or events that can be cut out and used for ads, sales flyers, or promotional materials. Books of clip art are available at art and office supply stores as well as larger libraries.

consignment: Giving a product, at no charge, to a store, sales representative, or dealer, with the understanding that the product will either be returned at a later date or paid for when it is sold.

contract manufacturer: A manufacturer that agrees to make another manufacturer's or an inventor's product for a fee.

co-op advertising: A promotional program in which manufacturers and retailers split the cost of ads promoting the manufacturer's products. A co-op advertising allowance is the percentage of a customer's purchases that a manufacturer will pay for ads. For instance, when a manufacturer offers a 10 percent co-op advertising allowance, it will pay for ads costing a dollar amount equal to 10 percent of a retailer's purchases.

copy: All the words used on an ad, package, or promotional display.

direct mail: Any type of promotion in which materials are mailed or delivered to homes, apartments, or businesses.

distributor: A company that buys products from a supplier and later resells them to retailers, other companies, or consumers. A distributor owns the products it sells, in contrast to a manufacturers' representative, who never buys the product.

due diligence: A thorough company evaluation completed by an investor or venture capitalist prior to deciding whether to invest in a company.

factoring: The practice of selling receivables for immediate cash. For example, if a manufacturer ships a $20,000 order to a customer, the invoice or statement is a receivable. If the manufacturer needs immediate cash, it will sell the receivable or factor it to a commercial finance company. The charge for factoring ranges from 4 to 10 percent of the receivable's value.

focus group: A market research term for a group of 5 to 15 people brought together for the sole purpose of evaluating a product.

four-color artwork: Another term for full color. Printing is done with only black, yellow, red, and blue ink. All colors are produced by mixing these four. One-color artwork means only one color of ink is used. Two-color artwork uses two colors. Four-color artwork is expensive because it requires (1) a color separation (the process that turns a photograph into four printing plates, one for each color ink) and (2) a larger printing press.

guaranteed sales: A manufacturer's or distributor's promise to issue a refund for any unsold merchandise.

injection molding: A common way of making small plastic parts. An injection mold shoots plastic into a mold, cures it (heats and then cools the plastic so that it becomes a solid), and then pops the part out of the mold. Ideal for high-volume, automated production. The process has high start-up costs because of expensive tooling charges.

in-kind investments: Investments of free services or materials rather than money. Examples are free rent, working without pay, or use of a prototype laboratory.

letter of credit: A statement from a bank that it will transfer money to a supplier's bank once a shipment has been received. Sometimes required by suppliers before they will ship products. Before a letter of credit will be issued, a manufacturer needs either a line of credit or an escrow account equal to the amount of the letter of credit.

license: A contractual arrangement in which an inventor agrees to allow a manufacturer to produce his or her idea in return for a royalty (a predetermined share of either the manufacturer's sales dollars or its profits). A 5 percent royalty based on sales will give an inventor an amount equal to 5 percent of a company's net sales of the inventor's product.

manufacturers' representative: A person who acts as a sales representative for several manufacturers, never taking possession of a product, but funneling orders to the manufacturers in return for a commission (usually 10 to 15 percent). Manufacturers' representatives are used by companies whose sales are too low to justify having their own sales forces.

margins: The percentage of profit that a company makes. Gross profit margin is equal to the selling price minus the manufacturing cost, divided by the selling price. Net margin is the selling price minus all costs—manufacturing, marketing, administration, and so on—divided by the selling price.

markup: The percentage a retailer or distributor increases the price of a product. If a retailer buys a product for $1 and sells the product for $2, the retailer has a 100 percent markup. The formula for determining markup is:

$$\frac{\text{Dollar amount increase in the product's price} \times 100\%}{\text{Purchase price of the product}}$$

mock-up: A crude model of a product that helps an inventor to visualize what the final product will look like. Often made out of cardboard, papier-mâché, or other easily shaped materials.

model: A representation of what the product will be like, usually structurally sound and functionally similar to a production unit. A model is different from a prototype in that a model will not be quite like the final product; it may have different materials, a different size, or some other different feature. A prototype is very close to, if not exactly like, the final product.

niche market: A small segment of a large market. For example, Mercedes-Benz targets people with incomes of over $100,000, a market that is a small segment, or niche, of the total car market. Chevrolet appeals to buyers looking for $7,000 to $25,000 cars, a very big part of the market.

option: A contract conveying a right to buy shares of a company at a specified price during a specified period. Other stipulations may also apply.

overhead: Any expense that occurs regularly—rent, salaries, utilities, telephone, and so on. Sometimes referred to as *fixed expenses*.

per-unit surcharge: A charge by which a contract manufacturer recovers tooling or other costs. If a manufacturer has absorbed $10,000 in up-front setup costs, those costs might be recovered by charging 25¢ per unit over and above a product's manufacturing cost.

placement: Refers to the process by which manufacturers or inventors put their products in locations where customers can see and buy them.

point-of-purchase display: A display located near where a product is placed for sale in a store. Liquor-store displays promoting certain brands of liquor are point-of-purchase displays.

positioning: A marketing term that relates to the practice of adding features and benefits to a product so that target customers will perceive it in a certain way, such as technologically advanced or as a value leader.

private-label manufacturing: A manufacturer's production of an item that is then sold under another company's name. For example, manufacturers that make the products sold under the Sears brand name are producing private-label products.

private-placement memorandum: A legal document used by small companies when they have more than 35 nonaccredited investors.

pro forma: A projected income and cash flow statement. Most loan documents require an income and cash flow statement for at least 12 months in the future.

promotional allowance: A type of price discount that pays for a customer's promotional programs. A 10 percent promotional allowance, for instance, gives a retailer reimbursement for its promotional costs in an amount equal to 10 percent of its purchases.

promotional mix: How a company spends promotional money. Sales brochures, trade shows, advertising, promotional allowances, and coupons are only a few of the promotional tactics a company might use. The promotional mix refers to how much a company uses each tactic.

prototypes: A sample of what a product will look like once it's produced. Prototypes are usually manufactured with a different technique than will be used for the final production unit.

public domain: When an idea becomes known to the public, it is said to be in the public domain and it loses its confidential status. Selling the product, publishing press releases, and attending trade shows are means of placing a product in the public domain.

rack jobber: A distributor who contracts with stores to furnish all of a certain type of product, such as hair care products, stationery products, or toys. Rack jobbers can typically put whatever they want on the rack, but they agree to charge the store only for what is sold. Because of their contracts, rack jobbers often control certain markets.

receivables: The money that is owed by customers to a manufacturer or distributor.

right of first refusal: A contract term that offers one party to a contract the right to match any offer from another person or company to the first party in the contract. For example, a company might have the right to match a license agreement from another company in return for a $30,000 advance.

rotational molding: A manufacturing process in which plastic is charged into a mold, and the mold is then rotated so that centrifugal force will push the plastic into the proper configuration. Typically used for large parts, such as plastic drums.

royalty: A payment made to an inventor based either on a percentage of sales or on the unit volume of products sold.

shrink-wrap: A common packaging technique in which a sheet of thin, usually transparent, plastic is placed around a product, and then pulled tightly over it and held with a heat-seal. The wrapping looks like thick cellophane.

slotting allowance: A payment to a store that is required before a manufacturer can obtain shelf space. Grocery stores are among the stores that require this payment.

subscription agreement: This is a formal document whereby the investor, in effect, applies to buy shares of stock in a company. The agreement needs to comply with security agreements for formal stock offerings. You should always have a formal document when acquiring investors, to avoid later lawsuits.

targeting: A process in which a manufacturer or inventor identifies a small segment of the market as having potential customers, and then directs all of its promotion at that segment. *Targeting* and *niche marketing* are often used interchangeably.

temporary tooling: Tooling that is expected to last for only a short production run.

terms: A period of days after which payment is due. For example, "30-day terms" means payment is due for a product or service 30 days after the product is shipped or the service performed.

trade shows: Conventions that are geared toward one market, such as tire wholesalers, gift galleries, novelty distributors, or semiconductor manufacturers.

turnover: How long it takes for a store to sell its inventory. If a store sells out a product in two months, then the product has a two-month turnover.

vacuum-forming: A manufacturing process in which a sheet of plastic is placed over a mold. Then the plastic is heated and a vacuum is applied to draw the plastic tight over the mold. Used for fairly large products where high strength is not required.

vendor: Another term for *supplier.*

virtual company: A company that outsources most or all of its functions, including manufacturing, R&D, customer service, and sometimes sales and marketing. A virtual company might have three or four employees with annual sales of over $1 million.

wholesale price: The price at which a product is sold to distributors.

HELPFUL SOURCES

ACCU Data, 1326 Cape Coral Parkway, Cape Coral, FL 33904. Source of mailing lists.

American Color Printing, 8031 N.W. 14th Street, Miami, FL 33126. Low-cost color printer.

Artmaster, 500 N. Claremont Blvd., Claremont, CA 91711. Supplier of a wide range of clip art.

Bar Codes Systems, 7000 Central Parkway, Suite 1210, Atlanta, GA 30328. Offers assistance in obtaining bar-code numbers.

Castolite Inc., P.O. Box 391, Woodstock, IL 60098. A great source of liquid plastics, fiberglass, and mold-making compounds. Its catalog is informative, and I recommend it for anyone interested in making models or prototypes.

Color Graphics Press, 11-20 46th Road, Long Island City, NY 11010. Printing source for low-cost catalog sheets.

Creations Unlimited, 2939 Montreal Drive, N.E., Grand Rapids, MI 49505. Source of small tools and files for producing prototypes.

Direct Marketing magazine, 224 Seventh St., Garden City, NY 11530-5771. Contains numerous sources for mailing lists, catalog houses, and card packs.

Dremel, Division of Emerson Electric, 4915 21st St., Racine, WI 53406. Source of miniature power tools.

337

Edmund Scientific Co., 101 E. Gloucester Pike, Barrington, NJ 08007. One of my favorite catalogs. The first place I look for small motors, optical parts, and miscellaneous parts.

Fair Times magazine, P.O. Box 455, Arnold, MO 63010. Targeted at people who sell products at fairs and flea markets. Has a fairly complete list of upcoming shows. Also has ads for flea market–type products.

Fine Scale Modeler magazine, Kalmbach Publishing Co., 21027 Crossroads Circle, P.O. Box 1612, Waukesha, WI 53187. Contains numerous ads for small parts and small-scale modeling equipment.

Graphic Products Corp., 1480 South Wolf Road, Wheeling, IL 60090. Source of clip-art books.

Great Catalog Guide, Consumer Affairs Dept., Direct Marketing Association, 11 W. 42nd St., P.O. Box 3861, New York, NY 10163. Available for $3, it lists virtually every catalog sold in the country.

Hobby Stuff, Inc., 11239 9 Mile Road, Warren, MI 48089. Manufacturer of a small vacuum-forming machine. Also has a line of small hardware parts.

Hysol Electronic Chemicals, 15051 East Don Julian Road, Industry, CA 91746. Supplier of casting and laminating compounds that are ideal for an inventor. Catalog #T 6-15, 5/88 is especially helpful.

Light Machine Corp., 669 East Industrial Drive, Manchester, NH 03103. Manufacturer of small lathes, machining centers, and milling systems.

MANA, P.O. Box 3467, Laguna Hills, CA 92654. An association of manufacturers' representatives that publishes a newsletter along with a list of representatives looking for lines.

Marketing Magic: Innovative and Proven Ideas for Finding Customers, Making Sales, and Growing Your Business, by Don Debelak (Holbrook, MA: Bob Adams, 1994). Excellent source of ideas for solving difficult marketing problems.

MDIS, Inc., P.O. Box 120861, New Brighton, MN 55112. Send $10 for a hardbound Engineering Notebook. Also has videos available on the new-product introduction process.

Micromark, 340-835 Snyder Ave., Berkeley Heights, NJ 07922. Source of modeling tools.

Model Maker's Handbook, by Albert Jackson and David Day (New York: Alfred A. Knopf, 1981). Excellent book for anyone interested in making models or prototypes.

Morgan Industries, 3311 East 59th St., Long Beach, CA 90805. Manufacturer of a small prototype and short-run injection-molding machine.

Patents, General Information Concerning, U.S. Department of Commerce, Patent and Trademark Office, Washington, DC 20231. This helpful pamphlet is available for only $2.

PDI, P.O. Box 130, Circle Pines, MN 55014. Produces Plasti Dip, a product that will coat metal or other materials with a protective plastic layer.

Pyramid Products, 3756 South 7th Ave., Phoenix, AZ 85041. Makes small foundry furnaces and supplies.

QVC, 1365 Enterprise Drive, West Chester, PA 19380. Home Shopping TV network.

Rapid Color Corp., 101 Brandywine Parkway, West Chester, PA 19380. Will print as few as 100 color catalog sheets.

Response TV, 201 East Sandpoint Ave., Suite 600, Santa Ana, CA 92707. Magazine for the direct-response TV industry, including infomercials and one- and two-minute ads, which ask you to call an 800 number and place an order.

Start-Up Money: Raise What You Need for Your Small Business, by Jennifer Lindsey (New York: John Wiley & Sons, 1989). Sources of financing for sales expansions.

Stock Model Parts, Division of Designatronics, Inc., 2101 Jericho Turnpike, New Hyde Park, NY 11040. Great assortment of small parts, such as gears and drives, and prototype kits. Excellent source for small, hard-to-find parts.

Total Marketing: Capturing Customers with Marketing Plans that Work, by Don Debelak (Homewood, IL: Dow Jones-Irwin, 1989). This has been called an excellent book to help you map out a marketing strategy.

Uniform Code Council, 8163 Old Yankee Road, Suite J, Dayton, OH 45458. Organization that assigns bar-code numbers. Send for free information pamphlet.

U.S. Press, P.O. Box 640, Valdosta, GA 31603. Source of inexpensive color printing.

Wal-Mart Innovation Network, Center for Business Research, College of Business Administration, Southwest Missouri State University, 901 National Ave., Springfield, MO 65904. Provides low-cost product evaluation services. Write for an information packet.

INDEX